John McCarthy

Fantasy and Reality

An Epistemological Approach to Wieland

European University Papers

Europäische Hochschulschriften
Publications Universitaires Européennes

Series I
German language and literature

Reihe I   Série I
Deutsche Literatur und Germanistik
Langue et littérature allemandes

Vol./Bd. 97

John McCarthy

Fantasy and Reality

An Epistemological Approach to Wieland

Herbert Lang Bern
Peter Lang Frankfurt/M.
1974

John McCarthy

Fantasy and Reality

An Epistemological Approach to Wieland

Herbert Lang Bern
Peter Lang Frankfurt/M.
1974

ISBN 3 261 01357 5

For Mecki

CONTENTS

When Christoph Martin Wieland was born in Oberholzheim near Biberach in 1733, the German Enlightenment was coming into full swing. Brockes published his Irdisches Vergnügen in Gott from 1721 to 1748, Haller's Die Alpen appeared in 1729. The stage was set for the famous literary dispute between Leipzig and Zürich with the puplication of Gottsched's Versuch einer critischen Dichtkunst vor die Deutschen in 1730. Furthermore, the decade of Wieland's birth as well as the one following it were characterized literarily by the rising popularity of the Anacreontic poets, Hagedorn and Gleim, by the sentimentality of Gellert, the enthusiasm of Klopstock, and by the emerging critical acumen of young Lessing. When Wieland died eighty years later, in 1813, the intellectual climate in Germany had changed radically.

The philistine concepts of Wolff, Gottsched, and Nicolai had been decisively altered by Herder's relativism, Shakespeare's titanism, Heinse's vitalism, Goethe's morphology, and Lenz' social outcry. On the other hand, the narrow confines of the Enlightenment had been expanded by Winckelmann's apotheosis of the Greeks and Lessing's humanism; both of which prepared the way to the idealism of the Classical-Romantic period. At the same time, as a reaction to the ratiocination of the age, irrationalists and intuitivists of the type of Hamann and Lavater, or of St. Germain and Cagliostro, or of Swedenborg made their appearance. By the year of Wieland's death the Romantic movement had already begun to succumb to darker, demonic forces; and the esoteric Classical movement had just passed its peak, surviving somewhat in the works of Jean Paul, Friedrich Hölderlin, and the late Goethe.

Wieland's life obviously spanned some of the most momentous years in German literary history. And the year of his death, 1813, saw the birth of representative figures of a new generation: Büchner, Hebbel, Kierkegaard, Richard Wagner. In the light of these considerations, the stereotype of Wieland as the "typical man of the Enlightenment" seems a bit shallow indeed. Critics have failed to note the similarities in style and thought between Wieland and Jean Paul (concept of man), Wieland and Tieck (levels of reality), and Wieland and Wackenroder (importance of re-ligio), for example. As editor-in-chief of a widely circulated journal, Wieland naturally shared the spiritual climate which shaped these and other writers.

Those who base their opinion on the Komische Erzählungen (1762), Don Sylvio von Rosalva (1764), or Musarion (1768) tend to see Wieland exclusively as a master of the titillating Rococo art. Those who have studied Agathon (1766-67), on the other hand, know him as an originator of the Bildungsroman and as a moral educator. For yet other readers, Die Geschichte der Abderiten (1774 - 80) portrays Wieland as an accomplished humorist and satirist. The precision, virtuosity, and perfection of verse and expression in Oberon (1780) still charm all comers and reveal another facet of the author.

The views of Wieland are, therefore, numerous. One speaks of his Kulanz, for example, and the term seems to leave a bad aftertaste in the speaker's mouth. The disparagement implied in pointing to Wieland's social and journalistic behavior is really uncalled for. I cannot here go into an in-depth analysis of this particular aspect of Wieland's character (that will be treated in a future study); but the basic reasons for the unjust deprecation must be, at least briefly, pointed out. In the most famous instances of the author's accomodating manner (Zürich Serapherei, Biberach frivolity, and Weimar journalism) a plausible psychological or business explanation is profferable.

Bodmer wanted a seraph and Wieland needed a patron so Wieland "accomodated" Bodmer. The call to Zürich was the desired excuse for the budding poet to leave off his wearisome jurisprudence studies in Tübingen and to pursue a career compatible to his interests. No one can say that this religious enthusiasm was feigned; it was part of his character as we well know from reports on his upbringing. Unfortunately, Wieland discovered that the puritanical household in Zürich was as restrictive as the academic Faberei in Tübingen. Ten years later Wieland found the provincial atmosphere of Biberach oppressive after the excitement of Zürich and Bern. Naturally he sought the cosmopolitan and cultural society of Count Stadion's estate, Warthausen, and "obliged" the group with works like the Komische Erzählungen and Don Sylvio. Here too it cannot be denied that wit and playfulness were part of Wieland's makeup. Yet critics tend to "play down" the fact that the idea of Agathon was nurtured at the same time. Robert Minder's incisive observation concerning the deeper significance of Warthausen as a formative experience is a rarity in Wieland studies: " Warthausen, résidence d'un de ces aristocrates éclairés, annonce Weimar. " [1]

Finally, Wieland's journalistic activities in Weimar seem to perpetrate the image of him as a kulanter Mensch. The "Popularisator im Schneckenhaus" [2] is supposedly characterized by "Standpunktlosigkeit" and by "Unbestimmtheit und Unsicherheit seines Wesens. " [3] Der deutsche Merkur (1773-1810), founded and nurtured by Wieland, owes its tremendous success and extensive influence to his personal efforts and to his ability to capitalize on the changing topical questions of the day. In order to insure the success of this "public" undertaking, he could not afford to take an offensive stand publicly. [4] Wieland had to be many things to many people: cajoling, urging, fawning, threatening, reprimanding as the situation required.

The ready temptation is to assume that this outwardly accomodating manner is applicable to his "personal" work; that is, to his poetic writings and to his novels. Sengle aptly notes that Wieland "never finished with a work" ; [5] but he fails to distinguish clearly between Wieland's journalism and his belles lettres. Frequently Wieland was forced to compose an article in the last moment in order to fill an issue of the Merkur. In such instances one can justifiably characterize the author's work as superficial and pedestrian. His Kernwerke, however, are another matter. We need only call to mind the fatiguing formation of Agathon or Agathodämon to recognize this fact. True, a complete picture of Wieland is only possible "when we consider both the core and the outer surface. " [6] However, we must first learn, as Lucian does in Peregrinus Proteus, to pare the outer layers of appearance in order to lay bare the essence of convictions. We must, therefore, guard against considering Wieland to be "characterless" because he wears many masks. His chameleon-like appearance can be and often is deceptive.

A chief concern of this study will be to counteract the specious transference of
Wieland's social and journalistic Kulanz to works treating his profound experience of the condition humaine. Thus I will endeavor to elucidate and stress a
common element of the varied impressions Wieland has given his readers. I also
hope to convey the image of Wieland as a sensitive, alacritous individual and a
serious, if not original, thinker. Ever since Sengle's biography of Wieland appeared in 1949, more and more scholars have turned their attention to this ver-
satile poet. It is evident that the stereotypes of Wieland as a moral educator, sybaritic faun, or rational skeptic do not do him complete justice. The dawn of Wieland criticism is growing lighter. Students of the author are becoming aware that
the essence of this writer is not to be found in the individual products of his mind
and imagination, but rather in the aggregate of these particulars.

My approach to Wieland, therefore, will be phenomenological and hermeneutical.
His works will not be considered solely as self-contained, artistic expressions,
but as successive contributions to his view of man and man's condition. Each work
must be seen as a dialectic interplay between the author and the reader. Irony and
dialogue, features so representative of Wieland's style, are indicative of this constant re-evaluation of one's position. The individual works of art not only invite
the reader to re-examine his view of the world; they also reveal Wieland's own
continual struggle for certitude, for the right answers. Those who would criticize
him for not taking a stand must bear in mind that he was too honest to form a definite opinion before he had viewed questions of life and death (for those are concerns
closest to his heart) from all perspectives. In a very positive sense the majority
of Wieland's works can be seen as reflections of a religious experience. "Religious,"
according to the etymological roots of the term: re-ligio, that is, a reunification
of the particular with the universal.

Some recent Wieland research has noted this positive aspect of the author's apparent indecisiveness. Wieland's remark that his style, his complicated coda, were
determined by his "Bestreben nach Deutlichkeit und Bestimmtheit," [7] has not gone
unnoticed. In fact, in the wake of Friedrich Beissner's tone-setting analysis, "Poesie des Stils," [8] Wieland's verse and prose style has become the focus of an increasing number of studies. So, for example, Jürgen Jacobs demonstrates the
urbane-cosmopolitan basis of Wieland's novels which accounts for the characteristic
structural and formal elements of dialogue, irony, active reader role, narrator
intrusion, etc. As variations of dialogic interplay they can be viewed as intrinsic
to Wieland's search for certitude. Jacobs has gone beyond Beissner and Kausch [9]
by pointing out the occasional breaks in the structure and style of Agathon (1794)
and Danischmend which seem to connote the inadequacy of the "rococo synthesis
of bourgeois and aristocratic cultural elements" as the means to overcome the
restrictions of middle class sentimentalism and to solve the problem of ethical
behavior in society. [10] Thus Jacobs is able to uncover a further characteristic of
Wieland's style, which promises to be of great moment for the future direction
of Wieland research: the element of irrationality. However, this discovery is not

pursued any further by Jacobs in his own investigation. He concludes his study by correctly asserting that Wieland's unresolved inner conflict between ethical aprior- ity and the empirical orientation of ratiocination gives his novel of the "schöne Gesellschaft" a uniquely human dimension. [11]

Since 1969, other critics have occupied themselves with this particular irrational aspect of Wieland's work; the most successful and provocative of the studies are Klaus Oettinger's Phantasie und Erfahrung, Hermann Müller-Solger's Der Dichter- traum, and Jan-Dirk Müller's Wielands Späte Romane. Each of these undertakings attempts a different solution to the problem exposed by Jacobs. Thus Oettinger is concerned with Wieland's poetological views, Müller-Solger with the role of the dream in Wieland's writings and with the interacting of fantasy and reality evident in it. Müller's work demonstrates the inescapably individual and relative develop- ment of man in Wieland's writings.

Oettinger's point of departure is Wieland's poetics, which Oettinger sees as empir- ically oriented; thus he tends to depreciate the irrationality noted by Jacobs. His basic thesis is that Wieland as an enlightener subscribed to the empirical thought of de l'Ambert, Diderot and Locke. Oettinger argues that this materialistic slant gives rise to the de-mythologization of fantasy constructs in favor of the historicity of empirical fact. "Medium der Erkenntnis, " Oettinger claims, " ist für Wieland allein der Verstand, der gesunde Menschenverstand." [12] Therefore, Wieland's poetological views are decidedly disparate from the Romantic view of Poesie. Oettinger's contention seems to be valid for Don Sylvio, Agathon (first edition), Danischmend, and Der goldene Spiegel (the novels he concentrated on and which were written before 1775); but his reasoning begins to break down with later works such as Peregrinus Proteus, Agathodämon, Aristippus (which he fleetingly mentions) for he is unable to answer the questions raised about the irrational characteristics of Peregrinus and Appolonius. The weakness and resultant inadequacy of Oettinger's supposition is even more apparent in his digression on Wieland and Locke. Nowhere does Oettinger note that Wieland rejected Locke's tabula rasa theory. [13] This theory is the cornerstone of Oettinger's argument. Thus, although Oettinger does scrutinize the relationship between form and content, he fails to shed light on the reason for the increasing evidence of irrational forces at work in Wieland's writings after about 1775, and remains entrapped in the stereotyped view of Wieland as a faithful advocate of gesunder Menschenverstand all his days.

Müller-Solger's exhaustive consideration of the dream motif in Wieland's writings does greater justice to the element of irrationality. On the basis of his investiga- tion Müller-Solger provides a more plausible explanation for Wieland's use of fantasy and for his views of the role of poetry. Whereas Oettinger's main concern was with the formation of Wieland's aesthetics prior to 1775, Müller-Solger effec- tively demonstrates that fundamental changes in the estimation of fantasy and reality occured during the 1770s. Wieland's distancing from English and French empiri- cism is announced in a letter to Gleim on October 2, 1769, where he states he is going to renounce his hedonistic manner of writing in order to give himself over to his "penchant for the ideal." [14] In the essay of 1777, "Gedanken über die Ideale der

Alten, " this idealizing trait is so pronounced that Müller-Solger can justifiably
assert: "Nicht die Gestalt, sondern die Kraft, nicht das Auge, sondern das Herz,
nicht die Realität, sondern die Idealität sind die tragenden Elemente seiner Aesthe-
tik." [15] This insight emphasizes the closer relationship of Wieland to the Romanticists (which Oettinger does not entirely deny) [16] and stresses the divine nature
of the fantasy, which plies the course between the realms of phenomenal reality,
the human soul, and the Eternal One. [17]

Müller-Solger's work goes far beyond Jacob's study. It not only provides an answer
to the question of irrationality in Wieland's thought posed by Jacobs, but also demonstrates that the so-called "breaks" in continuity of style discovered by Jacobs
are - from the new point of view - not "faults" at all but completely consistent with
the author's poetics and philosophical conviction. Hermann Müller-Solger's study
can, therefore, be viewed as a substantive contribution to Wieland research. However, the thrust of Müller-Solger's undertaking is on the evolution of Wieland's
poetic theory to about 1780. Oberon figures as the culminating point of the study.
Little is said about the "antiquarian" novels and no attempt is made to place the
early, middle and late works in (otherwise) closer conceptual proximity to one
another.

In a sense, Jan-Dirk Müller's Wielands Späte Romane (1971) represents a regres-
sion in view of Müller-Solger's accomplishments. For example, he holds with
Klaus Oettinger that Wieland's conception of poetics remained empirically oriented, denying the fantasy powers of divination. As a result he encounters similar
difficulties in reconciling the newly recognized demands of innere Form with the
principle of goldene Mittelmässigkeit, [18] which is considered to be Wieland's
inalterable ideal. Müller's argument does not satisfactorily explain why, for example, Lukian is justified in obeying the dictates of his "inner form" whereas the
Schwärmer Peregrinus is not. Thus Müller is presented with the same enigmatic
problem of irrationality that Jacobs encountered. Obviously, both men suffer from
the restrictions of their empirical views.

The true significance of Müller's study lies in his serious treatment of the oft-
neglected novels Peregrinus Proteus, Agathodämon and Aristipp. As part of his
investigation, Müller successfully demonstrates the continuity or evolution of
style from Don Sylvio to Peregrinus Proteus which he sees in the use of dialogue,
subjectiveness and polyperspective. [19] For this attempt, Müller is to be lauded,
yet his contributions to Wieland research would have been greater had he been able
to consult Müller-Solger's work. As it stands, Müller's study goes beyond Jacob's
Wielands Romane only regarding the shift of emphasis to the late novels and a
reaffirmation of the significance of "inner form" for Wieland. [20]

In the significant studies by Jürgen Jacobs, Hermann Müller-Solger and Jan-Dirk
Müller, strides are made toward a fuller understanding of Wieland's Kunstwollen
and toward a greater elucidation of his style. Yet each undertaking is wanting in
one respect or another. The above critics attempt to delineate the connection between form and content. I propose to examine the form-content nexus as well, but

I trust that my analysis will not merely be a rehash of the above works. Rather, I intend to complement the empirical approaches of Jacobs and Müller and to expand Müller-Solger's explanation of the fantasy. What is needed is a methodology which can be applied to the majority of the author's works in order to gain a deeper insight into the complex interplay of style and idea. At the same time, this study should draw into clearer focus the common basis underlying those considerations of Wieland's style [21] and those of his geistesgeschichtlicher position. [22]

The approach necessary to accomplish these goals is latent in the analyses considered above. It is a philosophical one: the question of epistemology. Occasionally an awareness of the theory of knowledge as an interpretive tool surfaces in Wieland research (particularly with Müller-Solger); but this consciousness is not total and no serious attempt has been made to determine Wieland's epistemology and its relationship to his literature. [23] I am convinced that epistemology is the key to a deeper understanding of Wieland's personality and accomplishments and of his medial position between the Enlightenment and Romanticism.

For purposes of convenience as well as out of consideration for the added dimensions of Wieland's narrative style, I have decided to limit myself to the author's novelistic writings. A number of the novels could have been chosen: Der goldene Spiegel, Danischmend, Die Abderiten, or (particularly) Aristipp. But I have elected to restrict myself primarily to three novels: Don Sylvio von Rosalva, Die Geschichte des Agathon, and Die geheime Geschichte des Peregrinus Proteus. Agathodämon will be briefly analyzed as part of a definitive statement of the findings of this study.

The question naturally arises: Why these novels and not the others? One consideration was the period of inception. Don Sylvio is a product of the Biberach period, when Wieland seemed overwhelmed by the rococo atmosphere of Graf Stadion's country estate, Warthausen. Agathon, likewise from this period, was revised twice in the ensuing thirty years. It is widely considered Wieland's lifework and must be included if only for that reason. Furthermore, by comparing the three versions the metamorphosis as well as the continuity of Wieland's thought might be revealed. Peregrinus Proteus is representative of the religious concerns of Wieland's final period of creation. It is time to correct the misconception that it and Agathodämon are the antiquarian, historical novels that they have been considered to be. [24] In addition to Müller's study there have been others in recent years with a concentration on the late novels. [25] However, they have centered more on content than on style, making little effort to understand the artistic merits of these neglected works. There is still need, therefore, for a study that will further the appreciation of the novels as poetic as well as provocative creations. An effort will be made to see these "antiquarian" novels in a common light with the Cervantes-like and Fielding-like achievements of the Biberach period.

The primary concern in the selection of the above writings, however, has been the central role the Schwärmer plays in each one. The Schwärmer is a somewhat ambivalent figure in the eighteenth century. He is discredited as the victim of de-

lusion by the rationalists and is acclaimed as a prophet by the emotionalists. [26]
In him the interplay of fantasy and reality is reflected most saliently. He is guided
more by his heart than by his head. Judging by the many outsider-types who serve
as protagonists in the author's novels (Diogenes, Danischmend, Democrit, etc.),
it seems apparent that Wieland sanctions the outsider-figure rather than deprecates
him. In fact, Wieland once explicitly stated that Socrates and Harlequin were his
favorite characters, and even more so was Sterne's Yorick because he embodied
the spirit of both. [27]

In Don Sylvio , Agathon and Peregrinus Proteus the psychogenesis of the Schwärmer, who is viewed positively as a quester and would-be reformer, is followed
in detail. In Agathodämon only the results of the protagonist's development are
communicated, not the process. That is the primary reason why this novel is not
given equal consideration with Don Sylvio, Agathon and Peregrinus Proteus. On
the other hand, Agathodämon must be considered at least in passing because it
contains the succinct results of Wieland's long years of contemplation and because
the relationship of its hero to Peregrinus is similar to Archytas' relationship to
Agathon. [28] Finally, these three novels were chosen because they can be seen as
a kind of trilogy that depicts in three distinct stages the evolution of the outsider
from a Schwärmer to an enthusiast. In the course of the study it will become increasingly evident that the Schwärmer is the focal point of Wieland's epistemological deliberations.

The initial chapter is devoted to an elucidation of the epistemological problem per
se, to a tracing of the major philosophic influences on Wieland, and to an examination of Wieland's minor writings with regard to his theory of knowledge. The
ensuing three chapters contain an analysis of Don Sylvio, Agathon and Peregrinus
Proteus, respectively. The Peregrinus chapter is followed by a cursory investigation of the epistemological problem in Agathodämon.

All citations in the text refer, unless otherwise noted, to J. G. Gruber's edition
of Wieland's collected works (Leipzig, 1818-1828). The volume number is designated by Roman numerals, the page numbers by Arabic. The Gruber edition available to me lacked Volume I. Therefore, the Göschen edition (Leipzig, 1855-1858)
was consulted when necessary. The following abbreviations designate various edi-
tions of Wieland's correspondence and works:

A	Geschichte des Agathon (editio princeps)
AB	Ausgewählte Briefe von C.M. Wieland
DB	Auswahl denkwürdiger Briefe
Göschen	Wielands Sämtliche Werke
Gruber	Wielands Sämtliche Werke
Hassencamp	Neue Briefe C.M. Wielands
Jacobi	F.H. Jacobis auserlesener Briefwechsel

| Keil | Wieland und Reinhold |
| Seiffert | Wielands Briefwechsel |

The original orthography has been retained in all instances.

NOTES

1. Robert Minder, "Réflexions sur Wieland et le Classicisme," Un Dialogue des Nations (München: Max Huber Verlag, 1967), p. 36. Minder sees several parallels between Wieland and the German classicists. Italics mine.

2. Friedrich Sengle, Wieland (Stuttgart: Metzler, 1949), pp. 382-393. Sengle's formulation still holds sway today. As yet no one has challenged his explanation that Wieland retreated to his "Schneckenhaus" in order to immerse himself in work and thus not be reminded of the "horror vacui" experienced as a result of the "collapse of his idealism" (p. 389). This study implicitly rejects Sengle's widely accepted opinion.

3. Sengle, p. 393.

4. Cf. Hedwig Weilguny. Das Wieland-Museum im Wittumspalais zu Weimar (Berlin und Weimar: Aufbau Verlag, 1968), p. 59. When a particular stance proved to be too unpopular, Wieland made every effort to blunt the abrasive edges; so, for example, his early support of Napoleon. Cf. Fritz Martini, "Wieland, Napoleon und die Illuminaten," Un Dialogue des Nations (München: Max Huber Verlag, 1967), p. 73, et passim.

5. Sengle, p. 390.

6. Sengle, p. 393.

7. Karl August Böttiger, Literarische Zustände und Zeitgenossen I (Leipzig: Brockhaus, 1838), p. 259.

8. Friedrich Beissner, "Poesie des Stils," Wieland: Vier Biberacher Vorträge (Wiesbaden: Insel Verlag, 1954).

9. Karl H. Kausch, "Die Kunst der Grazie," Schillerjahrbuch II (Stuttgart: A. Kröner Verlag, 1958).

10. Jürgen Jacobs, Wielands Romane (Bern und München: Francke, 1969), pp. 102-105.

11. Jacobs, p. 108.

12. Klaus Oettinger, Phantasie und Erfahrung (München: Fink, 1970), p. 127.

13. Oettinger, pp. 141-145. Cf. below p. 36.

14. Cf. Hermann Müller-Solger, Der Dichtertraum (Göppingen: A. Kümmerle, 1970), p. 179.

15. Müller-Solger, p. 220.

16. Oettinger, p. 126.

17. Müller-Solger, p. 318.

18. Jan-Dirk Müller, Wielands Späte Romane (München: Fink, 1971), p. 81, 119, 193.

19. Müller, pp. 19-31.

20. Cf. below pp. 147-149.

21. In addition to Jacobs and Müller, recent stylistic studies of Wieland include: Charlotte Craig, Christoph Martin Wieland as the Originator of the Modern Travesty in German Literature (Chapel Hill: University of North Carolina Press, 1970); Steven R. Miller, Die Figur des Erzählers in Wielands Romanen (Göppingen: A. Kümmerle, 1970). Cf. also the chapters dealing with Wieland

in: Liselotte E. Kurth, Die Zweite Wirklichkeit (Chapel Hill: University of North Carolina Press, 1969); Jörg Schönert, Roman und Satire im 18. Jahrhundert (Stuttgart: Metzler, 1969).

22. In addition to Müller-Solger und Oettinger: Wolfram Buddecke, C.M. Wielands Entwicklungsbegriff und die Geschichte des Agathon (Göttingen: Vandenhoeck und Ruprecht, 1966); Barbara Schlagenhaft, Wielands "Agathon" als Spiegelung aufklärerischer Vernunft- und Gefühlsproblematik (Erlangen: Palm und Enke, 1935); Hans Wolffheim, Wielands Begriff der Humanität (Hamburg: Hoffmann und Campe, 1949).

23. For example, Müller-Solger, p. 212, asserts: "Selbstverständlich können wir von Wieland keine systematische Abhandlung zur Erkenntnistheorie erwarten ..." For whatever reason, Müller-Solger does not attempt a methodical investigation of Wieland's theory of knowledge, although his interpretation of the dream and of the fantasy are integral aspects of the epistemological question.

24. Sengle, p. 479.

25. Gerhard Reimer, "The Schwärmer in the Novelistic Writings of Christoph Martin Wieland", Diss. Michigan State University, 1968, proposes to "pursue Wieland's treatment of Schwärmerei from work to work, especially in light of the solutions (if any) he proposes" (p. 1; see also pp. 46, 62-63). Margrit Wulff, "Wielands späte Auseinandersetzung mit Schwärmerei und Aberglaube," Diss. University of Texas, 1966, investigates Wieland's attitude toward religion in general and Christianity in particular. They, as well as Müller, still consider the eccentric hero to be a negative figure.

26. Cf. Victor Lange, "Zur Gestalt des Schwärmers im deutschen Roman des 18. Jahrhunderts," Festschrift für R. Alewyn (Köln: Böhlau, 1967), p. 154.

27. C.M. Wieland, Auswahl denkwürdiger Briefe, ed. L. Wieland (Wien: Gerold, 1815), I, 234 (letter of December 5, 1768). Peter Michelsen, Laurence Sterne und der deutsche Roman des 18. Jahrhunderts (Göttingen: Vandenhoeck und Ruprecht, 1962), pp. 202-212 et passim.

28. Müller-Solger, p. 77.

Chapter 1

AESTHETICS AND EPISTEMOLOGY

Nous connaissons la vérité non seulement par la raison
mais encore par le coeur. - Pascal, Pensées, frag. 110

Le coeur a ses raisons que la raison ne connaît point.
- Pascal, Pensées, frag. 423

Christoph Martin Wieland was above all an eclectic thinker who viewed epistemological problems in moral, utilitarian, and aesthetic terms. The concepts of the
True, the Beautiful, and the Good are manifest in almost all of the author's writings. Germane to these concerns is Wieland's depiction of man's quest for the
Highest Good. This study of Wieland proposes to investigate his conception of
ultimate Truth and man's ability to comprehend it. Because Wieland was a poet-
philosopher one can reasonably expect his theory of knowledge to be poetic as
well as philosophic. For this reason, the term "ultimate Truth" will be synonymous with the term "Highest Good." The content of this good can be ambivalent
if one omits the distinction between empiric and transcendent. On the experiential
plane the Highest Good is eudaimonistic, but on the metaphysical level it is tanta-
mount to a mystical union with God. I will endeavor to demonstrate that the Highest Good in a mystical sense is the decisive factor in ascertaining the nature of
ultimate Truth, since Wieland gradually became more aware of an inherent relationship between the Epicurean and the Christian points of view.

Fundamental concerns of epistemology are the limitations and the validity of
knowledge.[1] The traditional epistemological debate involves the dualism of perception and cognition. These are mediated respectively by Verstand (intellectus
passivus) and Vernunft (intellectus agens). A further Dichotomy. especially in
Wieland's case, is that of Kopf and Herz. Kopf entails for Wieland the per-
ceptive and cognitive functions of the mind which supply man with non-moral and
non-aesthetic knowledge.[2] Herz is, in Wieland's theory, man's autonomous
moral and aesthetic guide which is unrelated to either Vernunft or Verstand.
The mind can convince the individual of phenomenal reality only, whereas the
heart can persuade a person of the legitimacy or moral rightness of an act or a
thing. The highest organizing body which evaluates the data of Verstand and
Herz is Vernunft. The interaction of these faculties, and particularly the
ancillary relationship of the rational processes of the mind to the intuitive appre-
hensions of the heart, are central to Wieland's epistemological view. It must be
kept in mind that his epistemological and ontological attitudes will have very
strong moral overtones.

Traditionally, theoreticians have noted the subjective nature of perception.[3] Generally speaking, man is incapable of definite knowledge concerning the nature of things. Sense sensations are ipso facto subjective, since man has no guarantee that his perception of the world is necessarily coincident with those of other men. What man acknowledges as phenomenal reality is the sum total of each individual perception of that world. Each man must subscribe to a consensus of the divergent views in order to be able to interact harmoniously with other men.

A priori truths have been posited which concern only the realm of ideas, not the realm of things. These a priori truths are distinct from and independent of a posteriori conclusions, which are by definition contingent on sense experience. Thus, in many epistemological views a transcendental world is postulated in an attempt to overcome the inherent subjectivity and relativity of sensual perception. Definite, objective knowledge is possible only with respect to ideas. Wieland subscribed to this dualistic conception of the world (noumenal and phenomenal), as well as to the consensus of sense perception as central to social harmony. This will be demonstrated later on the basis of the novels under investigation.

It is evident from a letter to Schinz in May 1752 that Wieland was not concerned with subtle proofs of the existence and essence of phenomena. Man should concentrate, in his opinion, on the moral truths emanating from the godhead, because man can have certain knowledge only of them. All other knowledge is inadequate and superfluous. Man need not be concerned with the essence of phenomena per se because all things have their origin and design in God. These thoughts are implied in Wieland's response to his friend's criticisms. Wieland asserts: "Meine Hypoth[ese] de aeternitate mundi, gründet sich auf diesen Satz. Gott ist der Grund oder die Quelle aller Realitäten; die Welt aber ist ein Inbegriff aller Realitäten ausser Gott. Diese Realitäten müssen also würklich seyn, sonst wären sie keine Realitäten sondern Chimeren."[4] Thus we should not expect Wieland to become involved in the philosophical dispute concerning the existence or non-existence of phenomena as entities distinct from our mental impressions of them. He obviously considers reflections of this sort to be senseless and inconsequential. In the same letter, Wieland states further: "Ich werde gewiss niemalen in einen philosoph[ischen] Streit geflochten werden können über metaphysische Subtilitäten, worüber mann schon etliche tausend Jahr raisonnirt, und doch nicht weiter gekommen ist als Plato oder Pythagoras."[5] This passage gives further evidence that Wieland's epistemological concern is directed at understanding the Highest Good and not at empirical reality. He accepts the external world as truly existent but will not claim that man can necessarily perceive it objectively.[6]

In order to determine how Wieland conceived of the Highest Good, let us turn to a consideration of those two thinkers who exerted the greatest influence on him: Plato and Shaftesbury.[7] Plato's influence apparently contributed significantly to the particularly mystical character of Wieland's first phase, from 1749 to 1755. This period is typified by a nexus of religious mysticism and Platonic idealism. These years are marked initially by an almost total lack of interest in mundane affairs. Critics have frequently pointed out, for example, the Platonic relation-

ship between Wieland and his engaging cousin, Sophie Gutermann, or the spiritual
relationship between Wieland and Frau von Grebel-Lochmann.[8] That aspect of
Platonism which affected Wieland generally was its metaphysical emphasis of
noumenal reality. Specifically, the young writer seemed to be influenced by the
doctrine of Forms.

Philosophically speaking, Plato's Forms are eternal, immutable ideas of which
objects are imperfect copies. The perfect Forms are the ultimate metaphysical
realities and are therefore the proper object of true knowledge. They might be
known by reason but not by the senses. In Plato's view man can only form opinions
about sensible things. "We cannot be said to perceive the real properties of things
because of the possibility of illusion and because of the causal aspects of perception itself."[9] This doctrine is evidently the intended reference in the above-men-
tioned letter.[10] J.G. Gruber, Wieland's early biographer, describes the interrelationship between the noumenal and phenomenal as follows: "Die Welt entstand,
indem die Gottheit die Materie mit diesen Ideen verband, oder sie ordnete nach
ihren ewigen Urbildern. Das Weltideal, sofern es von Gott gedacht wird, macht
die Verstandeswelt aus, nach welcher die sichtbare dadurch, dass die Materie
mit den Ideen verbunden wurde, gebildet ist."[11]

From a theological and psychological perspective, Plato thought of the human soul
as of divine origin. Its nature is to struggle for reunification with the godhead,
since its original state was oneness with God. This theory accounts for the notion
that the human soul has experienced all things in previous existences. Plato uses
this concept in the Phaedo to explain how sensible things are able to remind man
of what he already knows and of what he is incapable of ascertaining through sense
experience.[12] The body is conceived of as a prison in which the soul is detained
as a form of punishment. The body and the senses are incumbrances to the aspirations of the soul. Man can only achieve felicity here on earth if he is able to
renounce the terrestrial demands of his corporeality and return to an undisturbed
view of the innate, invisible truths. In order to fulfill his true destiny man must
continually strive to become more divine and less bestial. This process is described by Gruber:

Um noch Glückseligkeit hienieden zu erlangen, muss man das
Irdische fliehen, die Seele vom Körper abziehen, und die ewige
Wahrheit des Unsichtbaren unverwandt mit dem Auge des reinen
Verstandes anschauen, worin die wahre Weisheit, die Mutter
aller Tugenden, besteht. Des Menschen Glückseligkeit besteht in
der Aehnlichwerdung Gottes, wozu die Tugend, die Anerkennung des
Elendes der eingekerkerten Seele und die Reinigung derselben
die Mittel sind.[13]

Crucial to the progressive spiritualization of the human being in Platonic theory
are the concepts of love and kalokagathia. Kalokagathia means "nobleness and
goodness," a derivation from kalòs kai àgathós, which means "beautiful and good."

The interconnection of the concepts of love and kalokagathia is lucidly explained in Plato's Symposium, in which Socrates relates Diotima's theory of love. This emotion is defined generally as "the love of the everlasting possession of the good."[14] In his desire for eternal possession of the good, man can progress from love of corporeal beauty to love of spiritual beauty and finally to love of Absolute Beauty. Diotima maintains:

> He who from these [perishable beauties] ascending under the
> influence of true love begins to perceive that beauty is not
> far from the end. And the true order of going, or being led by
> another, to the things of love is to begin from the beauties
> of earth and mount upward for the sake of that other beauty,
> using these as steps only, and from one going on to two, and
> from two to all fair forms, and from fair forms to fair practices,
> and from fair practices to fair notions, until from fair notions
> he arrives at the notion of absolute beauty, and at last knows
> what the essence of beauty is. ... But what if man had eyes
> to see the true beauty — the divine beauty, I mean, pure and clear
> and unalloyed, not clogged with the pollutions of mortality and
> all the colors and vanities of human life — thither looking, and
> holding converse with the true beauty simply and divine? Remember
> how in that communion only, beholding beauty with the eye of the
> mind, he will be enabled to bring forth, not images of beauty,
> but realities (for he has hold not of an image but of a reality),
> and bringing forth and nourishing true virtue to become the
> friend of God and be immortal, if mortal men may. Would that
> be an ignoble life?[15]

In the analysis of Wieland's novels it will become readily apparent to what degree the Platonic notions of the Forms, previous existences, love, and kalokagathia have influenced the author's Weltanschauung.

Shaftesbury's impact on Wieland can be viewed as an intensification and expansion of the more important Platonic conceptions. In Die Weltanschauung des jungen Wieland, Emil Ermatinger asserts that Shaftesbury became for Wieland the key to a more proper and deeper understanding of Platonic philosophy.[16] In a sense, Shaftesbury becomes for Wieland the juncture of Greek idealism and European Enlightenment.

Shaftesbury seems to represent for Wieland a synthesis of the fermenting rationalistic, religious, moral, and aesthetic views of the age. Shaftesbury's concept of the virtuoso (together with the notion of kalokagathia) becomes Wieland's ideal.[17] The virtuoso is the Enlightenment's designation for the refined, cultured gentleman whose inner harmony is reflected in external beauty.[18] The virtuoso is able to harmonize the two opposite poles of human nature: the spirit and the flesh. The spiritual aspect of human nature is the nobler; its needs -- for example, truth, righteousness -- are beneficial to both sides of human nature. On the other hand, excesses of man's lower nature are detrimental to the whole man, and for this reason the animal nature must be subordinated to the spiritual.[19] The complete harmony of these two constituent aspects of human nature becomes the ideal which man must strive to attain.

The two mainstreams of eighteenth-century thought -- social consciousness (Enlightenment) and individualism (Pietism, Sentimentalism, Storm and Stress) -- come together for Wieland in Shaftesbury's dualistic concept of man. This juncture becomes obvious when the innate dichotomy of human nature is described as a tension between man's inherent drive to be free of all restrictions and his equally intrinsic need of other men's society. This need for companionship nec - essarily restricts individualism. [20] Furthermore, Wieland envisions in this tension a conflict between man as a free agent who can impose his will on the world and man as a plaything of external forces. Victor Michel defines these opposing tendencies in the following manner: "Ce sont donc d'abord deux conceptions qui s'affrontent: le déterminisme d'Helvétius, qui fait dépendre les idées morales et la conduite des influences extérieures, du milieu social, de l'occasion, et, d'autre part, l'individualisme de Shaftesbury, pour qui l'homme impose sa forme au monde."[21] These tensions prove to be decisive in determining the import and form of the three novels under investigation.

One feature of Shaftesbury's philosophy which had a profound impact on Wieland was the identification of aesthetics, morality, and truth. The beautiful is good and true; virtue is beautiful. For Shaftesbury the question of the nature of Truth is inseparable from that of the nature of Beauty.

To him "truth" signifies rather the inner intellectual structure of the universe, which cannot be known in terms of concepts alone or grasped inductively by means of an accumulation of individual experiences, but which can only be immediately experienced and intuitively understood [cf. Spinoza]. This form of experience and of intuitive understanding is available in the phenomenon of the beautiful. Here the barrier between the world within and the world without disappears; both worlds are governed by the same all-inclusive law, which each expresses in its own manner. [22]

The beautiful is not a concept abstracted from experience. Rather, it partakes of the Divine and expresses the Divine in an original way. In fact, divinity is the source of all beauty. God is described as the "substance of all beauty," the "eternal beauty," and the "everlasting prototype of the beautiful." [23]

Man has a propensity for perceiving beauty (and therefore Truth, in the Shaftesbury-Wieland view), but man can be deceived if reason and feeling do not stand in the proper relationship to one another. Feeling of course plays the major role in the perception of the True, Beautiful, and Good because they are immediately comprehended by the intuition. Nevertheless, feeling can deceive man if it is not accompanied by salubrious reason. In Shaftesbury's view, the interaction of the heart and mind is decisive for right perception. [24] This doctrine could very well be the source of Wieland's own aversion to the dominance of either reason or feeling. It will be seen in the course of this study that Wieland attempts to hold the mind and the heart in delicate balance. Excessive leaning to either side results in deception. It must be stressed that Shaftesbury requires feeling to function together with salubrious reason (gesunde Vernunft), since reason too is fallible. Wieland does not interpret feeling in quite the same manner as Shaftesbury. For Wieland feeling is always more reliable than reason, even if there is conflict between the two; yet, the ideal is a harmonious balance of the two forces. [25]

The standard to which man must orient himself is Nature because of its divine quality; i.e., proportion, harmony, and delicate balance. [26] Each individual has an inner voice which indicates to him what is natural or unnatural. [27] Man needs only to hear and obey that inner voice of Nature in order to remain on the path of Truth. This voice of Nature can be likened to the voice of the divinity, "since the gods are either the cause of Nature or are Nature herself." [28] In fact, it can be asserted: "In allem kann man sich auf die Stimme der Natur verlassen." [29] Wieland holds a similar view in his semiphilosophic theory.

However, should the individual not be attentive to the inner voice of Nature or should he not be in possession of salubrious reason, then scepticism and mockery should be employed as the touchstone of Truth. By means of mockery one can distinguish the natural ("das Naturgemässe") from the unnatural ("das Naturwidrige"). [30] This point is also crucial, as will be seen in later chapters.

Another indicator of Truth is "intrinsic experience." Intrinsic experience is the object of self-observation, which Shaftesbury (and Wieland) so highly recommends, and which is always correct. This type of experience is contingent upon the intense involvement of one's passions and affections and is true because "we cannot doubt of what passes within ourselves." [31] Wieland expresses basically the same thought in a letter to Gessner: "Die Sentimens eines Menschen bleiben immer, wenn er einmal welche gehabt hat, aber die Begriffe ändern sich von Zeit zu Zeit." [32]

Finally, a word about Shaftesbury's concept of enthusiasm. According to the English philosopher, enthusiasm is a spiritual exaltation which is capable of raising the individual above sensible reality and of gaining actual access to Truth. [33] Enthusiasm enhances the feeling of community. It induces sublime thoughts and noble deeds. Religio-philosophic enthusiasm leads one to beauty and purity of soul and enables man to renounce the things of this world for the eternal values of the next. [34] This specific point will become clear, especially with regard to Peregrinus Proteus. It should be noted that there is a certain affinity between this concept of enthusiasm and Plato's interpretation of love as a desire to attain everlasting possession of the Beautiful.

There is little reason to distinguish between the distinctive features of Platonism

and Shaftesbury's moral philosophy in the discussion of Wieland's semi-philosophic works. The two philosophic systems have become so synthesized in Wieland's mind that it is often impossible to trace a given thought infallibly to its
actual originator. The reason for this fusion of ideas in Wieland's mind is perhaps the fact that the English philosopher was both a Christian and a rationalist.
Thus Shaftesbury was better able to apply metaphysical concepts to the practical
world and to demonstrate how man can live in this world but be of the next. Man
is confronted on the one hand with the problem of satisfying physical needs. On
the other, he senses a certain dissatisfaction and inadequacy in a life which is
arranged merely to expedite a comfortable existence. By synthesizing the dictates
of the Enlightenment -- best expressed in the concept of gesunde Vernunft [35] --
with the yearnings of the heart for deeper significance and fulfillment, Shaftesbury formulated the philosophy that immediately and completely appealed to Wieland, who was becoming ever more disillusioned with the abstract Platonic concepts which appeared to have little relevance to the actuality of life. In fact, it
can be aserted that Shaftesbury provided Wieland with a philosophic explanation
for the disillusioning experience he underwent with Frau Amtmann Grebel. Although Shaftesbury's postulation of the nature of the transcendent was still abstract, it nevertheless had meaningful application for men rooted in the sensual
world. It was this harmonizing of the rational and irrational, spiritual and bestial
forces in man for the purpose of experiencing the unified whole of phenomena and
noumena in the form of the Beautiful which intrigued Wieland. Wieland's identification with Shaftesbury's thought was so intensive that Goethe called him the
Englishman's "Zwillingsbruder im Geiste."[36] Through Shaftesbury's influence
significant aspects of Platonic thought took on new and deeper significance for
Wieland in his philosophy of life.

The extent of the transformation in Wieland's attitudes toward metaphysical realities in the late 1750's has, in my opinion, been overestimated. Too much stress
has been placed on Lessing's famous remark: "Freuen Sie sich mit mir! Herr
Wieland hat die ätherischen Sphären verlassen, und wandelt wieder unter den Men-
schenkindern."[37] Attempting to underscore the contrast between Wieland's first
and second phases, critics have interpreted this comment as a substantiation of
the Swabian's abandonment of ethereal realms. The impression has been given
that this was a total renunciation of Platonic idealism.[38] Indeed, Wieland himself
has supplied material that augments and confirms this unduly monistic position.
Many references in his correspondence in support of this particular argument
could be cited.[39] Let it suffice to quote only a representative passage from one of
the author's letters to his confidant Zimmermann, written in November of 1762.

Non sum, qualis eram, mon cher Zimmermann; sans m'étonner d'avoir
été enthousiaste, hexametriste, ascéte, prophète et mystique, il y a bien
du temps que je suis revenu, grace à Dieu, de tout cela, et que je me
trouve tout naturellement au point d'où je suis parti il y a dix ans. Platon
a fait place à Horace, Young à Chaulieu. . . . J'y ai senti le néant de tous
ces grands mots et de tous ces brillants Fantômes, qui, dans une douce et
agréable solitude ou à coté d'une Me Guyon ou Rowe ont des charmes si sé-

duisants pour un coeur aussi sensible que le mien et pour une imagination d'autant plus active, qu'elle étoit obligée de me dédomager de tout ce qui manquoit du coté des sens.[40]

The affirmation of the radical nature of the change wrought in Wieland is lucid enough, especially in the statement about "the inaneness of all those grand words and brilliant chimeras."

Despite all the contrary evidence, it is not justifiable to assume that Wieland truly renounced all the Platonic ideals he had subscribed to during the previous decade. Given the author's pietistic upbringing and his mentality, such a dramatic change would seem psychologically improbable. Wieland himself has given us an oblique warning to be wary of judging him too quickly. As early as 1759 he cautions his friend Zimmermann against rashness in forming an inalterable opinion about him. Wieland states that he is not the person Zimmermann presumes him to be, and he uses the metaphor of the chameleon to stress this point: "Je ressemble pour mon malheur au Cameleon; je parois vert aupres des Objets verts, et jaune aupres des jaunes; mais je ne suis ni jaune ni vert; Je suis transparent, ou blanc come veut Mr de la Motte." [41] The literary allusion to De la Motte further underscores the intended point. In De la Motte's fable, the chameleon itself resolves the dispute concerning his color by exhorting the disputants to be tolerant of each other's views because each perceives the chameleon from a different perspective.

Allez, enfants, allez, dit le Cameleon;
Vous avez tous tort et raison.
Croyez qu'il est des yeux aussi bons que les vôtres;
Dites vos jugemens; mais ne soyez pas fous
Jusqu'à vouloir y soûmettre les autres.
Tout est Cameleon pour vous. [42]

With this metaphor in mind, we will be less prone to misjudge the degree of change Wieland underwent. Instead of closing our eyes to the similarities of the author's pre- and post-1759 views for the sake of contrast, we must be simultaneously aware of the similarities and contrasts in order better to evaluate the significance of the transition. If we do this, then we will not overlook those passages in the author's correspondence which indicate that he has not totally rejected Platonism. In October of 1760 Wieland writes to Sophie von La Roche that he is no longer a "downright Platonist." The use of the English word "downright" seems to insinuate that his Platonic view of the world has been altered but not obliterated. [43] Four years later, in a letter to Zimmermann, the author complains again of being misunderstood. He objects to Zimmermann's intimation that he has become wanton and lascivious. Wieland exclaims that it is not necessary to become a degenerate Epicurean in order to be jolted out of Platonic reveries.[44] The piqued tone of this passage also indicates that Wieland is not as radically and fundamentally changed as his contemporaries assumed.

The change that actually occurred was that of humanization. This humanization was partially effected by exposure to Shaftesbury's philosophy and its exhilarating effect on Platonism,[45] and partially by enlightening intercourse with the Zürich and Bernese societies.[46] Wieland did not suddenly and irrevocably deny Platonic idealism, as it seems at first sight. Rather, he was awakened to the legitimate claims of terrestrial existence. He acknowledged and accepted the existential world in addition to the metaphysical. To be sure, his initial reaction against the Platonic "follies" of his youth did tend to be an overreaction which, however, later subsided and was superseded by an attempt to harmonize man's dualistic nature: the spiritual and the animal. This oscillation between the dual demands of human nature will become particularly transparent in the discussions of Don Sylvio, Agathon, and Peregrinus Proteus.

In June 1760 Wieland returned to his hometown of Biberach, where he had been elected senator. In the ensuing decade he reached the first zenith of creative activity while attempting to give poetic expression to his world view. Indicative of this world view is a description of his convictions and aspirations contained in a letter to Zimmermann dated April 26, 1759. Wieland's chameleon-like character, the misunderstanding surrounding his person, his own disillusionments and ideals are all indicated.

> Je sens que j'ai dû paraitre un homme merveilleux, inconcevable, enigmatique, fanatique aux yeux des uns, hypocrite aux yeux des autres, inconsequent aux Esprits graves et lents, lunatique aux Hommes du Monde, poëte aux philosophes, philosophe aux poëtes, superficiel aux Pedans, ridicule ou peut etre meprisable aux Esprits mediocres que sai-je moi? On m'a pris pour tout ce que je ne suis pas on m'a condamné pour des defauts imaginaires, on m'a prisé pour des perfections imaginaires. C'est Vous, mon Ami, qui me connaissez; je ne me contente pas de cet avantage; J'aspire à l'approbation de tous les Sages, de tous les Vertueux, et je tacherai de la meriter. Je vois tous mes egaremens -- je les éviterai; j'ai fait des experiences, j'en tirerai profit; je connais assez moi même pour me defier de mes foiblesses, et pour faire valoir ce que j'ai de talens et de vertus; je connais assez les hommes, pour n'en avoir ni trop bonne ni trop mauvaise opinion. J'étudierai la grande maxime d'Horace Virtus est Vitium fugere. J'ai toujours aimé avec passion le Vrai, le Bon, le Beau, je m'efforcerai de devenir ce que j'ai aimé. En un mot, car je parle au Dr. Zimmermann, j'ai passé 25 anns. [47]

Not only does this letter indicate where Wieland has been, so to speak, but it also indicates where he is going. It is important to note that, despite his failings, he has always loved the True, the Good, and the Beautiful and has attempted to live according to their dictates. The insinuation is that Wieland intends to continue his endeavors at self-perfection, now that he has acquired the necessary maturity ("j'ai passé 25 anns"). The implication that he had been an honest Schwärmer tends to mitigate his culpability. Thirty years later the concept of the "honest dreamer" will turn up again in its full force. Honesty and integrity are crucial to Wieland's epistemological view, as will become evident in the course of this study.

The purpose of the foregoing discussion of Wieland's "transformation" was to indicate that the change in epistemological and ontological attitudes is not as radical as one might expect.[48] The Plato-Shaftesbury philosophic nexus supplied Wieland with a concept of ultimate reality (the object of true knowledge) and the means for discerning it. In his long life Wieland never wavered in his attempt to gain the Highest Good, although he did vacillate at times in the choice of instrument to be used in the perception of this good. Wieland's view of the object of true knowledge and the means for acquiring it can be collated from his shorter works written between 1751 and 1787. This collation will serve as a prelude to the investigation of the novels. Because of the constancy of his epistemological position it will not be mandatory to adhere to a strict chronological order of the works. The novels under consideration will be especially valuable in providing an accurate depiction of Wieland's attitudes in their development and flux.

In 1751 Wieland published his first work, a didactic poem, "Die Natur der Dinge." Although this composition precedes the predominant influence of Platonism (it bears the mark of Leibnitz' theories), it introduces a number of themes which later come into full bloom under the nurturing effect of Plato. Of foremost importance is the dualism of reality expounded and the intrinsic bond between the human soul and God.[49] The poem expounds the postulation that all phenomena are but concrete reflections of abstract realities. At this point the young poet seems to feel that experiential objects are exact replicas of ideas (Göschen, XXV, 69). Of further significance is the assertion that perception is subjective and relative. Sense perception is not only contingent upon restricted intellectual acumen but is also subordinate to emotional prejudice. For these reasons, Wieland says, we are and will always be prone to err. "Der Sinn muss trügerisch seyn, der Stoff muss uns verführen, / So lange wir in uns der Schöpfung Schranken spüren; / Und diess wird ewig seyn" (Göschen, XXV, 109).

Wieland, however, distinguishes between Verstand (intellectus passivus) and Vernunft (intellectus agens). Whereas the Verstand is liable to error, the Vernunft is more reliable and is capable of guiding man safely through the labyrinth of sense deceivers. Wieland labels reason "die selbstleuchtende Vernunft" and maintains that its astuteness enables it immediately to discern the essence of things: "Ein Geist, der Stoff und Bild von seinem Kleid entblösst, / Und, was zufällig ist, vom Wesentlichen lös't" (Göschen, XXV, 110). At this point in his development Wieland ascribes no special powers of discernment to the imagination. Or rather, he does not know if the fantasy is able to intuit essences (Göschen, XXV, 72). These concepts -- as well as the theories of animated monads and of harmonious spheres which pervade the poem -- are altered and subsumed by the Plato-Shaftesbury synthesis.

Among the first works to be affected by Platonism is the poetic composition "Briefe von Verstorbenen" (1753). The doctrines of the perfect Forms, kalokagathia, intuition, and absolute Beauty all function as integral parts of the young author's new view. Wieland seems to revel in his newly gained insight in such passages as the following, in which these Platonic concepts are alluded to.

Freund, der Vorhang ist weg, die Nacht ist vom Tage verschlungen,
Dein Theagenes sieht! Die Wahrheit unter den Menschen
Kaum im Bilde bekannt, die himmlische Göttin der Schönheit,
Gibt sich mir willig zu sehn; ich schaue die ew'gen Ideen,
Sie, die in eure Gruft durch die engen Ritzen der Sinne
Gleitende Schatten nur werfen, die ihr für Wesen umfasset.
Mein erweiterter Geist entfaltet höhere Kräfte,
Die, auf Erden unbrauchbar, im Grunde der Seele verborgen,
Schlummerten; innere Sinnen, auch weite Behälter der Wahrheit,
Augen für hellere Gegenstände, erhabne Begierden,
Denen die Erde zu leicht, der Cirkel des Menschen zu eng ist.
(Göschen, XXVI, 42)

Here too is the intimation that sensible things can provide man with only vague and imperfect knowledge of the absolutes. The initial results of Wieland's study of Platonic philosophy are apparent in "Briefe von Verstorbenen." But it was not until a year later that the first mature fruits of his intellectual maturation were reaped.

The year 1754 saw the appearance of a number of short semi-philosophic essays, all of which were concerned with one or more of the Platonic-Shaftesbury concepts. One of the most fertile (for present purposes) is the discourse "Sympathien" (1754). This essay sounds a number of leitmotifs which are central to Wieland's epistemological and ontological views. Earlier in this chapter we discussed Plato's belief that all experience is nothing more than a process of remembering what has occurred in a previous existence. The same notion is reiterated by Wieland in the introduction to the "Sympathien." The affinity between certain souls as a result of a previous existence is emphasized.

Wie glücklich, wenn sympathische Seelen einander finden!
Seelen, die vielleicht schon unter einem andern Himmel sich
liebten, und jetzt, da sie sich sehen, sich dessen wieder
erinnern, wie man eines Traums sich erinnert, von dem nur eine
dunkle angenehme Empfindung im Gemüthe zurück geblieben ist.
. . . Ein geheimer magnetischer Reiz nähert sie einander, sie
schauen sich an, und lieben sich immer mehr, je länger sie sich
anschaun. (XXX, 7 - 9)

This passage not only indicates Wieland's attraction to the theory of previous existences but also to the concept of instinct ("eine dunkle angenehme Empfindung. . . . Ein geheimer magnetischer Reiz"). This instinct is innately related to the eternal yearning for transcendence each man is conscious of in his heart. That which is capable of satisfying him completely is not to be found in the mundane world but in the metempirical. Yet man does not realize that his visions are of realities and are not chimeras, as he supposes. Sympathie connotes for Wieland the interconnection of ideals, instinct, and yearning.[50] The author further states in the essay:

Kaum erwachen die schwesterlichen Seelen wieder von der Betäubung, worein der Fall in den irdischen Klumpen sie stürzte; kaum fühlen sie sich selbst wieder recht, so erwacht auch eine geheime Sehnsucht, die ihnen selbst fremd ist. Sie athmen nach einem Gute, das ihnen fehlt; sie staunen; oft sinken sie, in einsamen Schatten, oder unter den Flügeln der Nacht, in ernste Träume. Tausend Gestalten der Dinge gehen vor der denkenden Seele vorbei, ohne sie zu rühren; sie erfindet sich zuletzt ein liebenswürdigers Bild, sie mahlet es aus und liebt es, und wünscht, wie Pygmalion, dass es leben möge, unwissend, dass dieses Bild ein Urbild hat, und dass sie sich nur wieder auf seine Züge besinnt. (XXX, 8)

This instinct nexus -- particularly with respect to its unconscious operation -- will be seen as crucial to the perception of reality in the novels.

The role that instinct plays in Wieland's theory of knowledge is underscored and further explained in the essay "Das Gesicht des Mirza" (1754). Wieland is convinced that instinct has been given to man by God so that man might find the path that leads to the reinstatement of his original greatness and happiness (XXX, 93). And the intrinsic relationship between this instinct and man's insatiability is intimated in yet another essay which appeared in 1754. In "Platonische Betrachtungen über den Menschen," Wieland claims that man is destined for eternity: "Nur diese Wahrheit löset das sonst unbegreifliche Räthsel der menschlichen Begierden auf, die unter den unendlichen Dingen keinen Gegenstand finden, der sie erschöpfen könnte" (XXX, 142). He goes on to state that this vague feeling of our destiny and the tendency to think in terms of eternity are common to all men. All reality and truth has its origin in God (XXX, 139, 163). Man alone -- unique among all creatures -- can have awareness of himself and of his world, and therefore of God. Just as instinct in beasts leads to their fulfillment and preservation, so too does instinct in man lead to the realization of his destiny -- which transcends experiential reality.

The notion that these insatiable human desires imply ultimate, transexperiential realities is repeated and elaborated upon in "Theages. Ueber Schönheit und Liebe," written in the late 1750's.[51] Wieland asserts that the objects of these desires are not chimeras but realities. These yearnings can be stilled if man learns how to go about it properly (XLIV, 62 - 63). (The solution Wieland offers here will be important in another context).

Twenty years later, in the discourse "Ueber das Verhältnis des Angenehmen und Schönen zum Nützlichen" (1775), these same concepts of instinct, longing, and transcendent realities are re-expressed. This time the influence of Plato's Symposium is transparent. Instinct is now seen as the innate sense of beauty and propriety (XLIV, 85), which draws man forward to ever-increasing self-perfec-

tion and realization of his relationship to the whole of creation. Wieland refers to
the various stages of progress man undergoes as "Fortschritte der Menschheit."
As in Diotima's theory of love, man advances from love of the corporeal to love
of the spiritual and moral.

> Durch alle diese Stufen erhebt er sich endlich bis zu der
> höchsten Vervollkommnung seines Geistes, die in seinem
> gegenwärtigen Leben möglich ist, zu dem grossen Begriffe des
> Ganzen wovon er ein Theil ist, zum Ideal des Schönen und Guten,
> zu Weisheit und Tugend, und zur Anbetung der unerforschlichen
> Urkraft der Natur, des allgemeinen Vaters der Geister, dessen
> Gesetze zu erkennen und zu thun zugleich ihr grösstes Vorrecht,
> ihre erste Pflicht und ihr reinstes Vergnügen ist. (XLIV, 85)

The significance of this interpretation of life for Wieland is even more pronounced
in a letter to Zimmermann written nineteen years earlier in September 1756.
Wieland feels called upon to defend the unjustly defiled and reviled mystics. His
contention that mystics are not fanatics or fantasts is reminiscent of the chameleon fable. Like Wieland's picture of mankind, the mystic is drawn onward and
upward by irrational and intuitive forces. Even so, the efficaciousness of their
irrational belief is greater than that of the rational powers exerted by philosophers. [52] Wieland writes:

> Sehr vermutlich kennen Sie die wahren Mysticos nicht durch sich Selbst
> und aus ihren Schriften; ohnezweifel halten Sie dieselben mit grossen
> Hauffen der Gelehrten und Ungelehrten für Phantasten und fanatiques;
> aber wissen Sie auch dass es würklich in meiner Gewalt ist Ihnen zu be-
> weisen, dass Armelle mehr Weise war als alle Philosophen zusammenge-
> nommen, und dass der unfehlbare Weg zum höchsten Grad der Glükselig-
> keit in dieser Welt zu gelangen, der Mysticismus ist, welcher ohne eine
> gäntzl[iche] Verläugnung aller irdischen Dinge und unsrer Selbst nicht
> bestehen kan, und daher zieml[ich] nahe mit dem Eremiten-Leben zusam-
> menhängt. [53]

One might be understandably startled to see the intensive mystical nature of
Wieland's view of mankind in light of the temporal proximity of this "confession"
to his "transformation." Yet it will become clear that Wieland remained true to
a fundamentally mystical interpretation of life. Peregrinus Proteus will be especially revealing in this respect.

In the above letter to Zimmermann Wieland touches upon a theme which figures
in all of the novels under consideration: the hermit's way of life. Don Sylvio grows
up almost totally isolated from his fellow man. Agathon ends his life in a city
which might be likened to a community of monks. Peregrinus Proteus wanders
from city to city and from country to country almost as a solitary and ascetic
pilgrim. The justification for Wieland's assertion that mystics are wiser than

philosophers has already been supplied in the essay "Sympathien." Mystics are very conscious of the spiritual bond between the human soul and the Divine. An image of the mystic is projected in that essay, and Wieland is unequivocal in his claim that the sensitive soul is not chasing fantasms when it prefers metempirical stimuli to sensual stimuli:

> Tausend Gestalten der Dinge gehen vor der denkenden Seele vorbei, ohne sie zu rühren; sie erfindet sich zuletzt ein liebenswürdigers Bild, sie mahlet es aus und liebt es, und wünscht, wie Pygmalion, dass es leben möge, unwissend, dass dieses Bild ein Urbild hat, und dass sie sich nur wieder auf seine Züge besinnt. (XXX, 8)

This is the justification for saying that mystics are wiser than philosophers although they appear to be dreamers and visionaries. Mystics are aware, however vaguely or lucidly, of an ultimate reality which operates behind the visage of this world.

Despite the humanization and relaxation of his ascetic views effected between 1757 and 1768, Wieland clung to his ideal of the mystic. This attitude is evinced by an essay on the concepts of Schwärmerei and Enthusiasmus written in 1775. [54] Schwärmerei generally denotes aberration from the norm, lack of contact with reality, and loss of gesunde Vernunft. On the other hand, in Wieland's terminology (obviously influenced by Shaftesbury's definition) enthusiasm denotes the ability immediately to perceive the Beautiful, the True, and the Good. [55] In the essay, "Schwärmerei und Enthusiasmus," Wieland contends that the two states are similar but not identical. [56] He asserts that it is high time that the terms Schwärmer and Enthusiast be no longer used interchangeably and equally disparagingly. To be sure, both the Schwärmer and the Enthusiast are inspired; yet there is a crucial distinction between the types of inspiration. "Der Schwärmer ist begeistert wie der Enthusiast; nur dass diesen ein Gott begeistert und jenen ein Fetisch" (XLVII, 184). To this comment the author appends a note:

> Man kann wohl Begeisterung zum Mittelpunkt machen. Dem Begeisterten zur einen Seite steht der Enthusiast, zur andern der Schwärmer. Jener erglüht für eine Idee, dieser für eine Schimäre. Jeder will sie anerkant, realisirt wissen, und ist eifrig darin; der Enthusiast wählt nur gute Mittel, dem Schwärmer wird das Mittel durch den Zweck geheiligt. Der Enthusiast ist allezeit mit der Vernunft harmonisch, der Schwärmer nicht. Enthusiasmus ist ein Affekt, Schwärmerei eine Leidenschaft, und daher das Schwärmen, d.i. mit lautem Getös umherschweifen, und zwar in Masse: der Schwärmer will auch Schwarm machen. (XLVII, 184)

Wieland attempts to make this distinction even more meaningful and vivid: "Schwärmerei ist Krankheit der Seele, eigentliches Seelenfieber: Enthusiasmus ist ihr wahres Leben!" (XLVII, 183).

Schwärmerei is defined as "an excitation of the soul by objects which are either not present at all in Nature or are at least not what the intoxicated soul believes them to be" (XLVII, 181). Wieland explains that fanaticism can be equated with Schwärmerei, although the former term is normally reserved for religious Schwärmerei. On the other hand, Enthusiasmus is defined as the "effect of the absolute perception of the Beautiful, the Good, the Perfect, and the Divine in Nature and in our soul, Nature's mirror" (XLVII, 181-182).

Wieland chose the term "enthusiasm" because of its etymology. It designated that state of the soul in which exceptional powers are present. The ancients interpreted these powers to be the result of the presence and activity of a god in the soul. "Diesem Zustande der Seele weiss ich keinen schicklichern angemessneren Namen als Enthusiasmus. Denn das, wovon dann unsre Seele glüht, ist göttlich; ist (menschenweise zu reden) Strahl, Ausfluss, Berührung von Gott; und diese feurige Liebe zum Wahren, Schönen und Guten ist ganz eigentlich Einwirkung der Gottheit, oder (wie Plato sagt) Gott in uns" (XLVII, 182).

It should now be evident that Wieland's understanding of the mystic is coincident with this view of the enthusiast. The object of the enthusiast's yearning is the True, the Beautiful, and the Good: concepts which have been transmitted by Plato and Shaftesbury. It is this longing for the True, the Beautiful, and the Good which differentiates the enthusiast from the Schwärmer. The distinction between Schwärmerei and Enthusiasmus will become crucial in the interpretation of the three heroes: Don Sylvio, Agathon, and Peregrinus. Each figure reflects Wieland's preoccupation with these inspired states. A true appraisal of his interpretation of Schwärmerei and enthusiasm is the key to a proper understanding and evaluation of the style and structure of the three novels with which we are concerned.

The state of enthusiasm indicates the innate relationship between man's intuition of the absolutely True, Beautiful, and Good and his attempt to still the insatiable longing for them. We have seen that Wieland was convinced that man would not have these desires if they could not be satisfied. In "Theages" Wieland suggests that man can placate these longings if he goes about it properly. The question now posed is "What is the proper procedure?" The answer further underscores the distinction between Enthusiasmus and Schwärmerei. The clue to the answer is inherent in the dualism of human nature: spirit and animal. As long as man confuses the insatiable longings of the spirit with the bestial appetites of the flesh, man cannot attain that happiness to which he has been predestined.

According to the author, Nature herself points a finger at this seemingly obvious truth. "Die Stimme der ganzen Natur, die mir Gott offenbarte, brachte mich unmittelbar auf den Gedanken: 'in einer Welt, wo Gott gleichsam die Seele ist, müsse die Glückseligkeit, für einen jeden, dem die Natur ein Recht gegeben sie zu verlangen, weder schwer zu erwerben noch weit zu suchen seyn'" (XLIV, 63 - 64). The solution to the problem does not lie far off and the attainment of felicity is not difficult once man recognizes the character of his yearning. The solution lies in the recognition of the higher demands and nobler sentiments of the human spirit. Wieland complains that the majority of people and even of philosophers impetuously pursue the satisfaction of their desires without any thought for the nature of these desires. Man must turn his inquiring eye inward and discover there his "wahres Selbst." Once this discovery has been accomplished, then Nature can provide man with the guideline which will assure felicity. It is important to point out that Nature fulfills two functions in this theory. She first directs man's gaze inward so that man can attain the perspicacity of vision necessary to interpret Nature in her true context; then she directs man's attention outward so that he may see the reflection of God in Nature (cf. "Theages"; XLIV, 64 - 68). Wieland's high estimation of Nature is reflected when he says: "Die Natur ist das, was uns fähig macht, den Endzweck unsers Daseyns zu erfüllen; der Endzweck unsers Daseyns ist eben das, was ich Glückseligkeit genennt habe; man muss also der Natur gemäss leben, um glückselig zu seyn" (XLIV, 66).

Theages, the chief figure in the dialogue, has retired from the bustle of the world with his only daughter to live the life of a hermit. He endeavors to instruct his daughter in the principles of life he has gleaned from Nature. ("Theages . . . hat sich seit dem Tod einer geliebten Gemahlin diese Gegend ausgewählt, um daselbst . . . die einzige Tochter . . . nach einem Plan zu erziehen, den er der Natur selbst abgelernt hat" [XLIV, 53].) The individual who has been so instructed and who is true to these principles is described as "a soul full with goodness, uprightness, and love" (XLIV, 53).

Theages is aware that his daughter will lack polish ("Weltklugheit") because of her cloistered life, but he is unconcerned. Inculcated with these fundamental principles of Nature, she can go out into the world and learn this "politische Tugend," which after all has no place in man's truly natural state (XLIV, 54). These principles of Nature, so important to the formation of man's character, are referred to as symmetry and perfection (XLIV, 54). The full impact of this man-Nature nexus is given in the definition of Enthusiasmus: the "effect of the absolute perception of the Beautiful, the Good, the Perfect, and the Divine in Nature and in our soul, Nature's mirror" (XLVII, 181-182).

This high estimation of the effectiveness of the "natural" way of life is evident in the other semi-philosophic essays dating from the mid-1750's, the "end" of Wieland's "seraphic" phase. For example, in "Sympathien," Wieland recommends that the reader turn to Plato or Shaftesbury to learn what Nature and virtue are (XXX, 39). In "Platonische Betrachtungen über den Menschen" (1754), Wieland states that it is man's destiny to live according to the laws of Nature, which are in effect the laws of God (XXX, 165). Finally, in a letter to Sophie La Roche about ten years after the publication of these writings, Wieland confides: "Cependant comme moi je suis philosophe, et grand Clerc en fait de Platonisme, je suis persuadé qu'il faut interroger, écouter et suivre la Mere Nature en tout." 57

The Plato-Shaftesbury influence on Wieland's view of Nature is obvious from the above explication. One final point of comparison between Wieland and the two thinkers is the understanding of the respective roles of reason and intuition in the pursuit of the True, the Beautiful, and the Good.

As early as 1754 Wieland points out the necessary cooperation of the head and the heart in the pursuit of genuine felicity. In the dialogue "Timoklea. Ein Gespräch über scheinbare und wahre Schönheit" (1754), Wieland relates an imaginary discussion between Socrates and the beautiful and charming Timoklea. Socrates directs the discussion to a consideration of the source of beauty. He is pleasantly surprised to discover that Timoklea is not the thoughtless, frivolous lass he expected her to be. He sees that she is on the way to becoming an enthusiast. Hoping to facilitate her progress toward a life of genuine happiness and virtue, he explains:

> Die Weisheit ist nicht schwer. Alles hängt bloss davon ab, dass
> man eine kleine Reihe von Wahrheiten deutlich einsehen lerne,
> und von ihrem unschätzbaren Werth, von ihrer göttlichen
> Schönheit so eingenommen werde, dass man sie zu beständigen
> Regeln seines Lebens mache. Das meiste hierbei thut ein
> gefühlvolles und redliches Herz; dieses kommt dem Verstand
> allezeit zu Hülfe; und wie die Exempel nicht selten sind, dass
> jemand durch die Liebe mit einer bewundernswürdigen Behendigkeit
> zur Vollkommenheit in einer Wissenschaft oder Kunst gestiegen
> ist: so ist kein Zweifel, dass man in der Bestrebung nach
> Weisheit und Tugend viel weiter kommen wird, wenn die Seele
> schon mit edeln Begierden nach dem Schönen und Vortrefflichen
> angefüllt ist. (XLIV, 15; italics mine)

The heart is comparable to a sixth sense organ or receptor which is "programmed" to receive only certain sensations. The heart, or intuition, is capable of "perceiving" the True-Beautiful-Good complex without rational mediation. [58] It is this psychic receptor which makes man aware of his higher nature and conscious of his moral destiny. It is obvious from the quoted passage that this moral sense is considered to be more important than reason. ("Verstand" clearly means "Verstand" and "Vernunft" in this context.) The priority of the heart is further underscored in the dialogue when Socrates claims that psychic health is even more mandatory than physical health in the fulfillment of true human destiny. Body and soul are said to be healthy when they are in a natural state (XLIV, 20).

Yet the heart alone is not enough; reason is also necessary. The heart without the head is like a lodestar without a ship to guide. The head without the heart is like a seaman who must navigate his vessel through dangerously raging seas without this celestial aid. The seaman must evaluate myriad phenomena which only imperfectly reflect the distant brilliance of the obscured lodestar, and on the basis of this faulty knowledge plot the ship's course. And even as the seaman can misjudge the wind and the waves and so be driven from his course, or even as the radiant star can be obscured by clouds, so too can man lose sight of his destiny and be deceived by phenomena or appearances. Nor can a ship reach its destination

-- even under the most favorable circumstances -- if it does not set sail. So too is it with man's destiny. It is not enough to be aware of his moral calling; man must attempt to cross the sea. Thus reason is just as crucial in the fulfillment of man's spiritual objective. In "Theages," Wieland gives further expression to the necessity of harmonious integration of the heart and the mind, as well as to his rejection of one-sidedness with respect to either.

Of primary importance to this question of the mind and the heart in the perception of the Highest Good is the essay "Was ist Wahrheit?" (1776). Wieland emphasizes the danger that arises when man makes either reason (XXX, 183) or feeling (XXX, 186) his sole guide in life. The abuse and misuse of reason has produced such skeptics as Karneades, Pyrrho, Sextus, Le Bayer, Bayle, and Hume. Wieland asserts that it is this abuse of reason which "has always been most intent on undermining and overturning the only supports of our miserable existence: faith and love" (XXX, 183). Although the author also considers rule by feeling alone to be erroneous and improper, he does not deal as harshly with it. He states quite explicitly that the individual who is guided by feeling alone should be left undisturbed as long as he does not annoy his fellow man. (This is particularly true in connection with metaphysical and aesthetic questions). However, if the "aberrant" individual attempts to force his opinion on others, as Don Quixote did, then action must be taken to counteract the deleterious views of the individual (XXX, 187).

Despite his repugnance for one-sidedness, [59] Wieland stresses the fact that the heart is more reliable than the head. He writes (Shaftesbury's concept of intrinsic experience is transparent here): "Ich kann von der Natur, von unsichtbaren Mächten, kurz von Ursachen, die ich nicht kenne, getäuscht werden: aber so lange ich mir bewusst bin, dass ich etwas gefühlt, beschaut, betastet habe, -- so glaube ich meinem Gefühl mehr als einer ganzen Welt die dagegen zeugte, und als allen Filosofen, die mir a priori beweisen wollten ich träume oder rase" (XXX, 186). The heart is the primary perceptor of the Highest Good in Wieland's epistemological view because of this aspect of intrinsic experience. Once man is convinced of the reality and validity of the metaphysical and moral values for the fulfillment of his ultimate destiny, he cannot be persuaded that this intrinsic experience is fallacious. In other words, once moral awareness is cultivated it cannot be lost.

The capability for moral awareness is inborn in all men, but some men neglect to develop this sense.

> Man hat sich schon lange über die Leute aufgehalten, die ein unerklärliches inneres Licht zum Leitstern ihres Glaubens und Lebens machen; man hat sie in Schimpf und Ernste bestritten, zu Boden gespottet und zu Boden räsonirt: und dennoch haben unläugbar alle Menschen etwas, das die Stelle eines solchen innern Lichts vertritt, und das ist -- das innige Bewusstseyn dessen, was wir fühlen. (XXX, 184)

Wieland's concept of this inner consciousness is reminiscent of the Sympathie motif discussed earlier, which derives from Plato's doctrine of previous existences. The author states further in the passage that this inner consciousness is always right, is infallible -- provided the individual is aware of the difference between his conceits and his experiences: "Unter allen Kennzeichen der Wahrheit ist diess unläugbar das sicherste; vorausgesetzt, dass ein Mensch überhaupt gesund und des Unterschieds seiner Empfindungen und Einbildungen sich bewusst ist" (XXX, 184). The investigation of the novels will show that this distinction between "Einbildungen" and "Empfindungen" is crucial for their philosophical content. A further connotation of the above passage is that the healthy person can distinguish between that which he has merely imagined and that which he has actually experienced. The converse assumption is of course that the unhealthy person cannot.

Even in an ideal state of harmonious cooperation of mind and heart man is not capable of definite and conclusive knowledge in the empirical sense. Wieland explicitly states in this essay on truth that each man's perception of Truth is subjective. Because each individual perception of Truth is contingent upon a multitude of factors, Wieland is repulsed by the idea that men can consider their opinions to be axiomatic and irreproachable (XXX, 189). Truth is not a physical object which can be easily isolated, studied, and comprehended. Rather, Truth is a nebulous complex of intrinsic relationships harmoniously united in the godhead. These divine principles are reflected in the laws of Nature. Yet, because of his finiteness, no man is capable of complete apprehension of the affinity between natural and divine laws. Thus Truth, although ubiquitous in Nature, can be apprehended only in part. Each individual perceives it from constantly limited perspectives. ". . . jeder sieht sie [Wahrheit] nur stückweise, nur von hinten, oder nur den Saum ihres Gewandes, -- aus einem andern Punkte, in einem andern Lichte; jeder vernimmt nur einige Laute ihres Göttermundes, keiner die nämlichen" (XXX, 188 - 189). This relativity of the perception of Truth is of prime importance for Wieland. [60] In fact, it is a leitmotif in the three novels under analysis.

We should bear in mind that in Wieland's view the heart intuits Truth (i.e., the Highest Good), whereas the mind receives and evaluates sensations occasioned by phenomena (which are imperfect representations of the absolutes). Therefore, when Wieland speaks of the relativity of the perception of Truth, he is referring to the rational functions of the head, not to the intuitive processes of the heart.

In conclusion, it can be asserted that Wieland's epistemological theory relies heavily on the intuitive processes of the heart. It is the "intrinsic experience" aspect of human intuition which reveals to man the affinity of the human soul to God and of Nature to God. Thus God, Nature, and man form a pyramid, the apex of which is God. The intuition discloses the indisputable supremacy of the spirit over the flesh, of altruism over egoism, of the world to come over the present world. Intuition supplies man with a vague awareness of this triangular relationship. Reason, in cooperation with this vague awareness, can discern the specifics of the intrinsic connections and thus better approximate definite knowledge. Without this intuitive consciousness reason is at the mercy of myriad phenomena and the resultant dangers of skepticism and sophistry. Thus it should be evident that Wieland was not merely an empiricist. His epistemological theory demands both detailed observation of the external world (perceived and evaluated by the Verstand-Vernunft nexus) and attentiveness to the vibrations of the internal world (emitted by the intuition). Wieland's oft-repeated disparagement of Locke's strictly empirical theory of knowledge stresses the duality of rationality and irrationality in his own epistemology. For example, Wieland asserts in his essay "Ueber die Ideale der griechischen Künstler" (1777):

> Ich trage für Herrn Johann Locke und seinen grossen Grundsatz
> nihil est in intellectu etc. alle gebührende Achtung. Die Epikuräer
> und viele andre ehrliche Leute haben ein paar tausend Jahre vor
> ihm eben so viel davon gewusst als er. Aber, trotz diesem grossen
> Axion, womit man . . . auf einmal so grosse Stücke herunter hauen
> kann, wird auch von der kleinen Welt in unserm Hirnkasten ewig
> wahr bleiben, was Shakespeares Hamlet von Himmel und Erde sagt:
> 'Es giebt gar viele Dinge da, wovon sich unsre Filosofie nichts
> träumen lässt.' (XLV, 217)[61]

Let us turn to the first of the three novels, Die Abenteuer des Don Sylvio von Rosalva, for an elucidation of Wieland's epistemological views as formulated shortly after the author's "transformation."

NOTES

1. Sources for the discussion of epistemology are: Ernst Cassirer, The Philosophy of the Enlightenment (Boston: Beacon Press, 1955); Frederick Copleston, S.J., A History of Philosophy: Modern Philosophy, VI, Part 1, "The French Enlightenment to Kant" (Garden City, N.Y.: Doubleday & Co., 1960); Philosophie, ed. A. Diemer and Ivo Frenzel (Hamburg: Fischer Bücherei, 1967); Encyclopedia of Philosophy (New York: Macmillan, 1967), "The History of Epistemology", III, 8-38; Hans M. Wolff, Die Weltanschauung der deutschen Aufklärung in geschichtlicher Entwicklung, 2nd ed. (Bern & München: Francke, 1963).

2. Eric A. Blackall, The Emergence of German as a Literary Language 1700 - 1775 (Cambridge: Cambridge University Press, 1959), pp. 387-390, discusses the literary significance of Kopf and Herz and their refinements Witz and Empfindung.

3. Encyclopedia, III, 10, 25, 29.

4. Wielands Briefwechsel, I, "Briefe der Bildungsjahre (6.1.1750 - 6.2.1760)," ed. Hans Werner Seiffert (Berlin: Akademie Verlag, 1962), 80. Cited hereafter as Seiffert.

5. Ibid.

6. Cf. Encyclopedia, III, 17; Friedrich Sengle, C.M. Wieland (Stuttgart, 1949), p. 476. Cited hereafter as Sengle.

7. To be sure, Plato and Shaftesbury were not the only philosophical influences on Wieland. There is ample evidence to the contrary in Wieland's correspondence. Cf. Seiffert, I, 50 (to Bodmer, 3.6.1752); C.M. Wieland, Sämmtliche Werke, ed. J.G. Gruber (Leipzig, 1818-26), V, 220. Hereafter references to this edition will be cited in text; footnote references will be cited as Gruber. Leibnitz' early influence on Wieland has been discussed by Emil Ermatinger, Die Weltanschauung des jungen Wieland (Frauenfeld: Huber, 1907), but need not be incorporated here because Leibnitz' influence was soon overshadowed by Plato's. H. Wollfheim has investigated the influence of the moral philosophers, Socrates and Christ, on the formation of Wieland's Humanitätsbild, in Wielands Begriff der Humanität (Hamburg: Hoffmann & Campe, 1949), pp. 153-201 et passim.

8. Cf. Ermatinger, Die Weltanschauung, pp. 96, 98, 101; Sengle, pp. 73-74.

9. Encyclopedia, III, 11.

10. Ermatinger also indicates Wieland's concurrence with Plato and Leibnitz concerning the subjectivity of sense sensation. Die Weltanschauung, p. 50.

11. Gruber, XXX, 206-207n.

12. Encyclopedia, III, 10.

13. Gruber, XXX, 207-208n.

14. Plato, Symposium, trans. Benjamin Jowett (New York: Bobbs-Merrill, 1956), p. 47.

15. Ibid., pp. 52-53.

16. Ermatinger, Die Weltanschauung, p. 112.

17. In March 1758 Wieland wrote to Zimmermann: "Je vise au Caractère du Vir-
    tuoso, que Shaftesbury peint si admirablement dans tous ses écrits; j'en suis
    bien éloigné encore, mais j'y vise pourtant." Seiffert, p. 326 (3.12.1758).
    Ermatinger, Die Weltanschauung, pp. 138-139, clarifies the difference be-
    tween the concept of the virtuoso and kalokagathia which Wieland fused into
    one concept.
18. Ermatinger, Die Weltanschauung, p. 127.
19. Leo Stettner, Das philosophische System Shaftesburys und Wielands "Agathon"
    (Halle / Saale, 1929), pp. 177-178.
20. Cf. Ermatinger, Die Weltanschauung, p. 112; Charles Elson, Wieland and
    Shaftesbury (New York, 1913), p. 121.
21. C. M. Wieland: La formation et l'évolution de son esprit jusqu'en 1772 (Paris:
    Boivin, 1938), p. 284.
22. Cassirer, p. 314; see also p. 152.
23. Elson, pp. 58-59.
24. Stettner, pp. 91-92.
25. It must be understood in this context that the dualism of feeling and reason
    does not parallel the dichotomy of sensuality and asceticism. The nexus head
    and heart is interpreted solely in relation to their cognitive functions. Thus
    Wieland's claim that "Musarion" is an articulation of his philosophy (cf. DB,
    I, 186; letter to Riedel, 6.2.1768) does not necessarily disprove the episte-
    mologic premise of this study. He is obviously referring to an avoidance of
    the extreme moral positions of Theophon (a Pythagorean) and Kleantes (a
    Stoic). It is intresting that, although Wieland dismisses Kleantes entirely
    (cf. XII, 62), he does not treat Theophon disparagingly (cf. XII, 57, 61-62).
    Musarion explicitly affirms: "Der Mann, nicht seine Lehren; / Das Wahre
    nicht, obgleich (nach aller Schwärmer Art) / Sein glühendes Gehirn es mit
    Schimären paart. / Nur diese trifft der Spott" (XII, 57). The verse narrative
    does reflect, however, the author's penchant for balance, for a harmony of
    the extremes. Cf. also Charlotte Craig, Christoph Martin Wieland as the
    Originator of the Modern Travesty in German Literature (Chapel Hill: Univer-
    sity of North Carlina Press, 1970), pp. 72-73.
26. Stettner, p. 88.
27. An interesting discussion of the concept of the inner voice in the eighteenth
    century is found in Norman Hampson, The Enlightenment (Baltimore: Penguin
    Books, 1968), chap. 6, pp. 186-217. Hampson points out both the indepen-
    dence and the superiority of man's intuitive powers. With regard to the first,
    he says: "Sentiment came to be accepted as a source of a kind of knowledge
    to which intelligence could not aspire, and as an arbiter of action" (p. 186).
    With regard to the second, he writes: "The superiority of the intuitive power
    was not confined to ethics. Even as a source of ideas, the imagination was
    felt to be quicker and bolder in perception than plodding reason" (p. 193).
28. Stettner, p. 173.
29. Ibid.
30. Ibid., pp. 89-90.
31. Shaftesbury, quoted by Stettner, p. 88.

32. C. M. Wieland, Auswahl Denkwürdiger Briefe, ed. Ludwig Wieland (Wien, 1815), I, 7 (letter of 11.7.1763). Hereafter cited as DB. See also David Hume's statement concerning the effect of sentiment as expressed in "Of the Standard of Taste," in Essays Moral, Political and Literary: "All sentiment is right; because sentiment has a reference to nothing beyond itself, and is always real, wherever a man is conscious of it. But all determinations of the understanding are not right; because they have a reference to something outside themselves, to wit, real matter of fact; and are not always conformable to that standard." Cited in Cassirer, p. 307. Cf. also Goethe's assertion Sophienausgabe, XXXVI, 335: "Der geistreiche Mann [Wieland] spielte gern mit seinen Meinungen, aber ... niemals mit seinen Gesinnungen."

33. Lange, "Zur Gestalt des Schwärmers," p. 155.

34. Stettner, pp. 182-183.

35. Wolff, Die Weltanschauung, p. 30, defines gesunde Vernunft thus: "Nur soweit die Vernunft sich auf die Probleme dieser Welt und dieses Lebens beschränkt und sich dem Gesichtspunkt der Nützlichkeit unterwirft, kann sie zu positiven Resultaten führen, nur dann kann sie als 'gesunde Vernunft' gelten."

36. Goethe, Werke, ed. Auftrage der Grossherzogin von Sachsen (Weimar: Hermann Böhlau, 1887-1912), XXXVI, 323.

37. Gotthold E. Lessing, Gesammelte Werke (München: Hanser, 1959), "Briefe die neueste Literatur betreffend," II, 185.

38. See, for example, Ermatinger's unequivocal comment in Die Weltanschauung, p. 112, or Sengle, p. 90: "Nicht nur eine Abkehr vom christlichen Mystizismus, sondern auch vom platonischen Idealismus." Cf. also Paul Kluckhohn, Die Auffassung der Liebe in der Literatur des 18. Jahrhunderts und in der deutschen Romantik (Tübingen: Niemeyer, 1966), p. 175: "Wielands Entwicklung von mystischer Schwärmerei zu nüchterner epikuräischer Auffassung." Ermatinger later gives a succinct and accurate account of the vicissitudes Wieland underwent between 1746 and 1768 in Deutsche Dichter: 1750-1900 (Bonn: Athenäum, 1961), pp. 38-40, Ermatinger's conclusions substantiate my own argument.

39. Cf. Seiffert, I, 333 (letter to Zimmermann, 4.17.1758); C. M. Wieland, Neue Briefe: vornehmlich an Sophie von La Roche, ed. Robert Hassencamp (Stuttgart, 1894), p. 11 (letter to Sophie von La Roche, 10.25.1760). Hereafter cited as Hassencamp. C. M. Wieland, Ausgewählte Briefe von C. M. Wieland, an verschiedene Freunde in den Jahren 1751-1810 geschrieben und nach der Zeitfolge geordnet (Zürich, 1815), II, 241-242 (letter to Julie Bondely, 7.16. 1764). Cited hereafter as AB. DB, I, 150-151 (letter to Sophie von La Roche, 3.20.1770); AB, III, 385 (letter to Leonhard Meister, 12.28.1787).

40. AB, II 194-195 (11.8.1762).

41. Seiffert, I, 415 (3.27.1759).

42. Seiffert, II, 374.

43. Hassencamp, p. 10 (10.25.1760).

44. Wieland writes to Zimmermann on March 8, 1764: "Je vois cependant par les petites questions que vous me faites dans votre dernière lettre, que vous vous avez mis dans la tête, que pour être revenu des rêveries de Platon et de la frivolité sublime des spéculations de l'autre monde, il faut absolument que je

fusse devenu Epicuri de grege porcus, en quoi vous vous trompez assurément."
AB, II, 224.

45. Sengle, p. 90.

46. Ibid., p. 75.

47. Seiffert, I, 431.

48. Hermann Müller-Solger, pp. 72-77, also argues that Wieland's "grosse Wand-
    lung" was not as radical as Sengle (p. 92) would have us believe. Müller-Sol-
    ger bases his contention on the intellectual relationship between the Cyrus
    fragment and Agathon and introduces further evidence in the form of the simi-
    lar relationships between the heroes Araspes and Cyrus, Agathon and Archy-
    tas, Peregrinus and Agathodämon. He sees the depiction of the first member
    of each pair as "analytic" and that of the second as "synthetic." The continui-
    ty of Wieland's thought of the pre- and post-"transformation" periods is effec-
    tively revealed for Müller-Solger in the constant vacillation between the ana-
    lytic description of experience and the culminating synthetic realization of the
    ideal.

49. C.M. Wieland, Sämmtliche Werke (Leipzig: Göschen, 1857), XXV, 23. Cited
    hereafter as Göschen.

50. Emil Ermatinger, "Das Romantische bei Wieland," Neue Jahrbücher für das
    klassische Altertum, Geschichte und deutsche Literatur (Leipzig: Teubner,
    1908), XXI, No. 3, 223-227, examines Wieland's use of the concept of Sym-
    pathie. He not only demonstrates its relationship to Plato's thought but indi-
    cates its affinity to Leibnitz' theory of pre-established harmony (pp. 225-227).
    Ermatinger concludes that "Sympathie for Wieland, even in his old age, was
    a thoroughly irrational, symbolic, and therefore romantic concept" (p. 227).

51. Gruber dates the work 1760, but B. Seiffert believes it was written before
    1758. See "Prolegomena zu einer Wieland-Ausgabe," Abhandlungen der könig-
    lichen Preussischen Akademie der Wissenschaften (Berlin, 1904), I, 49.

52. Plato had already indicated the efficaciousness of true belief -- at least in
    connection with its practical effects. Encyclopedia, III, 10.

53. Seiffert, I, 279.

54. The essay is part of a controversy over enthusiasm and Schwärmerei which
    aroused much interest in the mid-1770's. Cf. Gruber, Wielands Leben, LII,
    179-282, esp. 184-214, 226-232.

55. Wieland himself did not consistently differentiate between these terms prior
    to 1775, as is evinced by his use of "Enthusiasmus" and "Enthusiast" in his
    correspondence. Cf. AB, II, 241-242 (letter to Julie Bondely, 7.16.1764);
    and AB, III. 5 (letter to Gleim, 8.15.1770). According to Wieland's definition,
    the condition referred to in these instances should properly be described as
    Schwärmerei.

56. Even when this distinction is observed by critics it is not always consistently
    pursued. See Reimer, pp. 63, 106, 110. For a discussion of the distinction,
    see Lange, "Zur Gestalt des Schwärmers," and Ermatinger, "Das Romanti-
    sche bei Wieland," pp. 276-279.

57. Hassencamp, p. 94.

58. Oettinger, p. 127, contends that reason is the sole cognitive agent for Wieland.
    Oettinger's study is based on the assumption that Wieland rejected all specu-
    lative philosophy in favor of a strict empirical method.

59. Wolfram Buddecke, C. M. Wielands Entwicklungsbegriff und die "Geschichte des Agathon" (Göttingen: Vandenhoeck & Ruprecht, 1966), p. 64, reaches the same conclusion when considering the function of the mind in Wieland's thought.
60. See also "Magnetismus," ed. Gruber, XLVIII, 92-120.
61. Hamlet's comment, "Es giebt gar viele Dinge da, wovon sich unsre Filosofie nichts träumen lässt," is also alluded to in the first edition of Agathon (1767; rpt. Berlin: Akademie Verlag, 1961), p. 274; in Gruber, X, 245; in "Magnetismus," ed. Gruber, XLVIII, 92; and in "Eine Lustreise ins Elysium," ed. Gruber, XL, 252. Klaus Oettinger completely overlooks this rejection of Locke's strictly empirical epistemology and as a result misjudges the extent "Erfahrung" modifies "Phantasie." Cf. his concluding chapter "Wieland und Locke," pp. 141-145.

Chapter 2

DON SYLVIO: THE QUESTION OF FANTASY AND REALITY

Tu si hic esses, aliter sentias.
-- Terence, Andria (Act II, Scene 1)

Having completed the course of study at Klosterberg near Magdeburg in the spring
of 1749, Wieland stopped off in Erfurt en route to his home in Biberach. His stop-
over was to last a year. During that period Wieland associated with Johann Wilhelm
Baumer, who introduced him to contemporary philosophy. These studies intensi-
fied Wieland's interest in Bayle, Voltaire, and Wolff which he had privately pursued in Klosterberg. More significant for the author's later poetic development,
however, was his introduction to Cervantes' masterpiece, Don Quixote, a work
which impressed him deeply.

Wieland's first completed novel, Die Abenteuer des Don Sylvio von Rosalva, is
written in the manner of Don Quixote. Although Don Sylvio seems at first glance
to be merely a delightful product of rococo satire, evidence of Wieland's philosophical nature is at once apparent beneath the novel's frivolous façade. That Don
Sylvio is philosophically serious is attested in the author's correspondence. In
August 1763 Wieland wrote his friend and publisher, Solomon Gessner: "Es [Don
Sylvio] ist eine Art von satyr[ischem] Roman, der unter dem Schein der Frivolität
philosophisch genug ist." [1] In a subsequent letter to Gessner, Wieland is even more
explicit concerning the latent earnestness of his work: "Man scheint manchmal zu
spassen und narriren, und philosophiert besser als Chrysippus und Kreantor. Ich
zweifle sehr daran, ob Sie . . . bei einer zwoten Durchlesung sich in der Idee be-
stärkt finden werden, dass der Autor des Don Sylvio keine bessere Absicht gehabt
habe, als dem geneigten Publico, wie Sie sagen, einen Spass zu machen." [2] There
is evidently more to Wieland's first novel than meets the eye. Korff's later comment about Wieland's novels can be accepted as entirely accurate, even for Don
Sylvio. Korff characterized them as an "Aufbau einer romanhaften Handlung um
einen philosophischen Mittelpunkt." [3]

Because Wieland described his first novel as a "satiric work which is philosophic
enough," we can reasonably expect a two-pronged approach: one satirical, destruc-
tive, and negative; the other philosophical, constructive, and positive. On the one
hand, he subjects vice or folly to ridicule and reprobation. On the other, he investigates the facts and principles of reality and of human nature. Criticism of Don
Sylvio's naive belief in wondrous beings and of Pedrillo's primitive superstition
has been sufficiently noted. With this in mind, I will concern myself primarily
with the philosophic content of Don Sylvio and with its impact on the structure and

style of the novel,[4] without, however, neglecting the satirical aspects. Indeed, it would be difficult to overlook the satire, since Wieland uses it to point the way to the deeper significance of this novel.

The novel recounts the quixotic adventures of young Don Sylvio, raised by his spinster aunt, Donna Mencia, in almost complete isolation from the world on their modest estate at Rosalva in Spain. The boy was an avid reader of fairy tales. The almost continuous perusal of fantastic adventure stories, coupled with the youth's isolation from the world, turned his head even as chivalric romances had so intensly influenced Cervantes' hero.

One day, while pursuing a blue butterfly,[5] Don Sylvio happens upon a medallion in the forest. To his inflamed imagination this butterfly is by no means ordinary. Rather, it is an enchanted princess longing for release. Don Sylvio associates the picture of the beautiful woman on the medallion with the blue butterfly and convinces himself that the butterfly is a princess who has been magically transformed. The medallion seems to be a sign of her favor, and he feels chosen to release his beloved princess (love at first sight!) from the power of the wicked witch Fanferlüsch. During these flights of fancy the butterfly indifferently flies off.

Impelled by the desire to find his princess, Don Sylvio sallies forth into the world with his servant-companion Pedrillo (modeled after Sancho Panza).[6] In the course of their adventures they help rescue a young woman, Jacinte, from the hands of abductors. The two men accompanying Jacinte are Don Eugenio, who is in love with her, and his friend Don Gabriel. It becomes known later that Jacinte is Don Sylvio's long-lost sister and that Don Eugenio is Donna Felicia's brother. Donna Felicia proves to be the woman pictured on the medallion; in fact, she had lost the portrait only shortly before Don Sylvio found it. After several quixotic experiences, Don Sylvio and Pedrillo stumble upon Donna Felicia's summer house at Lirias. In effect, the search for an imaginary princess ultimately leads Don Sylvio to true love and a recognition of his folly. The novel traces the transition from a state of profound naiveté to one of budding cosmopolitanism. At the tale's end, Don Sylvio sets out on the prerequisite extended travels throughout Europe before returning to marry his beloved Donna Felicia.

In the encounter of the dreamer with the world, the nature of both imagination and reality are more closely examined. The strange and fantastic events are so depicted as to appear not only probable in their context but also natural.[7] This discussion of <u>Don Sylvio</u> is an attempt to elucidate the relation between imagination and reality. "Denn," to speak with Wolfgang Preisendanz, "nicht die Abenteuer des Don Sylvio als solche, nicht der Zusammenhang der Begebenheiten an sich sind wesentlich; erzählenswert sind sie nur, sofern sich in ihnen ein subjektives Wirklichkeitsverhältnis manifestiert."[8]
Early in the novel the author draws attention to an aspect of reality which is of the utmost importance for the problem of reality as expressed in this work.

So wie es nehmlich allen <u>Egoisten</u> zu Trotz, Dinge giebt die wirklich <u>ausser</u>

uns sind, so giebt es andre, die bloss in unserm Gehirn existiren. Die erstern sind, wenn wir gleich nicht wissen dass sie sind; die andern sind nur,
in so fern wir uns einbilden dass sie seyen. Sie sind für sich selbst— nichts;
aber sie machen auf denjenigen der sie für wirklich hält, die nehmlichen
Eindrücke, als ob sie etwas wären; und ohne dass die Menschen sich des-
wegen weniger dünken, sind sie die Triebfedern der meisten Handlungen des
menschlichen Geschlechts, die Quelle unsrer Glückseligkeit und unsers El-
ends, unsrer schändlichsten Laster und unsrer glänzendsten Tugenden. (V,
67 - 68)

According to this statement, there is a twofold aspect to reality: there is the inner psychic world as well as the external physical one. Furthermore, a certain
paradox is involved in the nature of these two worlds. Wieland asserts that the external world exists even though man may be incapable of knowledge concerning it:
"Die erstern sind, wenn wir gleich nicht wissen dass sie sind." On the other hand,
the constituents of the inner world are completely subjective and exist only in the
imagination: ". . . die andern sind nur, in so fern wir uns einbilden dass sie sey-
en." Despite its imaginary character the subjective world proves to be in effect
the real motivating factor in man's life. Man can be spurred on to the heights of
humanity as well as dragged to the depths of depravity by this subjective reality.

The nature of the intellect and the possibility of knowledge concerning the phenomenal world have been discussed earlier. In regard to Don Sylvio, it is necessary
to point out another function of the intellect which can affect the ordering of sensations: the faculty of imagination. The imagination is capable of forming mental objects not present to the senses. It is the power to synthesize new ideas from elements experienced separately. The inner reality, therefore, has its origin through
the mediation of the imagination, and its continuing existence is dependent upon
this force. The phenomenal world mates with man's fertile imagination to create
a subjectively valid reality. This process is vital to the epistemological concept
of the novel. Wieland alludes to this important phenomenon at the beginning of the
work:

Das angenehme Grauen, das uns beym Eintritt in die dunklen Labyrinth eines dichten Gehölzes befällt, befördert ohne Zweifel den allgemeinen Glauben der ältesten Zeiten, dass die Wälder und Haine von Göttern bewohnt
würden. Der süsse Schauer, das Erstaunen, die gefühlte Erweiterung und
Erhöhung unsers Wesens, die wir in einer heitern Nacht beym Anblick des
gestirnten Himmels erfahren, begünstigte vermuthlich den Glauben, dass
dieser schimmervolle mit unzählbaren, nie erlöschenden Lampen erleuch-
tete Abgrund eine Wohnung unsterblicher Wesen sey.

Aus dieser Quelle kommt es vermuthlich, dass die Landleute, denen ihre
Arbeiten keine Zeit lassen, die verworrenen Eindrücke, welche die Natur
auf sie macht, zu deutlicher Erkenntniss zu erhöhen, überhaupt abergläubi-
scher als andere Leute sind. Daher die körperlichen Geister, womit sie die
ganze Natur angefüllt sehen; daher die unsichtbaren Jagden . . . die Feen

. . . die freundlichen und boshaften Kobolde . . . der Alp, der die Mädchen drückt . . . die Berggeister, die Wassernixen, die Feuermänner. (V, 13)

Nature seemingly gives rise to all psychic realities. This "seemingly" will become increasingly important for Wieland's epistemological view. Nature is the source of superstition, tales of fantasy, and primitive religion. The preternatural and the miraculous are the result of man's biased interpretation of the phenomenal world. The author of Don Sylvio leaves no doubt as to the precise meaning of the above message. The reader is made aware that the author considers all figments of the imagination in the same light. He states, for example, that Alexander's desire for fame was just as chimerical as Don Sylvio's belief in supernatural beings (V, 68). In both instances illusion served as the motivating factor for the protagonist's actions. Wieland's irony is definitely manifest in this equation.

Wieland considers the relationship between Nature and illusion to be paradoxical, that is, ironical. Careful observation of natural processes should prohibit aberrations of the mind; yet under certain conditions Nature does prove to be the source of "erroneous" illusions. "Die Natur selbst, deren anhaltende Beobachtung das sicherste Mittel gegen die Ausschweifungen der Schwärmerey ist, scheint auf der andern Seite durch die unmittelbaren Eindrücke, die ihr majestätisches Schauspiel auf unsere Seele macht, die erste Quelle derselben zu seyn" (V, 12 - 13).

Insight into this crucial problem of fantasy and reality can be gained through structural and character analysis, aspects of satire. This point will be taken up later, but first we must concern ourselves with the perplexing question of how Truth can be ascertained at all. If man cannot trust his sense perceptions or if man cannot rely on the validity of judgments concerning these sensations, how can he know Truth? This is the problem Wieland poses in Don Sylvio.

The reader must constantly make a distinction between that which Don Sylvio has actually experienced and that which he has merely imagined. For Don Sylvio there is no twofold aspect to reality as explained above, because he does not distinguish between his chimeras and Nature. For him the subjective world and the objective one are identical. Don Sylvio's inclination to daydreaming -- of which he is often unaware -- attests his inability to discern a difference between the two spheres. Because he considers his fancies (Einbildungen) to be genuine sensations (Gefühle), and therefore evidence of his consciousness, he does not recognize his aberrations for what they are.

Unvermerkt verwebt sich die Einbildung mit dem Gefühl, das Wunderbare mit dem Natürlichen, und das Falsche mit dem Wahren. Die Seele, die nach dem blinden Instinkt Schimären eben so regelmässig bearbeitet als Wahrheiten, bauet sich nach und nach aus allem diesem ein Ganzes, und gewöhnt sich an, es für wahr zu halten, weil sie Licht und Zusammenhang darin findet, und weil ihre Fantasie mit den Schimären, die den grössten Theil davon ausmachen, eben so bekannt ist als ihre Sinne mit den wirklichen Gegenständen,

von welchen sie ohne sonderliche Abwechslung immer umgeben sind. (V, 11 -
12)

Because of his prejudices and predisposition the events of the external world seem
to confirm the subjective truth of his own personal illusions. Above all, the complete harmony between the psychical and physical realities for the young hero is
confirmed and strengthened through the discovery of the miniature portrait. The
likeness has the same significance for Don Sylvio as the glove did for Prince Friedrich von Homburg. Don Sylvio stumbled upon the portrait while in a state of daydreaming; Prince Friedrich found the glove immediately upon awakening from a
vivid dream. Both objects serve as the undeniable connection between their subjective
fantasies and external reality. Don Sylvio is ultimately led into the world of objective reality by means of the portrait. Because of Don Sylvio's prejudice for the illusory world and its correspondence for him with the external world, Wolfgang
Preisendanz can say: "Die äussere Wirklichkeit wird einem vorgegebenen Erwar-
tungshorizont eingeordnet, ihre Bedeutung von einer vorgängigen Sinnerwartung
statuiert und das auf solche 'Wahrgenommene' wird selbst wieder Bestätigung, Erweiterung und Verdichtung des statuierenden Systems: dies ist das vielfältig vari-
ierte Schema der Abenteuer des Don Sylvio."[9]

The complete agreement in Don Sylvio's mind between the imaginary and phenomenal worlds is above all the result of the hero's misunderstanding of the nature of
the wondrous. He considered it to be a function of Nature, not suspecting that it
was not coincident with the natural. Don Sylvio did not realize that imagination is
merely the intermediary between inner consciousness and sense perceptions. The
youth strikes upon the true relationship between the wondrous and the natural only
late in the novel after he has already begun to suspect that his view of the world
does not coincide with reality. As Wieland says, "Unser Held . . . kam beim ersten Eintritt in diesen anmuthsvollen Hain auf den Gedanken: dass die Fantasie
vielleicht die einzige und wahre Mutter des Wunderbaren sey, welches er bisher,
aus Unerfahrenheit für einen Theil der Natur selbst gehalten" (VI, 269 - 270).

Two thoughts of utmost importance are expressed in this passage: the imagination
as the mother of the wondrous, and Don Sylvio's inexperience. Don Sylvio's misconception of the function and nature of the imagination is understandable when one
considers his social isolation, his lack of sensible guidance, and his one-sided
view of life gained under his aunt's mentorship. How should he not be naive of the
ways of the world and unaware of the fictional character of fairy tales and tales of
knight-errantry! Don Sylvio's mistake is psychologically understandable and logical. Fortunately, the young man is released from his isolation. Through the newly won contact with other men and other opinions, Don Sylvio comes to realize that
his view of the world is subjective. Now he is able to arrive at a healthy concept
of truth and reality. The tone of the novel is set by the blending of the hero's fantasms with his sensations and his final recognition of their true interrelation.

Wieland's essay "Was ist Wahrheit?" addresses itself to this question of ultimate
Truth and its perception. Wieland contends that "Die Wahrheit ist, wie alles Gute,

etwas verhältnismässiges. Es kann vieles für die menschliche Gattung wahr seyn,
was es für höhere oder niedrigere Wesen nicht ist, und eben so kann etwas von
dem einen Menschen mit innigster Ueberzeugung als wahr empfunden und erkannt
werden, was ein andrer mit gleich starker Ueberzeugung für Irrthum und Blend-
werk hält" (XXX, 181 - 182). (Shaftesbury's influence on Wieland is evident here
with the equating of Truth with the Good).[10]

This idea of the subjective perception of Truth is encountered repeatedly in Don
Sylvio. One of the earliest direct allusions to this aspect of apperception is made
by the author in the frog episode. Don Sylvio rescues a frog from a stork because
he believes the creature is actually an enchanted being. Unfortunately, the hero
ends by falling face first into the pond and the presumed fairy ungratefully hops off
into the underbrush. Nonetheless, Don Sylvio's belief in the frog's supernatural
quality is unshaken. Wieland explains the hero's astonishing behavior as follows:

> Vermuthlich werden einige Leser sich wundern, wie es möglich sey, dass
> Don Sylvio albern genug habe seyn können, um aus dem widrigen Ausgange
> dieses Abenteuers nicht den Schluss zu ziehen, der am natürlichsten daraus
> folgte, nehmlich dass der Frosch keine Fee gewesen sey. Allein sie werden
> erlauben, ihnen zu sagen, dass sie die Macht der Vorurtheile und vielleicht
> ihre eigene Erfahrung nicht genugsam in Erwägung ziehen. Nichts ist unter
> den Menschen gewöhnlicher als diese Art von Trugschlüssen; das Vorurtheil
> und die Leidenschaft macht keine andre. (V, 26 - 27)

The influence of passion and prejudice becomes increasingly more manifest as the
reader becomes better acquainted with the various characters in the novel. Each
individual in the novel sees the phenomenal world with different eyes, since each is
predisposed through personal biases and preferences. For this reason Nature is
constantly seen, interpreted, and rendered from a changing point of view. In the
extreme case (e.g., Don Sylvio's), this alteration of Nature is totally unconscious.
Concurrent with an increase in the unawareness of subjective perception is an
increase in the individual's intolerance of differing opinions. Each character represents a different level of this perception-consciousness.

In the chapter "Gegenseitige Gefälligkeiten," Book V, Wieland interrupts the narration to reflect on the nature of the human psyche. He reproves man's tendency
to judge others according to personal standards. He simultaneously justifies subjectivity of perception and attempts to show that perception can only be subjective.

> Es ist wahr, unter allen diesen Egoisten ist keiner unverschämt genug die
> Forderung geradezu zu machen: aber, indem wir alle Meinungen, Urtheile
> oder Neigungen unserer Nebengeschöpfe für thöricht, irrig und ausschwei-
> fend erklären, so bald sie mit den unsrigen in einigem Widerspruche stehen;
> was thun wir im Grunde, anders als dass wir ihnen unter der Hand zu ver-
> stehen geben, dass sie Unrecht haben, ein Paar Augen, ein Gehirn und ein
> Herz für sich haben zu wollen? (VI, 44)

Also in the same chapter, Wieland puts the following words into the mouth of an objective arbiter in a hypothetical dispute. Not only does this reasoning yield the decisive argument for the imaginary controversy, but it also forms the basis of Wieland's own philosophical position.

Ihr Streit ist von einer Art, die nur durch einen gütlichen Vergleich ausgemacht werden kann. Gestehen Sie einander ein, dass Ich gar wohl berechtiget ist, nicht Du zu seyn; hernach setzen Sie Sich jeder an des andern Platz; ich will verloren haben was sie wollen, wenn Sie nicht eben so dächten wie Er, wenn Sie Er, oder in seinen Umständen wären; und so hätte der Streit ein Ende. (VI, 47)

This aspect of relativity is of the utmost significance for Wieland's epistemological view and for the structure of the fiction created. For example, Don Sylvio is remarkable for the various, distinctive roles Wieland assumes. The novel supposedly has an author, a translator, and an editor, each one representing a different point of view. Each of these roles enables Wieland to make a judgment appropriate to the role. Nor is that all: as soon as more than one character appears, the reader is forced to accept a still different judgment. Of course, each judgment originates in Wieland's imagination. Thus, Die Abenteuer des Don Sylvio has a multiplicity of "truths." Don Sylvio, Pedrillo, Donna Felicia, Donna Jacinte, Donna Mencia, Don Gabriel, and Don Eugenio each sees the world from a different perspective, and each has his subjective understanding of Truth.

Wieland's masks account for the unique structure of his shadowgraph-like work. Wieland as author allows each character to have his own opinion, although each opinion originates in the creator's own genius. Wieland as translator gains a certain freedom from the author; and as editor he is enabled to treat the work objectively. The predominant role is naturally that of Wieland as author. By means of this role Wieland creates a believable "real" world which eventually is shown to be a fantasy world. By acting as a commentator, Wieland can remain in the background to direct and criticize. Paradoxically, his comments enhance rather than disperse the illusion: the characters gain psychological depth, and thus the illusion becomes more probable and more plausible.

The role of author as commentator is manifested in the characterization of Donna Mencia. The disparity between the narrator's views and Donna Mencia's results in psychological credibility. Wieland's irony makes it apparent that her perception of the situation was quite different from fact.

Die Dame hatte die Hoffnung, sich durch ihre persönlichen Annehmlichkeiten zu unterscheiden, schon seit dem Sukcessionskriege aufgegeben, in dessen Zeiten sie zwar jung und nicht ungeneigt gewesen war, einen würdigen Liebhaber glücklich zu machen, aber immer so empfindliche Kränkungen von der Kaltsinnigkeit der Mannspersonen erfahren hatte, dass sie mehr als Einmal in Versuchung gerathen war, in der Abgeschiedenheit einer Klosterzelle ein

Herz, dessen die Welt sich so unwürdig bezeugte, dem Himmel aufzuopfern. . . . Sie wurde eine Spröde, und nahm sich vor, ihre beleidigten Reizungen an allen den Unglückseligen zu rächen, welche sie als Wolken ansah, die den Glanz derselben aufgefangen und unkräftig gemacht hatten. Sie erklärte sich öffentlich für eine abgesagte Feindin der Schönheit und Liebe, und warf sich hingegen zur Beschützerin aller dieser ehrwürdigen Vestalen auf, denen die Natur die Gabe der transitiven Keuschheit mitgetheilt hat, von Geschöpfen, deren blosser Anblick hinlänglich wäre, den muthwilligsten Faun — weise zu machen. (V, 3 - 4)

The expressions "persönliche Annehmlichkeiten," "würdig," "glücklich machen," "empfindliche Kränkungen," "Kaltsinnigkeit," "unwürdig," "aufopfern," "beleidigte Reizungen" reflect Donna Mencia's view. On the other hand, the terms "transitive Keuschheit," "den muthwilligsten Faun weise machen." are to be understood from the author's point of view.

The passage is typical of Wieland's involved and ornate style, which abounds in Verschachtelungen and ironic twists. Eric Blackall has pointed out that Wieland uses such involved periods "to characterise persons of a pedantic, hypocritical or affected nature (in speech and reflection), and also (in narrative or author's comments) with wider stylistic functions to contribute to the ironical atmosphere of the whole." [11] The intricate syntax can also be seen as expressing a desire for maximum clarity. [12] The massive verbiage of a Wieland sentence is, in this latter sense, an attempt to get to the heart of the matter, to expose the truth.

A subtle irony pervades the characterization of Donna Mencia. Wieland uses irony to impart to the reader a different, more plausible view of the facts. The narrator becomes personal. The quoted passage demonstrates a common stylistic method, the periodic sentence, which is used to win the reader's sympathy and confidence. The verb "hatte" of the first clause can be used either independently or as an auxiliary. It is not until the reader reaches the end of that clause that he realizes that "hatte" is not used in its own right. The presence of "aufgegeben" reverses the coda, causing the reader to smile to himself. Another example of the periodic sentence appears at the end of the quoted passage. The final three words after the hyphen revoke the positive declaration of the preceding baroque clause, culminating the sentence in a salient point. Rapport between narrator and reader is heightened here and elsewhere through the use of parenthetical intimations, footnotes, and the personal pronoun "unser." At times Wieland even interrupts the story to address the reader directly for a whole chapter. The primary purpose of these stylistic features is rapprochement between author and reader, since they are variations of direct address. These salient features of Wieland's prose highlight the all-pervasive irony.

The role of irony in the novel must not be underestimated. Wieland uses it to express his opinion concerning the nature of perception. Irony, of course, presupposes a common understanding between author and reader while it satirizes another point of view. Nevertheless, this semblance of objectivity does not suspend the basic subjectivity of perception. Even the perspective of irony has no claim to absoluteness.[13] Wieland's irony makes discernible -- in the language itself -- the polarity of fantasy and reality.[14] More precisely, the author is on the one hand the conscious creator of a fiction consistent in itself. The coherence of the creation is such that the reader perceives it as true and real. On the other hand, the author constantly underscores the fictional nature of this presumed reality by means of irony. For example, Don Sylvio's aberrations ultimately lead to his Lebensglück.[15] Irony is thus the moving factor in the novel. The reader is ever aware that the assumed reality of truth is actually the product of the imagination of the individual characters in Don Sylvio and, ultimately, of Wieland.

The ironic implications of the novel are heightened with the introduction of the translator, another of Wieland's masks. Wieland as translator offers us another vantage point from which to view the Romanwirklichkeit. This perspective calls into question the reliability of the author. Wieland as author satirizes his characters; Wieland as translator satirizes himself as author. The various perspectives become more complex. At the beginning of Book 2 the translator remarks:

> Aber nichts desto minder versichert unser Autor, (der sich mit seinem Talent in den Seelen zu lesen nicht wenig zu wissen scheint) dass Rodrigo Sanchez mit dieser Figur die Ehre gehabt habe, beym ersten Anblick über die Abneigung zu siegen, welche sie jederzeit gegen den Ehestand hatte spüren lassen. (V, 74)

The use of irony seemingly reaches a climax here. Simultaneous with the author's use of it against Donna Mencia is the translator's use of it against the author. A fictitious translator mocks an author who is both author and translator!

But Wieland carries irony even further when he dons the mask of editor. He appears in this role in the so-called epilogue, where a third opinion of the novel is offered. As author Wieland explains the logic of his narration; as translator he apparently stresses its delectare aspect; and now, as editor, he seems to emphasize prodesse. Editor Wieland points to several aspects of the novel which the reader might have overlooked. For example, while he maintains that the work is intended solely as innocent entertainment, he admits that a Jansenist acquaintance of his did not consider it harmless:

> Er wollte sichs nicht ausreden lassen, dass die Abenteuer des Don Sylvio eine Allegorie oder Parabola sey, wie er es hiess, deren geheimer Sinn und Endzweck auf nichts geringers als auf den Umsturz des Glaubens, des Evangelii des Pater Quesnell und der Wunder des Herrn von Paris abgesehen sey. 16

How does Wieland intend this comment? Is it a veiled warning of another philosophical or religious aspect concealed behind the façade of frivolity? Or does it merely anticipate the elucidation of Wieland's concept of reality? It is stated that the acquaintance is biased by his Jansenist beliefs. It is also seen later in the novel that occult religion and superstition are the result of fantasy and reality.

Wieland's philosophic view of reality has affected the form of the novel in still another way. For example, editor Wieland maintains in the witty "epilogue" (which by "mistake" appears as a prologue) that Don Sylvio's story is historically true. To give the work the appearance of reality, he attempts to prove its "historicity" by citing a manuscript.[17] However, in the course of Don Sylvio's adventures, the reader catches glimpses of this so-called "historical" truth. Finally, at the conclusion of the hero's adventures there is no longer any doubt about the "truth" of the novel. The country estate at Lirias proves to be the former estate of Gil Blas of Santillana (Lesage's famous fictional hero). Donna Felicia is revealed as the granddaughter of Gil Blas and Dorothea of Jutella. In fact, Donna Felicia closely resembles her grandmother. On the subject of the novel's historical lineage in fictional truth, Wolfgang Jahn says: ". . . im selben Augenblick, da Don Sylvio durch Felicias Hand ins Reich des Wirklichen einzutreten scheint, erklärt der Autor dieses 'Wirkliche' offen zu literarischen Fiktion."[18] The illusion of historical truth is poignantly lifted.[19]

And now, a final word about the structure of the novel as a reflection of the relativity of truth. In Part 2 the narration of Don Sylvio's adventures is twice interrupted by other narratives. One interruption is the Donna Jacinte episode; the other is the fantastic Biribinker tale. These two digressions reflect the polarity of fantasy and reality of which Don Sylvio is an intricate mixture. Donna Jacinte is a noble-minded girl of sixteen who had been constantly exposed to lasciviousness and bad company, yet who had preserved her innocence. Biribinker, on the other hand, is an easily seduced prince, who finds it impossible to be faithful to his beloved milkmaid. These two episodes constitute a comparison and a contrast to our hero. The point of comparison and contrast is not really that of sexual morality, although Don Sylvio himself is morally upright. Rather, the aspect of these two interludes which is of interest here is the "reality" of the respective tales or, more specifically, the setting in which the chief figure operates. Jacinte lives her life in the phenomenal world and is subject to the usual human needs.

Biribinker, however, exists in a purely illusory world. His is a fairy tale — and a fantastic one. (For example, he discovers a world complete with sun and moon in the belly of a whale). In the Biribinker episode, Don Sylvio's tale is elevated to the purely fantastic and all sham of intercourse with the "real" world is rejected. Nevertheless, Biribinker's exotic story is logical and plausible when viewed from Biribinker's standpoint. Donna Jacinte's "fantastic" story is likewise plausible from her point of view, though some readers may rebel at the notion that she could have retained her innocence in the face of so many contrary influences.[20] Thus in both episodes a parallel is drawn to Don Sylvio, since his unusual experiences are also credible from his perspective.[21] Taken together, the three tales can be considered as variations on a theme.

The various individuals in Don Sylvio seem to satirize the hero's subjective view of the world, in that each has his own subjectively valid view. The two interspersed episodes seemingly satirize the world depicted in the novel as a whole by offering the reader alternate composite "realities" which are just as valid according to their own innate laws. Thus does Wieland intensify the relativity of pragmatic truth. In other words, the fictional reality (Romanwirklichkeit) in Don Sylvio is the simultaneous projection of the real and the imaginary in their polarity. The sum of the personal convictions each character has about the validity of his view of Nature and the valid Weltanschauungen of the Don Sylvio, Donna Jacinte, and Biribinker episodes attests to the intersubjectivity of the reality depicted, which seems to form the philosophical basis of Don Sylvio.

At the close of Biribinker's story, the magician Karamussal reveals himself as the all-powerful and all-motivating figure in the narrative. He is actually the creator of Biribinker's fate and the instigator of the situations in which Biribinker becomes involved. Biribinker encountered his difficulties as a result of his name, conferred on him by Karamussal. This revelation of the magician as the creator of the fiction "Biribinker" has its parallel in Don Sylvio. Through the "historical" and literary connection with Gil Blas of Santillana, Wieland reveals himself as the creator and director of the fates of his own characters.

The relativity and subjectivity of truth for Wieland is evident. We should not overlook the fact, however, that Wieland considers Nature the point of departure for all relative views. The importance of Nature as a reflection of Truth for Wieland has already been noted in the preceding chapter. Nature can lead man to the possession of the Highest Good, if viewed in the proper perspective. Unfortunately, she does not reveal herself entirely to any one man. Each man's view of Nature is partial. In order to be reassured of the validity of his partial view of Nature's innate truths, each man must differentiate between his sensations (which affect his heart) and his fancies (which are a result of his mental processes). If one is aware of this distinction, then, in Wieland's words, one is healthy.

This question of a distinction between Empfindungen and Einbildungen and the reliability of the former in sensing Truth is a prime concern in Don Sylvio. For example, Wieland says in the chapter "Worin der Autor eine Tiefe Einsicht in die Geheimnisse der Ontologie an den Tag legt": "Man muss gestehen, dass der schlichte natürliche Menschenverstand, Vernunftinstinkt, Wahrheitssinn, oder wie man es sonst nennen will . . . seinem Besitzer zuweilen weit nützlicher ist als die subtilste Vernunft" (V, 219 - 220).

That the author makes a strict differentiation between the mind (Einbildung) and the heart (Empfindung) in the novel is further apparent in this same chapter. Pedrillo is still a bit stunned by his encounter with Donna Felicia and Laura. While in their presence there was no doubt as to their actual existence. But now that they have gone, he begins to wonder whether he has really experienced or merely dreamed the meeting. The author comments (note the distinction): "Die Verwirrung, die diese Erscheinung in seinem Kopf und in seinem Herzen zurück liess, war so gross, dass uns die blosse Bemühung, eine Beschreibung davon zu machen, beynahe in eine eben so grosse Verwirrung setzt" (V, 218; italics mine). "Kopf" and "Herz" seem to represent two entities for Wieland. He seems to say that the head is the habitat of ideas, the heart the receptacle of intensive personal experience. The confusion in his head refers to the encounter itself; the confusion in his heart refers to the stirrings of love for Laura. Wieland's choice of "Erscheinung" is further evidence of the centrality of the interplay of fantasy and reality in the author's style and thought. A literal translation of the term would be "appearance" or "apparition." In context, however, Wieland means "encounter." The use of the word here seems to say how easily man can confuse that which he has truly seen with that which he only thinks he has seen.

The same chapter also contains a reference to the double aspect of the intellect (passive and active) mentioned earlier. The distinction <u>Verstand-Vernunft</u> is of course crucial to the epistemological problem. Wieland's attitude toward the active aspect of the intellect is further clarified when he insinuates that its activity is actually sophistry (V, 221). And finally, Wieland makes Descartes the butt of his wit. Pedrillo has become so confused through his reflections on the actuality of his experience that he begins to doubt his own existence. Wieland comments that the famous "cogito, ergo sum" could have come to the youth's rescue by reassuring him of his existence had Pedrillo not been devoid of all thought. Indeed, Wieland restates in effect the Cartesian phrase in the negative: "Non cogito, ergo non sum" (cf. V, 219).

There is still some question as to the nature of the relationship between man's intuition and truth. Is intuition the result of certain mental processes or is it preterrational clairvoyance? [22] For example, after hearing Jacinte's story Don Sylvio suspects that she might be his sister who had been kidnapped at an early age. There are certainly some facts in Jacinte's story which are similar to Don Sylvio's recollection of her disappearance, but Don Sylvio is particularly moved by the affinity for her which he felt at first sight. He rationalizes the factual similarities between Jacinte and his sister to fit his preconceived notions of fantasy and reality. However, he cannot explain the irrational affinity that he intuitively senses.

> "Wenn der Instinkt nicht beträglich wäre . . . so würde ich geneigt seyn, die Anmuthung, die ich beim ersten Anblick für sie empfand, für die Stimme des <u>Blutes</u> zu halten. Aber ich besorge, Don Eugenio, dass ich mir mit einer unzeitigen Hoffnung geschmeichelt habe."
>
> -- "Und warum?" fragte Don Eugenio ungeduldig.
>
> -- "Ich finde einen Umstand in Jacintes Geschichte," antwortete jener, "der mich in Verlegenheit setzt." (VI, 121 - 122)

Wieland's irony is at work here, too. Don Sylvio considers instinct rather than reason to be fallible. The circumstance which induces Don Sylvio to reject the voice of instinct is his conviction that a witch had kidnapped his sister, not a gypsy as everyone else contended. A gypsy does not fit into his biased view, therefore Donna Jacinte cannot be his sister. His heart speaks the truth, but he will not listen because his "experience" seems to contradict that inner voice.

The treatment of the problem here reflects Wieland's treatment of it in his essay "Was ist Wahrheit?" If there is a discrepancy between one's own experience and a rational argument, the individual will always rely on the veracity of experience. Personal experience is always more convincing than the most conclusive syllogism. Wieland of course had one important reservation: ". . . vorausgesetzt, dass ein Mensch überhaupt gesund und des Unterschieds seiner Empfindungen und Einbildungen bewusst ist." Don Sylvio is in this case unaware that his "experience" is only a fantasm. The eventual cure for Don Sylvio's aberrations is initiated and culminated primarily through the enigma of human love (the heart), not by reason (the mind). The older view that he was cured by the effects of the extravagant Biribinker tale [23] is being gradually superseded by a recognition of the irrational causes. [24] Let us trace this development in Don Sylvio.

Don Sylvio is incapable of distinguishing between his sensations and his illusions because of his overwhelming naiveté and his fanatic belief in the fantasy world. In Chapter 3, Book V, the first doubts arise about the objective validity of his world view. The disastrous fiasco with the presumed nymphs has just ended, and he still smarts from the beating he received. He is dejected at the loss of the medaillon, taken by one of the peasant girls, and is angered by his patroness fairy, Radiante. She never helps him as other patrons have aided their protégés. Don Sylvio begins to wonder if she and her world are a figment of his imagination. In his rising confusion and dejection he can no longer think clearly. Yet there is one indubitable fact: his love for the shepherdess whose portrait was on the medallion. He exclaims: "Wenn auch alles andre Einbildung ist, rief er, so weiss ich doch gewiss, o du namenlose Unbekannte! dass es keine Einbildung ist, dass ich dich liebe" (VI, 21). His love is genuine, whether the loved one is of high or low station, living or deceased. His heart speaks the truth even when reason no longer functions clearly.

Wieland injects an ironic twist into this love story, since the girl in the portrait is Donna Felicia's grandmother. Yet the similarity between Donna Jutella and Donna Felicia is so striking that the two are practically identical. Later, meeting Donna Felicia, Don Sylvio is powerfully attracted to her. In short, it is love at first (second?) sight. He does not realize that she is his "princess"; no longer possessing the portrait he cannot establish a definite similarity between the twofold object of his love. In Donna Felicia's presence he is incapable of visualizing his princess. His heart tells him that his love for her is stronger than for his princess, which he refuses to believe since it does not fit into his preconceptions. Wieland of course resolves the imagined difficulty: "Der gute Sylvio hatte die Eindrücke, die das Bildniss seiner vermeinten Prinzessin auf ihn gemacht, und die Wünsche, die es in seinem Herzen erregt hatte, für Liebe gehalten: er hatte sich geirrt; es war nur eine schwache Vorempfindung, nur ein armes Schattenbild der Liebe, die ihm das Urbild selbst einflössen würde" (VI, 35).

In the chapter "Streit zwischen der Liebe zum Bilde und der Liebe zum Original," the struggle between the "two" loves becomes acute. His love for Donna Felicia proves stronger than his love for the portrait, naturally. However, Don Sylvio does not want to admit it, since he is convinced that his princess is still enchanted as a blue butterfly. Furthermore, he has sworn eternal fidelity to her. Despite his growing suspicions, he concludes that Donna Felicia cannot be his princess. Don Sylvio's heart tells him that Donna Felicia is his true love; but because it seems to him that his heart is not attuned to reality, he attempts to resolve his dilemma by attributing his plight to a sweet psychological delusion of his heart, which sees what it longs to see: ". . . es ist wohl gar nur ein süsser Irrthum meines Herzens, welches, von irgend einem ähnlichen Zuge verführt, diejenige zu sehen glaubt, die es überall zu sehen wünscht" (VI, 57). The similarity between the two women explains in his own mind why he is attracted to Donna Felicia. Thus Don Sylvio's illusions ironically twist the truth in his mind despite the telltale disquietude in his heart. [25]

In the following chapter Don Gabriel demonstrates Don Sylvio's conception of the world to be fallacious. He does this by means of sober reason. (Don Gabriel is the representative of salubrious reason in the novel.) As a last attempt to refute Don Gabriel's logic, Don Sylvio cites his personal experience as proof of the validity of his convictions. "Er schloss, dass Grundsätze, die seiner Erfahrung widersprächen, nothwendig falsch seyn müssten" (VI, 60). Nevertheless, Don Sylvio did not feel at ease with this argument; a certain disquiet remained in his soul (VI, 60). Once again Don Sylvio's heart, influenced by Don Gabriel's rational arguments, suspects the truth. However, since the hero is not rationally sound, that is, since he does not recognize his so-called experiences as founded in a fantasy world, he is unable to resolve the uneasiness.

There is one more passage that offers conclusive evidence that the heart is the primary factor in bringing about Don Sylvio's cure. Donna Felicia is aware that Don Sylvio is falling in love with her. She also realizes that she has a rival for his affection and, furthermore, she knows who the rival is. She has been informed that Don Sylvio found the medallion bearing the miniature portrait of her grandmother. Donna Felicia reasons that she can win the young man's heart completely if she can demonstrate that she is identical to the woman in the portrait. Having procured the lost medallion from the peasant girl who found it, she takes Don Sylvio into the gallery where portraits of herself and her grandmother are displayed. The pose and the shepherdess costume are the same in each painting. Don Sylvio, stunned by the similarity, is left alone to reflect upon his error. At tea the effect of the revelation is obvious. Don Eugenio's rational arguments to persuade Don Sylvio of his fallacy are no longer needed. The author makes the following remarks about this rapid development:

> Eine Weile darauf fand sich die ganze kleine Gesellschaft beim Theetische
> der Donna Felicia zusammen. Don Eugenio und Don Gabriel bewunderten die

sichtbare Verwandlung nicht wenig, die mit unserm Helden vorgegangen war. Der erste hatte sich schon mit einer ganzen Rüstung von Gründen gewaffnet, um die Feen aus ihren Verschanzungen in seinem Gehirn heraus zu treiben; allein er fand zu nicht geringer Beschämung seiner Filosofie gar bald, dass alle Arbeit schon verrichtet war, und musste sich selbst gestehen, dass ein Paar schöne Augen in etlichen Minuten stärker überzeugen und schneller bekehren, als die Akademie, das Lyceum und die Stoa mit vereinigten Kräften kaum in eben so viel Jahren zu thun vermöchten. (VI, 286 - 287)

Indeed, there is little doubt that Wieland uses the occasion even to ridicule pure reason abstracted from all sensation. How else is "zu nicht geringer Beschämung seiner Filosofie" to be understood? However, one is not justified in assuming that reason plays no role in Don Sylvio's rehabilitation to the practical world. Wieland's aversion to a one-sided emphasis of the mind is paralleled by his aversion to a one-sided emphasis of the heart, as has been established in the preceding chapter. Furthermore, the similarity between two objects is comprehended through the intellect, not through intuition. The similarity established in Don Sylvio's mind between Donna Felicia and the fairy is the turning point in his development, even though his heart had indicated the truth prior to that recognition. Love speaks directly to the heart; thus there is no room for error. Don Sylvio's cure could only be accomplished through the heart because his mind was completely closed to arguments contrary to his prejudices. As Gerhard Kaiser expresses it: "Don Sylvio wird durch Liebe, also echtes Gefühl, von der Empfindsamkeit, dem falschen Gefühl, befreit."[26]

The motif of the correspondence between the dictates of the heart and Truth (not necessarily moral truth)[27] is not characteristic of Don Sylvio alone. For example, Pedrillo refuses to believe that Donna Felicia and Laura are supernatural beings, although his master contends that they must be. It is interesting that it was Pedrillo who actually saw and spoke with the ladies, Don Sylvio having been asleep during the encounter. Pressed to accept his master's point of view, Pedrillo becomes confused and yields to some degree. Donna Felicia may be supernatural, but Laura is flesh and blood, Pedrillo insists:

> Wohl denn, gnädiger Herr, fiel ihm Pedrillo wieder ein; wenn die schöne Dame, die Euer Gnaden so aufmerksam betrachtete, Donna Schmergelina ist, so kann ich nichts dazu, ich muss es geschehen lassen; aber für die Kleine will ich gebeten haben! Ich weiss nicht wie es kommt, aber mein Herz sagt mir, die Gestalt, die sie hatte, war ihre eigene; ich will mir die Ohren abschneiden lassen, wenn Sie in der ganzen weiten Welt ein Paar Augen oder eine Nase oder ein kleines Schnäutzchen finden, die ihr besser liessen als ihre eigenen. (V, 239 - 240)

Pedrillo may not understand why his heart insists that the girl is human, but it is obvious to the reader: love. Here is another case of love at first sight. Love is a matter of the heart, not of the mind. Love is an experience, an Empfindung; it is not a syllogism, an Einbildung. For this reason, Pedrillo is willing to comply with his master's wishes and agree that Donna Felicia is a supernatural being, but he refuses to give ground when it comes to Laura. Laura touched Pedrillo's heart, Donna Felicia did not!

One can also cite Donna Jacinte's reliance on her instincts to tell her what is morally right or wrong. In some respects she is the prime example of Wieland's belief in the infallibility of the heart and its nobility. No one had imparted moral guidelines to her. On the contrary, practically everything she experienced should have prohibited such sentiments. Jacinte's heart alone was her lodestar in questions of moral rectitude. Her moral intuition can be equated with Wieland's "inneres Licht" (Shaftesbury's voice of Nature). Jacinte says:

> Die alte Zigeunerin, die nur darauf dachte, wie sie mich reitzend machen wollte, hatte sich wenig bekümmert, mich die Tugend kennen zu lehren; und wie hätte sie es sollen, da sie selbst weder Begriff noch Gefühl davon hatte? Dem ungeachtet war ich nicht gänzlich ohne sittliche Begriffe. Ein gewisser Instinkt, der sich durch meine Aufmerksamkeit auf die Handlungen unserer kleinen Gesellschaft und auf die Bewegungen meines eigenen Herzens nach und nach entwickelte, sagte mir, dass dieses oder jenes recht oder unrecht sey, ohne dass ich eine andere Ursache hätte angeben können, als meine Empfindung. (VI, 69)

The dictates of this instinct were confirmed for her by her scanty knowledge of the gentility in Toledo and even by acquaintance with romances and fairy tales.

It is this growing suspicion of her innate moral goodness which leads Jacinte to the supposition that she is not a blood relative of the old gypsy woman who had raised her. Without knowing anything about her family and origin, she senses the truth. She has little factual evidence to substantiate her claim, yet she exclaims: "O gewiss bin ich für einen so schmählichen Stand nicht geboren. . . . Wenn es auch meine Gestalt und Farbe nicht zu verrathen schienen, so sagt mirs mein Herz, dass ich keine Enkelin dieser schändlichen Kupplerin bin" (VI, 82). Her suspicions are of course later verified, since she is Don Sylvio's sister. In Jacinte's case, Wieland seems to say that man is basically noble and will remain so as long as he is loyal to his true nature. [28] Jacinte belongs in the society of Danae and Natalie, since she too is a schöne Seele. She is an obvious contrast to Biribinker, who is incapable of resisting temptation. Philosophically and historically speaking, she is evidently an example of the early Enlightenment concept that recognition of man's moral nature and destiny is sufficient for compliance to the demands of virtue.

The frequency with which the reader encounters the term Sympathie as a designation for the cause of love at first sight is another indication of the infallibility of the heart. In each case of love at first sight (there are four), like is unerringly drawn to like. [29] Don Sylvio is attracted to Donna Felicia, who also suffers from delusions, although less acutely than her admirer. Noble-minded Don Eugenio is irresistibly drawn to Donna Jacinte. Pedrillo is immediately attracted to his femi-

nine counterpart, and Biribinker instantly falls in love with the princess destined
to be his wife, though he is unaware that she is a princess. Each time, Sympathie
is offered as the cause of the mutual attraction. This psychic feeling is assumed
to be quite natural, according to Wieland.

> Es mag nun seyn, dass die Seelen solcher sympathischen Geschöpfe in einem
> vorherigen Zustande sich schon gekannt und geliebt haben; oder dass es eine
> natürliche Verwandtschaft unter Seelen oder . . . Schwesterseelen giebt; oder
> dass ihre Genii in einem besondern Einverständniss mit einander stehen . . .
> genug dass diese Sympathie sich eben so gewiss in der Natur befindet, als
> die Schwere, die Anziehung, die Elasticität, oder die magnetischen Kräfte.
> (V, 203 - 204)

Sympathie might be likened to the inner voice which is not susceptible to the error resulting from appearances. In Don Sylvio the meaning of this term is of course
synonymous with its meaning in the essay "Sympathie." [30]

Reference was made earlier to Wieland's two-pronged approach to the problem of
fantasy and reality in Don Sylvio. The approach is both philosophical and satirical.
Discussion has been centered primarily on the philosophical content of the novel
and its impact on form and structure. On the basis of the text, Wieland's conviction
of the relative validity of pragmatic truth and "reality" and his belief in the superiority of the heart over the mind in the apprehension of ultimate Truth has been
brought out. Attention will now be turned to the satirical aspect of the novel and
its relationship to the philosophical content.

Wieland as author is critical of several characters in the novel. His criticism of
Don Sylvio has already been indirectly treated in the discussion of subjective reality. Yet it must still be pointed out that author -Wieland's censure of his hero is
not entirely negative. Don Sylvio's naive belief in and total commitment to the truth
of fairy tales is not really rebuked. The exposition of the hero's folly, for example,
is not devoid of a warm understanding of its causes. In fact, it is even stated that
if Don Sylvio had not given rein to his inflamed imagination he might still be languishing in Rosalva.

> Wenn die Feen auch nur Geschöpfe unserer Einbildungskraft sind, sagte er,
> so werde ich sie doch immer als meine grössten Wohlthäterinnen ansehen,
> da ich ohne sie noch immer in der Einsamkeit von Rosalva schmachtete, und
> vielleicht auf ewig der Glückseligkeit entbehrt hätte, diejenige zu finden, die
> mein verlangendes Herz, seitdem es sich selbst fühlt, zu suchen schien. [31]
> (VI, 284)

This passage is also reminiscent of the Sympathie motif, since Don Sylvio inti-
mates that he has (unconsciously) sought for Donna Felicia ever since he became
aware of his own existence. In addition, a bridge is laid between that concept and
the dream world. Once again, therefore, the interplay of fantasy (dreams, fairy

tales) and reality (Sympathie) is exposed. The very fabric of the novel -- its structure and its atmosphere -- is the result of interweaving the two threads. Don Sylvio's belief in the fantasy world and his dreams are an expression of his inner
striving for happiness,[32] which he ultimately achieves because of them. The effects
on an individual can therefore also be beneficial. Victor Michel has noted the positive aspect of the hero's naive beliefs. He writes: "Que serait en effet la réalité
sans la part du rêve? Si trompeur qu'il soit le merveilleux n'en est pas moins le
présentiment du vrai."[33] However, he does not elaborate on the wondrous as a
presentiment of truth.

If the effects of fairy tales themselves on the individual are not criticized, then
one must look elsewhere for Wieland's reproof.[34] If Don Sylvio had not been solely
under his aunt's mentorship, and if he had not been physically isolated from the
society of his fellow man, the fantasms would not have been able to gain such massive influence over his character. It was easy for the youth to make no distinction
between the fantasy and phenomenal worlds, influenced as he was by an aunt who
accepted the validity of courtly romances and who was raising her nephew to be an
exemplary knight. Donna Mencia too suffers from delusions, although she simultaneously despises fairy tales. Don Sylvio recognizes no dissimilarity between the
two worlds and has as much confidence in the exploits of a Radiante or a Fanferlüsch as in those of a Roland or an Arthurian knight. Wieland's criticism seems
therefore directed at Don Sylvio's upbringing.[35] In order to avoid extremes, one
must be exposed to various influences. In Don Sylvio's case, his education actually
only begins when he comes into contact with other people. At the end of the novel
he sets out on a Bildungsreise to fill the vacuum left by the dispelled fantasms.
Yet the positive effect of the imagination in realizing Don Sylvio's destiny is significant.

A consideration of Donna Jacinte's fate underscores this important point in her
case as well. Unlike her brother she enjoyed no education. Donna Mencia, though
not an ideal mentor, was certainly better than none. Everything Donna Jacinte
learned was acquired through observation and intuition. In a sense, the girl's horizon was as restricted as Don Sylvio's. She too was exposed to only one type of
experience, though of a different kind. Her experiences did not appeal to and stimulate the imagination as did Don Sylvio's; hers were dissonant to her intuitive
apperception. Her moral integrity would have been undermined had it not been for
the decisive influence of her intuition and, paradoxically, fantasy.

The girl convinces herself that she is unique among her peers because of her moral
views and her sensitivity. She attempts to remember as far back as possible into
her childhood to find confirmation of her instinct-inspired sentiments. Although
her recollections are vague, her imagination supplies the details she so desperate-
ly desires to discover. She resolves to conduct herself in a manner befitting the
noblest blood in Castile even though she be of low station.

Ich bestrebte mich, so tiefe Blicke in meine Kindheit zu thun als mir möglich war, um in den schwachen Spuren erloschener Erinnerungen eine Bekräftigung meiner Wünsche zu finden; und so eitel und ungewiss auch die Einbildungen waren, womit ich mich selbst zu betrügen suchte, so dienten sie doch, mich in dem Vorsatz zu bestärken, in was für Umstände ich auch kommen möchte, meine Ehre eben so sorgfältig in Acht zu nehmen, als ob das edelste Blut von Kastilien in meinen Adern flösse. (VI, 82 - 83)

This resolve, consequent to a common effort by the heart and fantasy, gave her the fortitude to preserve her integrity during all her trials. Wieland's belief in the beneficial nature of the imagination (coupled with intuition) is thus evinced also in the person of Donna Jacinte.

Both Don Sylvio and Donna Jacinte have an inborn intuition which serves as their lodestar and which -- magnified by the power of fantasy -- leads them to the fulfillment of their destinies. The only difference here between brother and sister is the type of experience to which they were exposed. Jacinte never doubted as to how she should conduct herself, since the wantonness surrounding her was incompatible with her inherent moral sense. Fairy-tale adventures, on the other hand, are not ipso facto a source of ethical discord. Donna Jacinte's life history reads like a blatant confirmation of Leibnizian optimism. No matter what adverse experiences the girl undergoes, there is no despairing in her moral destiny. In fact, everything works out for the best. Voltaire's Candide and Wezel's Belphegor are stridently satiric of the popular theodicy of their age. Whereas these works ridicule the naively mechanistic "whatever is, is right" theory, Wieland's novel seems to uphold the theological view of the universe. Yet the difference between the works is even deeper: it is one of intent. Wieland is not attacking or defending a philosophical position as are Voltaire and Wezel; he is attempting to delineate the moral tissue of one of his characters. Thus, in Candide and Belphegor the emphasis is on the function of reason; in Jacinte's story it is on that certain instinct which leads the girl securely through a period darkened by lack of knowledge and sensible guidance. The inadequacy of human reason to solve the moral riddle of the cosmos is compensated for by the irrational presentiments of the heart. Are we to understand this shift in emphasis as a criticism of the excessive confidence in man's rational powers? The efficacy of the hegemony of reason is apparently called into question.

The principle of moderation became decisive for Wieland after his return to Biberach,[36] perhaps as a result of his growing skepticism of any and all claims to absoluteness.[37] It would be natural for Wieland to become wary of the complete dominance of either the head or the heart. In fact, throughout Don Sylvio Wieland appears to say that both the mind and the heart are needed to check the absolute supremacy of each other and to recognize and understand the nature of the world we live in.

This essential idea is revealed in the characterization of Don Sylvio and Donna Jacinte. He is fanatic; she is sensible. Yet they are brother and sister. By this means

Wieland implies that the mind and the heart are also complementary. Their true relationship is one of harmonious cooperation, not polarization. They are two sides of one coin. Only when both function together can man enjoy a "healthy" view of the world and of himself, for an overemphasis of the mind leads to rigid dogmatism and sterile pedantry (e.g., Pangloss). On the other hand, an overemphasis of the heart leads to myopic subjectivism. In Jacinte's case the heart guides her to rational action. Here the stress is to be interpreted positively (in contrast to Candide or Belphegor) as a rebuttal to the idea that reason alone is sufficient. Don Sylvio's heart also guides him, but he lacks the necessary contact with the world, which would act as a counterbalance. Thus by means of satire (Don Sylvio's extremism) and irony (the literary "parallel" of the Jacinte episode to Candide), Wieland points the way to the philosophic import of the novel.[38]

In the figure of Donna Mencia, Wieland seems to be criticizing self-imposed, feigned prudery.[39] Donna Mencia is not actually the venerable prude she seems to be. If she were, she would not have thrown herself at Rodrigo Sanchez nor would she have been so ready to arrange a marriage between her nephew and Rodrigo's malformed bourgeois niece for purely materialistic reasons. Wieland also criticizes her excessive passion for chivalric romances, which she takes as her model. Somehow these romances also seem to be a means of vicarious satisfaction necessitated by her prudery.

Pedrillo too is an object of the author's satire. Although Pedrillo usually acts reasonably and only believes in his master's fantasms in order to please him, the simple youth is also aberrant. Where Don Sylvio errs, Pedrillo sees clearly; but where Don Sylvio percieves correctly, Pedrillo goes astray. Don Sylvio's aberrancy is caused by fairy tales, Pedrillo's by superstition. For example, the latter is convinced that ghosts exist and he takes a huge oak to be a giant. Even after Don Sylvio lops off a branch of the tree to show Pedrillo that the imagined giant is only an oak, Pedrillo holds firmly to his belief. Offended at Don Sylvio, Pedrillo says: "Ich dächte, eine Höflichkeit wäre gleichwohl der andern Werth, und wenn ich Ihren Salamander gelten lasse, so könnten Sie meine Riesen wohl auch in ihrem Werthe beruhen lassen" (V, 127).

The parallel of this twitting behavior to that of Sancho Panza is obvious. However, a more important aspect of the interaction between Pedrillo and Don Sylvio is the aloof attitude of the omniscient narrator. From his perch high above the prejudices and finiteness of his characters, the author can treat objectively the faults of his unsuspecting creatures. One feels that the author is chuckling to himself at the foibles of his characters, even as does the reader.

Finally, Wieland as author criticizes Donna Felicia. Like Don Sylvio she too has a fertile and active imagination. However, Don Sylvio suffers from illusions, while hers are delusions. That is to say, Donna Felicia consciously plays the part of a shepherdess in an idyllic setting (especially designed for this purpose), whereas Don Sylvio is unaware that he is acting a part in a fantastic deception. Wieland seems to reprove Donna Felicia only indirectly for her rococo delight in masquerading as a shepherdess far from the cares of the world. He does not criticize her innocent play, but he does question the laudability of her method of attaining the financial freedom necessary to her way of life. For example, the narrator states that she was about sixteen when she married her sixty-eight-year-old husband, "who was considerate enough to die in his seventieth year, approximately two years after their wedding" (V, 198). The reason she married the aged gentleman is given as follows:

> Sie hatte sich den frostigen Armen so eines unpoetischen Liebhabers, als ein Ehemann von siebzig Jahren ist, aus keiner andern Absicht überlassen, als weil die Reichthümer, über welche sie in kurzem zu gebieten hoffte, sie in den Stand setzen würden, alle die angenehmen Entwürfe auszuführen, die sie sich von einer freyen und glücklichen Lebensart, nach den poetischen Begriffen, machte. (V, 199)

The butt of satire with respect to Donna Felicia, therefore, is the motivating factor which induced her to wed such an unlikely partner: rococo poets. Had it not been for their influence she would probably not have entered such a mismatch. Thus here too the influence of the fantasy on man is observed. Donna Felicia is gently reproved for her ignoble motivations regarding her marriage. And indirectly, therefore, Wieland satirizes the rococo vogue.

Of the many objects of satire in the novel -- Don Sylvio/fairy tales, Donna Mencia /chivalric romances, Pedrillo/superstition, Donna Jacinte/"reason supreme," Donna Felicia/rococo -- the last fares the best. The reason is apparently the fact that the young woman was conscious of her fantasies. Furthermore, her submission to illusion is the least dangerous and the least harmful. It is apparent from the preceding discussion that the author does not always agree in principle with what his characters say and do. In order to ascertain the author's personal opinion, the reader must understand the pervasive irony if he wishes to interpret the author's language.

Note that only Pedrillo suffers from superstition (Aberglauben) and not from degrees of Schwärmerei as do the others. The distinction between these two phenomena is important in understanding Wieland's evaluation of Schwärmerei and its relation to enthusiasm. In his letter to Zimmermann of November 7, 1763, Wieland explicitly states his conceptions of these two dispositions. He recognizes their influence on men's lives and the distinctive characteristics of each.

> Schwärmerey und Aberglauben erstrecken ihren Einfluss auf alle Zweige des menschlichen Lebens; beyde sind dem Menschen natürlich, indem jene sich in dem aktiven und diese in dem passiven Theile seiner Natur sich gründet; beyde bringen viel Gutes hervor; die Schwärmerey macht glänzende, kühne und unternehmende Geister, der Aberglaube zahme, geduldige, förmliche Thiere, die in dem ordentlichen Küh-Weg einher wandeln und für alles

ihre Vorschrift haben, von der sie nicht abweichen dürfen. Allein mit allen dem ist es doch jederzeit für sehr nöthig und heilsam geachtet worden, über jene Triebfeder der grossen Leidenschaften, und über diese plumpe <u>vis in-ertiae</u> der menschlichen Natur sich lustig zu machen.[40]

Of prime significance is the assertion that both phenomena evoke beneficial results for mankind. It is also noteworthy that the author uses the passive voice when he writes that it has always been considered necessary and salutary to ridicule these psychic occurrences. The overtones of the passive voice seem to intimate an ambivalent attitude. In the analyses of <u>Agathon</u> and <u>Peregrinus Proteus</u> this ambiguity will disappear. In <u>Don Sylvio</u>, the active aspect of <u>Schwärmerei</u> rather than the ossifying effect of superstition is the central philosophico-psychological concern. The relationship between <u>Schwärmerei</u> and enthusiasm is not a question in this work.

Wieland's statement to Gessner can now be seen as a genuine pronouncement of the author's intentions. <u>Don Sylvio</u> is a type of satirical novel which is truly philosophical (and psychological) despite its frivolous appearance. Fritz Martini has aptly summarized the main thrust of the novel: "Was als Scherz und Narrengeschichte mit gelenkiger Anmut des ironischen Stils begonnen war, erhielt in der Tat eine gewisse Tendenz zum 'Philosophischen,' genauer zu einer Psychologie der Liebe, die auf der Natur der 'Sympathien,' in der sich Geistiges und Sinnliches ununterscheidbar mischen, beruht."[41]

Wieland's philosophical convictions have not only influenced the content of the novel but also its form. In order to convince the reader of the relative perception of truth, the author must demonstrate the relativity of perspective. Wieland achieves this by forcing the reader to assume an active role in the novel. He becomes the author's confidant. The reader is taught to view the world through the eyes of the successive characters, while simultaneously recognizing to what extent the individual is aberrant.[42] The composition of the novel reflects Wieland's conviction of the relative perception of Truth because it is characterized precisely by the intersubjectivity of the views depicted.

In his first novel Wieland seems to be concerned primarily with the individual's integration into society, which promises to be reciprocally beneficial. Individuals "suffering" from degrees of (self) delusion are depicted, varying from harmless to chronic. The further one is from the social norm of reality, the more critical the problem. (The "norm" of reality is determined by a consensus.) To maintain a healthy relationship to society the individual must be exposed to the opinions of other men. This content, Wieland seems to say, will guard against overwrought subjectivism. Excessive <u>Schwärmerei</u> is considered an evil, because man is viewed essentially as a social being. Society is the greater good, and man's purpose is to become a useful member in it in order to expedite social progress. Any man who does not accept social dicta is a fool in the eyes of the majority.

As long as the individual is in harmony with society, reason is sufficient to maintain a healthy relationship between subjective and consensual opinion. However, if the individual becomes unaware that his view of the world is subjective, then he becomes aberrant. In this case reason is no longer sufficient to correct the error because reason is preconditioned by the totally subjective state to evaluate all sensations according to a bias. Thus the individual no longer perceives correctly; that is, according to the social norm. In the extreme situation, one's inborn intuition can still be relied upon to make the individual aware of his aberrancy. One gradually becomes aware that there is a disparity between what he _believes_ and what he feels (in an intuitive sense). Once the individual is again aware of a discrepancy between his view and the general one, then reason can resume its effective mediation between man, the phenomenal world, and social reality.

It should be noted that all the objects of satire in the novel have one common denominator: none is confined solely to empirical fact. All are products of the imagination and all represent to some degree (except perhaps Pedrillo's primitive superstition) a certain ideal. For example, fairy tales depict the idealism of good as opposed to evil; furthermore, Donna Jacinte reflects the Enlightenment's ideals of innate human goodness, perfectibility, and moral integrity.

The novel's conclusion is significant for an insight into its epistemological attitude because it indicates Don Sylvio's preparation prior to his becoming a useful and meaningful member of society. The emphasis in Don Sylvio is on urbanity; and there is little or no place for idealism in the active, practical life demanded of the harmoniously integrated member of society. For this reason, Emil Hamann is perhaps justified in interpreting Wieland's criticism of Schwärmerei in this novel as basically a criticism of all ideals, of anything which is not of this world of flesh and blood. "Im Don Sylvio verspottet er [Wieland] . . . nicht bloss die abergläubische Lust am Wunderbaren, sondern auch die schwärmerische Hinneigung zum Idealen, überhaupt jede höhere, über das Gewöhnliche hinausstrebende Empfindung und lässt nur den nüchternen, auf das platteste Wohlbehagen gerichteten Verstand als wahre Lebensklugheit gelten."[43]

Friedrich Sengle also refers to a lack of idealism. Although he does so in another context, his comment on the Schwärmer is applicable to Don Sylvio: "Schon ohne Gnade und noch ohne idealistisches Selbstbewusstsein, so steht bei Wieland der Mensch in einer Preisgegebenheit, aus der er sich nur spielend und spottend befreien kann."[44] Sengle writes "still without idealistic self-assurance" as if to insinuate that Wieland's fool-heroes eventually find an idealistic basis for action.

However, an argument can be made for idealism in Don Sylvio's case as well. Reference has been made to the ironic fact that Schwärmerei can lead to great benefit for mankind. A corollary was even drawn between Don Sylvio and Alexander the Great to indicate what achievements man is capable of if spurred on by his illusions or delusions. The whole concept of idealism is treated ironically -- but not disparagingly -- in Don Sylvio. Wieland's attitude toward idealism is ambiguous and demands clarification. The relationship between Schwärmerei and Enthusiasmus has been hinted at but not explained in this novel. The phenomenon of

Schwärmerei was a lifelong concern for Wieland and functions as a leitmotif in his novels. Agathon and Peregrinus Proteus will demonstrate that Wieland came to a better understanding of the causes of Schwärmerei and of the significance of Enthusiasmus for the meaning of life. Wieland leaves this essential question basically untouched in Don Sylvio. He chooses to concede to the demands of the Enlightenment and integrate his hero into society. Nevertheless, A. Marten's appraisal of Don Sylvio as "ein mit leichteren Strichen gezeichneter Agathon"[45] will be seen as quite accurate. It should become manifest that Agathon and Peregrinus no longer lack "idealistic self-assurance"; and that neither they nor their creator need revert to a "playful" or "mocking" attitude in order successfully to contend with the world, in order to reconcile the idealism of the individual with the practicality of society.

NOTES

1. AB, II, 221.
2. DB, I, 5-6 (11.7.1763); see also Wieland's letter to Leonhard Meister of December 28, 1787, in which he complains about the total misunderstanding surrounding Don Sylvio and restates the novel's true intent: "... da sein wahrer Zweck ist, dem Aberglauben einen tödtlichen Stoss zu geben." AB, III, 385. It is significant for this study that Wieland says "Aberglauben," not "Enthusiasmus."
3. Hermann August Korff, Voltaire im literarischen Deutschland des 18. Jahrhunderts (Heidelberg, 1917-18), p. 463.
4. For a discussion of Don Sylvio as an innovative novel form derived from satire and comedy, see Jörg Schönert, Roman und Satire im 18. Jahrhundert. Ein Beitrag zur Poetik (Stuttgart: Metzler, 1969).
5. Ermatinger, "Das Romantische bei Wieland," pp. 265-268, has elucidated Wieland's influence on Novalis' concept of the "blaue Blume" and the relatively insignificant import of the "blauer Schmetterling" as a symbol.
6. Other models could have been Fielding's Slipslop and Partridge. Sengle, p. 185; Michel, p. 333.
7. The original title of the work published anonymously in 1764 points forward to this "logical" aspect of the adventures depicted: "Der Sieg der Natur / über die Schwärmerey, / oder / die Abentheuer / des / Don Sylvio von Rosalva, / Eine Geschichte / worinn alles wunderbare natürlich zugeht."
8. "Die Auseinandersetzung mit dem Nachahmungsprinzip in Deutschland und die besondere Rolle der Romane Wielands (Don Sylvio, Agathon)," in Nachahmung und Illusion, ed. H. Jauss (München: Eidos, 1964), p. 84.
9. "Auseinandersetzung," pp. 82-83.
10. See Fritz Strich, Die Mythologie in der deutschen Literatur: Von Klopstock bis Wagner (Halle a/d Saale, 1910; rpt. Tübingen: Max Niemeyer, 1970), I, 75, 90, for Shaftesbury's influence on Don Sylvio.
11. Eric A. Blackall, The Emergence of German as a Literary Language 1700-1775 (Cambridge, 1959), p. 423.
12. Ibid., p. 421.
13. Cf. Cornelius Sommer, Christoph Martin Wieland (Stuttgart: Metzler, 1971), p. 27.
14. Dieter Kimpel, Der Roman der Aufklärung (Stuttgart: Metzler, 1967), p. 93.
15. Ch. M. Wieland, Werke, ed. Fritz Martini and Hans Werner Seiffert (München: Hanser, 1964), I, "Nachwort," 922. See also W. Buddecke, C.M. Wielands Entwicklungsbegriff und die "Geschichte des Agathon" (Göttingen: Vandenhoeck und Ruprecht, 1966), p. 86.
16. The witty, so-called "Nachbericht des Herausgebers welcher aus Versehen des Abschreibers zu einem Vorbericht gemacht worden" appeared only in the first edition of 1764. Quotation cited in Martini and Michel., I, 12.
17. Karl Heinz Kausch, "Die Kunst der Grazie: Ein Beitrag zum Verständnis Wielands," Jahrbuch der deutschen Schillergesellschaft, 2 (1958), 26, contends that Wieland's use of the fictive manuscript precludes objectivity. This state-

ment is made in connection with Agathon, but there is no reason why the same principle cannot apply to Don Sylvio which was composed at the same time. Besides, the fiction of the manuscript was a popular contrivance of eighteenth-century narrative and Wieland's consciously ironic use of the motif here would tend to discount any genuine attempt on his part to establish fact.

18. Die Abenteuer des Don Sylvio von Rosalva, ed. Wolfgang Jahn (München: Goldmann, n.d.), "Nachwort," p. 337. See also W. Kurrelmeyer, "Gil Blas and Don Sylvio," MLN, 34 (1919), 78-82, who demonstrated Wieland's borrowings from Le Sage.

19. The degree to which the fictional reality of this novel is dependent upon the fictitious worlds of other literary works is discussed by Lieselotte E. Kurth, Die zweite Wirklichkeit (Chapel Hill: University of North Carolina Press, 1969), pp. 141-157.

20. For a treatment of the Jacinte episode as a parodistic satire of Richardson's Pamela, similar to the intent of Fielding's Shamela and Joseph Andrews, see Guy Stern, "Saint of Hypocrite? A Study of Wieland's Jacinte Episode," Germanic Review, 29, (1954) 96-101.

21. Cf. V. Michel, C.M. Wieland, La Formation et l'évolution de son esprit jusqu'en 1772 (Paris: Boivin, 1938). Michel interprets the function of the Biribinker and Donna Jacinte episodes in the same manner: "L'histoire aventureuse de Jacinte va seulement montrer que l'existence peut l'emporter en extravagance sur la chimère, tandis que par le conte de Biribinker, le philosophe Gabriel prouvera avec facilité l'absurde peut être accepté comme vraisemblable" (p. 336).

22. Norman Hampson, The Enlightenment (Baltimore: Penguin Books, 1968), pp. 186-217, briefly traces the growing importance of intuition ("the inner voice") in all aspects of eighteenth-century thought.

23. Strich, I, 91.

24. Cf. Schindler-Hurlimann, Wielands Menschenbild: Eine Interpretation des "Agathon" (Zürich: Atlantis, 1964), p. 91; Lange, "Zur Gestalt des Schwärmers," p. 161.

25. The unimpeachable perspicacity of the heart (intuition) is not a phenomenon in eighteenth-century German literature unique to Wieland. For example, Christian Fürchtegott Gellert uses the theme in his sentimental comedy Die zärtlichen Schwestern (1747). A "house intrigue" is used to convince Julchen (one of the compassionate sisters) that she is indeed in love with her suitor Damis. Julchen is deceived by appearances; that is, by rational judgment, and believes that Damis is actually in love with her sister Lottchen. When the deception is revealed to her it becomes evident that her heart had not been deceived. Julchen exclaims: "Der Lohn? [d.i. für Damis's Liebe] Hassen Sie mich denn? Würde ich eifersüchtig geworden sein, wenn ich nicht. ... Also haben Sie mich nicht hintergangen? Ja, mein ganzes Herz hat für Sie gesprochen" (III, iii). Lustspiele (rpt. Stuttgart: Metzler, 1966), p. 77. Another example of unerring intuition (coupled with love) occurs in Schiller's Die Räuber (IV, iv) (1781). Amalia believes Karl to be dead; but when he returns disguised and unrecognizable, she is inexplicably attracted to him. She reproaches herself for this inclination because she has sworn eternal fidelity

to her "deceased" betrothed. The conflict between the intuitive cognizance of the heart and the syllogisms of the head becomes apparent in the garden scene in Act IV: "Horch! horch! Rauschte die Türe nicht? (Sie wird Karl gewahr und springt auf.) Er? -- wohin? -- was? -- da hat michs angewurzelt, dass ich nicht fliehen kann -- verlass mich nicht, Gott im Himmel! -- Nein, du sollst mir meinen Karl nicht entreissen! Meine Seele hat nicht Raum für zwei Gottheiten, und ich bin ein sterbliches Mädchen! (Sie nimmt Karls Bild heraus.) Du, mein Karl, sei mein Genius wider diesen Fremdling, den Liebestörer! dich, dich ansehen, unverwandt, -- und weg alle gottlosen Blicke nach diesem. (Sie sitzt stumm, das Auge starr auf das Bild geheftet.) "Sämmtliche Werke, I (München: Hanser, 1960), p. 582. The parallel to Don Sylvio's struggle between his love for the portrait and his love for the original is unmistakable. It is also interesting to note that the two examples are indicative of the Pietistic and Storm and Stress movements in eighteenth-century Germany with their emphasis on man's emotional and irrational nature. Critics have often not duly recognized the indebtedness of Wieland's philosophy to these two "irrational" movements.

26. Geschichte der deutschen Literatur (Gütersloh: S. Mohn, 1966), p. 66.

27. Cf. Hampson, p. 193: "This superiority of the intuitive power was not confined to ethics. Even as a source of ideas, the imagination was felt to be quicker and bolder in perception than plodding reason."

28. The same idea is expressed in Wieland's Theages, Gruber ed., XLIV, 50.

29. Cf. also the love at first sight between Aristipp and Kleone. Gruber ed., XXXIII, 209.

30. It would be interesting to investigate the possible influence of Wieland's concept of Sympathie on Goethe's Die Wahlverwandtschaften.

31. Cf. Don Sylvio's "confession" to Wieland's statement in a letter to Zimmermann: "Vollkommen erkenne ich alle vorigen Verirrungen meines Geistes und Herzens. Vermengen Sie aber nicht das schöne Ideal der Maler und Dichter, worüber Cicero so gut spricht, mit jenem Platonismus oder philosophischen Fanatismus, von dem Sie mich mit so viel Vernunft ablenken. Ohne jenes schöne Ideal kein Corregio, kein Raphael, kein Thomson, kein Leonidas, keine Alzire." Cited in Doering, C.M. Wieland (Sangerhausen: Rohland, 1840), p. 92. The benefit wrought by the transcendental and man's complete confidence in its reality for man's mundane existence is obvious in both cases.

32. Müller-Solger, p. 140.

33. Michel, p. 339.

34. Schönert, p. 140, n. 33, also does not consider Schwärmerei to be the foremost object of satire in the novel because of its innocuous effects in this case.

35. See Sengle, p. 183.

36. Sengle, p. 205. However, I do not believe that this principle of moderation ever became absolutely normative for Wieland. This point should become manifest particularly through a study of Peregrinus Proteus.

37. Sommer, p. 27.

38. Schönert, p. 135, sees the treatment of extreme subjectivism as satiric, whereas the treatment of pure rationalism is ironic.

39. Sengle, pp. 75-76, underscores the fact that Frau Amtmann von Grebel was the model for Donna Mencia, whom he wanted to expose as a sanctimonious prude.

40. DB, I, 6-7.

41. Martini, ed., I, "Nachwort," 928.

42. Schönert, p. 141, approaches this aspect in a different manner. He considers the novel specifically with respect to its form. Of prime importance for him is the narrator/reader relationship and the insight gained into the nature of literary "reality" by means of irony.

43. Emil Hamann, Wielands Bildungsideal (Chemnitz: H. Wilisch, 1907), p. 151. Hamann's purpose is to demonstrate that Wieland's ideal man is the urbane, refined individual versed in the ways of the world. Other works based on the same premise are Barbara Schlagenhaft, Wielands "Agathon" als Spiegelung aufklärerischer Vernunft- und Gefühlsproblematik (Erlangen: Palm & Enke, 1935); and Jürgen Jacobs, Wielands Romane (Bern & München: Francke, 1969). I would contend that Wieland's urbanity was only a stage in his search for Truth.

44. Sengle, "Von Wielands Epenfragmenten zum Oberon: Ein Beitrag zu Problem und Geschichte des Kleinepos im 18. Jahrhundert," in Arbeiten zur deutschen Literatur: 1750-1850 (Stuttgart: Metzler, 1965), p. 65.

45. A. Martens, Untersuchungen über Wielands "Don Sylvio" und die übrigen Dichtungen der Biberacher Zeit (Halle: E. Karras, 1901), p. 61.

Chapter 3

AGATHON: IDEALISM VERSUS MATERIALISM

Know then thyself, presume not God to scan
The proper study of mankind is man.
-- Pope, Essay on Man II, 1 - 2

Die Abenteuer des Don Sylvio von Rosalva can be considered a prelude to Wieland's
second, more elaborate and more philosophically ambitious novel, Die Geschichte
des Agathon. The chief concern of the two works is the same: the problem of fantasy and reality in the quest for Truth. The approach to the problem is different.
Don Sylvio was basically satirical and entertaining. Agathon is philosophic and didactic. Don Sylvio sought an enchanted sweetheart; Agathon seeks to know himself.
Wieland's intention in writing the two novels was also different. In Don Sylvio he
wanted to entertain the reader, whereas he intended Agathon to be essentially in-
structive. According to Martini: "Wieland schrieb diesen Roman [Agathon] um der
Wahrhaftigkeit, um einer Ehrlichkeit der humanen Vernunft, der Welterkenntnis
und der menschlichen Selbsterkenntnis willen. . . . Der Don Sylvio war als Scherz-
spiel der imaginativen Laune geschrieben."[1]

Yet Don Sylvio anticipates the basic problem and the distinctive style of Agathon.
In the first novel Wieland leads the reader to recognize the subjective nature of
perception and demonstrates that each individual enjoys only a partial view of Truth.
He also indicates in the person of Don Sylvio that the Schwärmer will come to his
senses once he is made aware of his aberrancy, of the discrepancy between his
view and the collective view of society.

Agathon's specific form of Schwärmerei, his dreamy adherence to the Platonic
ideals in the face of abrasive reality, is also considered detrimental to his effective functioning in society for the benefit of his fellow men.[2] Wieland's first novel
ends with the hero's recognition of his folly and his integration into society. Agathon is an intensification of the underlying problem in Don Sylvio. Wieland examines
more closely and minutely in Agathon the phenomenon of Schwärmerei. Here it is
expressed as idealism in philosophical and moral terms, whereas in Don Sylvio
the phenomenon was identified with an excessive concern for the world of fantasy.

It is significant for the relationship between the two novels that Don Sylvio was conceived while Wieland was struggling with the problems of Agathon and that Don Sylvio was a form of recuperation from the strenuous concentration demanded by the
"second" novel.[3] At the same time, we should remember that Agathon was written
under the influence of such philosophers and writers as Plato, Xenophon, and Lu-

cian.[4] This naturally added to the serious tone of the novel.

This relation between the content and intent of the two novels and the intensification of the underlying controversial issues in the second is referred to by Wieland in a letter to Gessner: "Dass ich in wenigen Jahren eine Apologie für mich und meine Schriften werde nöthig haben, sehe ich schon lange voraus; Agathon, der in allen Betrachtungen ärgerlicher ist als Sylvio, wird Murrens und Schreyens genug erwecken."[5] It can be anticipated, therefore, that many of the ideas concerning the subjectivity and relativity of perception and the respective roles of the mind and the heart will be encountered in this second novel. Our concern will be with how Wieland's attitude toward these philosophical questions has changed, if at all.

In Agathon Wieland's concern with ontological and moral problems is more clearly expressed than in Don Sylvio. This intensity is demonstrated by the altered structure of the three different versions of Agathon. The novel opens in medias res; more poignantly expressed, Agathon begins at the point at which Don Sylvio had arrived: contact with the wider world. (By the same token, Peregrinus Proteus begins where Agathon ends.) At the conclusion of Don Sylvio the hero departs on a Bildungsreise, but his further development is not depicted because Wieland was not primarily concerned with character development in his first novel. His attention was focused on the salvation of an aberrant Schwärmer.

At the conclusion of the third version of Agathon the hero also departs on an extended journey, but here it is not a question of filling a void caused by the dispersion of useless illusions. Agathon undertakes his journey to distract himself, to help himself overcome his passion for Danae to whom he has promised to be nothing more than a brother. During these travels Agathon learned nothing new; rather, his observations confirmed what he had already experienced and what Archytas in his wisdom had taught: ". . . dass die Menschen, im Durchschnitt genommen, überall so sind, wie Hippias sie schilderte, wiewohl sie so seyn sollten, wie Archytas durch sein Beispiel lehrte" (XI, 391).

Wieland's second novel stresses the evolution of a social being through interaction with the world. When we first meet Agathon he has already experienced disillusionment. He has learned that his idea of the world and the actual state of the world do not concur. In many ways Agathon resembles his spiritual brother, Don Sylvio. Agathon too is a Schwärmer, although not a naive one. He is aware of the discrepancy between his inner world and external reality. The Delphic adage "gnothi seauton" ("Know yourself") had been inculcated in him from early youth. Introspection led to an awareness of the disparity between mundane reality and ideality. The discrepancy between fantasy and reality in Don Sylvio could be resolved with relative ease because of the nature of that hero's Schwärmerei. The resolution was effected with the realization that das Wunderbare is not part of nature and that appearances are deceptive. In Agathon the recognition of subjective perception raises the more basic philosophical question: What is that Highest Truth which imparts meaning to life?[6]

This prime difference between Don Sylvio and Agathon can be expressed as the distinction between entzaubern and enttäuschen. Don Sylvio was entzaubert; that is, he was freed from overwhelming naiveté concerning the empirical world, from his belief in the all-pervasive reality of the fantasy world. Agathon, as we shall see, is enttäuscht; that is, he is deceived by mankind. He is disillusioned in the sense that, on the whole, mankind does not live up to his expectations. Nevertheless, Agathon does not renounce his ideals, does not become a Sophist or an Epicurean or a Cynic. This fact points to the concept of ultimate Truth in the novel.

Agathon is especially significant for a study of possible alterations in the poet's philosophical views simply because its composition covers three decades.[7] The first mention of the novel is in a letter to Zimmermann on January 5, 1762. Wieland writes that, despite the commotion and lack of time due to his obligations in Biberach, he had begun the novel several months ago.[8] Thirty years later Wieland writes his son-in-law Reinhold that he has been working on a revision of Agathon (the third version, published in 1794). Most of the revisions were stylistic. With respect to content, Wieland was either still in agreement with the novel's import or felt that major changes would destroy the work as a valid document of his literary and intellectual evolution. "An dem Inhalt dieses Werkes kann und darf ich nichts, oder doch nichts beträchtliches verändern (ausser dass ich ein paar Auswüchse ganz wegschneide)."[9]

It is ambiguous from this statment whether Wieland still agreed with the philosophical position of Agathon. Therefore, we will have to place more weight on Peregrinus Proteus, which is clearly the result of Wieland's intellectual fermentation in the late 1780's.

I base this discussion of Agathon on the third version, and refer to the earlier versions when necessary in order to ascertain if and how the intention of the novel has been altered. The differences between the various versions are as follows: the second (1773) includes "Ueber das Historische im Agathon" and "Geschichte der Danae." The third and final version (1794) adds Hippias' visit to Agathon in the Syracuse prison and the concluding dialogue between Archytas and Agathon. These additions are of special interest.

Hippias and Archytas are diametrically opposed in their philosophical views and for this reason are crucial to Agathon's development. Our major concern is the roles, the intellect and the heart play for them in ascertaining Truth. Hippias and Archytas consider the function of both in a decidedly different light.

The structure of the novel is intimately related to its epistemological and ontological import.[10] As in Don Sylvio, Wieland wears many masks in Agathon. He is omniscient author and congenial editor as well as creator of the fictive characters. However, unlike Don Sylvio, historicity in the form of a (dubious) manuscript is not claimed for the work. The opening paragraph of the preface to the first edition is ironic; Wieland does not expect to convince the reader of the "historic authenticity" of the events, nor does he care if the reader accepts the narrative as fact or fancy. His main concern is to relate a probable and believable story for the readers moral benefit. The essay "Ueber das Historische im Agathon," appended to the second version, emphasizes even more clearly the fictive but logical character of the events and development. For this reason one cannot expect -- and does not find -- the same kind of satiric and raucous irony evident in Don Sylvio. There are no sanctimonious prudes or superstitious knaves or bedazzled knights-errant to expose and ridicule. Thus the periodic sentence so common in Don Sylvio plays no major role in Agathon. [11] Nor do narrator and reader laugh at the follies of heroes and heels. The irony in Agathon is much more subdued, much more subtle. The general absence of playfulness signals the new psychological intensity in the German novel after 1767 and the work reveals Wieland as a master of psychological delineation.

The reader still enjoys an intimate relationship with the author and editor, who share special knowledge, even ignorance, with him. But the irony, which arises from the recognition of the disparity between fact and fantasy, provides an essentially comic relief from the labors of philosophic reflection and is not designed to ridicule. [12] An example of verbal irony common to both the first and third versions occurs shortly after the revelation of Psyche's true identity in Tarentum. The author chides his female readers: "Und nun, zärtliche Lesserinnen, was mangelte ihm noch, um so glückselig zu seyn als es Sterbliche seyn können, -- als dass Archytas nicht irgend eine liebenswürdige Tochter oder Nichte hatte, mit der wir ihn vermählen könnten?" (A, 390; C, XI, 186). [13]

One example of Wieland's light verbal irony is occasioned by the explanation of Psyche's presence in Italy. Wieland notes that a storm at sea is a convenient literary device to effect a sudden change in fortune for the hero or heroine.

Es war also ein Sturm (und wir hoffen niemand wird sich darüber zu beschweren haben, denn es ist, unsers Wissens, der erste in dieser Geschichte) der die liebenswürdige Psyche aus der furchtbaren Gewalt eines verliebten Seeräubers rettete. Das Schiff scheiterte an der Italiänischen Küste, einige Meilen von Kapua; und Psyche, von den Nereiden oder Liebesgöttern beschirmt, war die einzige Person auf dem Schiffe, welche vermuthlich auf einem Brete, wohlbehalten von den Zefyrn ans Land getragen wurde. Die Zefyrn allein wären hierzu vielleicht nicht hinreichend gewesen; aber mit Hülfe einiger Fischer, welche glücklicher Weise bei der Hand waren, hatte die Sache keine Schwierigkeit. (A, 393; C, XI, 191)

This same passage in Don Sylvio would have been related matter-of-factly and earnestly. But here Wieland expects no one to take das Wunderbare literally; thus he cannot treat the incident as raucously ironic. Furthermore, this type of chatty irony is restricted to non-essential aspects of the novel, e.g., those which have no bearing on the reader's moral edification.

At other times Wieland will use his guise as author or editor to protect himself from criticism for depicting immoral situations (A, 440; C, XI, 215) or for convincingly portraying a eudaemonistic philosophy (A, 4-5; C, IX, x ff.).

However, the chief type of irony in this novel is caused by the situations and is inherent in the structure. We should not expect the ironic parallel or contrasting episodic interspersion of the kind encountered in Don Sylvio. Wieland does introduce parallel interludes in the narration of Agathon's adventures, but these episodes serve to substantiate the hero's philosophical position. The situation irony in Agathon is the result of not achieving the intended objective. The effect of Hippias' visit to Agathon in prison is an example of this irony. The sophist appears personally in order better to win Agathon to his side, but succeeds only in defeating his purpose. It is further ironic that Danae refuses to enter into a marital relationship with Agathon -- a goal she had earnestly desired earlier. It is ironic that Agathon flees from Smyrna because of moral scruples and later learns that Danae is no less exalted than Psyche. We will also see that the conclusion of the novel is ironic, since the philosophical system explicated no longer corresponds to Wieland's conviction.

Finally, a word about the peculiar irony of the first version (which in some instances is carried over into the third). In the 1767 edition an omniscient author is postulated, but this author is exposed as being just as naive as Agathon. How could it be otherwise, since Wieland is attempting to depict himself and his own psychogenesis? (This point will be demonstrated later.) Wieland is too honest to portray a fully developed Agathon, since Wieland himself is not complete. Thus at the end of Book 9 (Book 11 in the third version) the author says:

> Ohne also eben so voreilig über ihn [Agathon] zu urtheilen, wie man gewohnt ist, es im täglichen Leben alle Augenblicke zu thun -- wollen wir fortfahren, ihn zu beobachten, die wahren Triebräder seiner Handlungen so genau als uns möglich seyn wird auszuspähen, keine geheime Bewegung seines Herzens, welche uns einigen Aufschluss hierüber geben kan, entwischen lassen, und unser Urtheil über das Ganze seines moralischen Wesens so lange zurückhalten, bis -- wir es kennen werden. (A, 321; C, XI, 44)

The connotation of this passage is obvious: Wieland does not know what Agathon's true essence is. As a result he procrastinates -- for thirty years! It is not until the dialogue between Archytas and Agathon is added in the third edition that the reader, the author, and Wieland achieve a full view of the hero's "distilled essence." The periodic sentence concluding the passage emphasizes the ironic twist. After the "bis" the reader expects some sort of encompassing explanation, but is confronted with the "omniscient" author's ignorance.

The irony of this passage is more pronounced in the first version than in the last. The reason is the radically different conclusion of the two versions. The attempt at a happy ending in the first version is in marked contrast to the exalted resignation of the final one. In the first edition Wieland admits that Danae's continence is improbable; yet he endeavors to convince the reader that he has done everything in his power to make Agathon happy (A, 408-409). The effect is nevertheless ironic because unconvincing. The irony gains another aspect when we consider that he did do all in his power to ensure his hero's felicity. The addition of Danae's story,

Hippias' visit, and the explication of Archytas' wisdom all preclude the possibility of an ironic ending in version three. The reader is no longer surprised that Danae and Agathon can so completely deny their erotic natures. [14]

The implementation of the time-honored technique of in medias res enables Wieland to capitalize on the advantages of present- and past-time narrative. Past-time narrative in the novel is restricted to flashbacks and retrospection. Wieland takes advantage of these opportunities to elucidate the psychogenesis of the major characters. Present-time narrative is confined, on the other hand, to the immediate situations in the novel. The hero's experiences are therefore not related in chronological order. This is also true of other characters in the book; for example, Danae and Archytas. In each case the reader makes the character's acquaintance at a certain stage in his development. Gradually, through the author's use of retrospection, the reader begins to understand why the character thinks and acts as he does. Wieland employs this method of retrospection, perhaps, in order to draw the reader's attention more vividly to certain stages or aspects of the character's evolution. [15]

If one could draw an analogy to a movie, one could say that the projectionist slows the film or stops it altogether in order to allow the onlooker an opportunity to scrutinize a crucial frame and to allow him time to reflect on the deeper significance. Then the film is rewound and replayed so that the psychogenetical factors can be better examined and apprehended. If the film is played through continuously from beginning to end at the normal speed, the viewer cannot fully comprehend some of the vital influences.

The reader is frequently confronted with this technique in Agathon. Because of its philosophical nature, the novel must give the reader the chance to pause and reflect on what has happened and what is happening. If Wieland had narrated Agathon's development chronologically and only in the present tense, he would have lost an additional and valuable perspective (a catchword in this study). Many pertinent influences in the psychogenesis of the chief figures would undoubtedly have gone unnoticed or at least unstressed. A few examples will clarify this point. The reason for Agathon's rejection of Hippias' eudaemonistic philosophy is explained in retrospect. Danae's ultimate decision to renounce her former way of life is elucidated post facto in the history of her early experiences. Finally, Archytas' philosophical position is clarified in depth after the reader has made his acquaintance. Even Psyche's true identity is revealed in retrospect.

We must therefore distinguish between two levels of narration. The first relates the events of present time and serves as the unifying factor of the novel. In all present-time narratives Agathon is an active participant. The second level of narrative is in past time, in the form of individual histories; for example, those of Agathon, Danae, Psyche and Archytas. The past-time narrative complements the second level of narration, causing a better understanding of present resolutions and action. It is particularly significant for the structure of the novel that a major portion of this second-level narrative was added in the second and third versions.

The retrospective examination of Danae's disposition and experiences vividly portrays her close spiritual relationship to her male counterpart, Agathon, as well as to her female opposite, Psyche. The third chapter of Book 16, "Darstellung der Lebensweisheit des Archytas," sums up the Weltanschauung that Agathon is gradually formulating for himself, and places Danae (Chariklea) in the proper spiritual perspective for the hero (cf. XI, 388).

These additions to the second-level narrative, therefore, serve as a further elucidation of Wieland's philosophical position, whereas the present-time narrative shows the genesis of the hero's world view. The interpolation of these two narrative levels also provides for variation. The present-time narrative frequently serves as a refreshing prelude to or respite from the philosophical discussions. In sum, the structure of Agathon is designed to highlight major confrontations with philosophical systems contrary or analogous to Agathon's own view.

When we examine Agathon's scenes of activity chronologically, a pattern emerges. The theaters of influence in his case are Delphi, Athens, Smyrna, Syracuse, and Tarentum. Here too there is an interspersion of types. Agathon's contact with the world is rather limited in Delphi, Smyrna, and Tarentum. He is in a more or less closed society and acts in a basically passive manner allowing external forces to influence him. (To a certain extent, the conclusion of the third version represents an exception because Agathon is depicted as co-ruler of the tiny republic of Tarentum.)

In Athens and Syracuse, on the other hand, Agathon takes an active part in directing the endeavors of large, influential republics. In these two theaters Agathon comes into contact with the world at large and attempts to leave his imprint on it.

In each of these spheres of action Agathon is on a quest. He is searching for the embodiment of his ideals in this world. He begins his search in the seclusion of the temple at Delphi and ends it in the seclusion of the ascetic court in Tarentum. In both cases his searching eye is directed inward into his own soul. Athens and Syracuse represent thwarted attempts to realize his ideals in the political realm. Smyrna -- the center of the novel and the most intensive of the experiences -- represents Agathon's attempt to harmonize the sublime desires of the spirit with the erotic passions of the flesh. A worthy adversary of Orphic philosophy is depicted in the sophist and epicure, Hippias. Hippias is able to present a strong case for materialism and exerts a tremendous influence on Agathon. Yet he is unsuccessful in winning the youth to his point of view. Agathon begins his Smyrnian adventures as a Schwärmer and ends them as a Schwärmer. This remark will be clarified later.

Let us turn now to an investigation of Agathon's epistemological and ontological views. The distinctive aspect of the ontological question in Agathon is the dichotomy of idealism and materialism (or transcendentalism and empiricism). In fact, the entire novel is devoted to depicting Agathon's vacillation between the Platonic ideals and the Epicurean pleasures of the senses in an attempt to harmonize his

head with his heart. Agathon's starting point in his quest for Truth is Nature.
(This is true as well of Hippias and Archytas, who arrive at opposite extremes of
the philosophical spectrum.)

Agathon begins his quest for Truth as an impressionable youth in Delphi. The education he received in the temple was conducive to an idealistic and metempirical
view of the world. Youth has a propensity for fantasy worlds and for delight in the
mysteries of Nature. This disposition is highly favorable to a philosophic system
which is able to explain everything to the young mind in vivid terms. Agathon
describes his state of mind during those years (note the tone reminiscent of the
introduction to "Sympathien"):

> Ich stand damals eben in dem Alter, worin wir, aus dem langen Traume der
> Kindheit erwachend, uns selbst zuerst zu finden glauben, die Welt um uns
> her mit erstaunten Augen betrachten und neugierig sind, unsre eigne Natur
> und den Schauplatz, worauf wir uns ohne unser Zuthun versetzt sehen, ken-
> nen zu lernen. Wie willkommen ist uns da eine Filosofie, die den Vortheil
> unsrer Wissensbegierde mit dieser Neigung zum Wunderbaren ... vereiniget,
> alle unsre Fragen beantwortet, alle Räthsel erklärt, alle Aufgaben auflöset!
> (X, 10)

Given this propensity of young people in such a state of mind as Agathon to project
their biases onto the phenomenal world, it is readily comprehensible why Agathon
viewed the world more with his imagination than with his five senses. He turns to
Nature for confirmation of his prejudices, and he finds it: "Vermuthungen und Wünsche werden hier zu desto stärkern Beweisen, da wir in dem blossen Anschauen
der Natur zu viel Majestät, zu viel Geheimnissreiches und Göttliches zu sehen glauben, um besorgen zu können, dass wir jemals zu gross von ihr denken möchten"
(X, 11). [16]

At first Agathon speaks hesitantly about the irrational perception of spiritual
reality ("zu sehen glauben"). But then he becomes more affirmative if still a bit
apologetic. It is obvious that the youth does not consider subjective, seraphic interpretation of Nature to be blameworthy when he confesses:

> ... selbst, itzt nachdem glückliche Erfahrungen mich von dieser hochfliegen-
> den Art zu denken zurück gebracht haben, glaube ich mit einer innerlichen
> Gewalt, die sich gegen jeden Zweifel empört, zu fühlen, dass die Ueberein-
> stimmung mit unsern edelsten Neigungen, die ihr das Wort redet, der echte
> Stempel der Wahrheit sey, und dass selbst in diesen Träumen, welche den
> sinnlichen Menschen so ausschweifend scheinen, für unsern Geist mehr Reali-
> tät, mehr Unterhaltung und Aufmunterung, eine reichere Quelle von ruhiger
> Freude, und ein festerer Grund der Selbstzufriedenheit liege, als in allem
> was uns die Sinne Angenehmes und Gutes anzubieten haben. (X, 11-12)

A fine distinction emerges here between material and spiritual reality, of which
the higher good is obviously the spiritual. Agathon does not deny the validity of

material reality as a basis for human behavior. But he does seem to assert that action resulting from an insight into spiritual reality is more desirable and morally of a higher nature. Man is composed of body and soul. And the soul is the decisive element in designating the essence of humanitas. The soul with its functions, not the body with its animalistic desires, is of paramount importance in this context.

There is a certain obvious parallel between Agathon in this state of mind and Don Sylvio. Both spent their early years in isolation and were exposed to only one interpretation of reality. For this reason Don Sylvio considered das Wunderbare to be part of Nature and not a product of his mind. In the above passages the insinuation seems to be that Agathon viewed das Wunderbare also as part of Nature. In Agathon's case, however, youth's innate attraction to the strange and mysterious is stressed more than in Don Sylvio's case. In his opinion man's preference for the marvelous is inborn, intrinsic to his very nature as a man. This appears to be the import of the fact that Agathon's biases are "substantiated" by Nature. Later, in the essay "Ueber den Hang der Menschen, an Magie und Geistererscheinungen zu glauben, " Wieland even asserts that the propensity for and delight in the marvelous is a basic trait of human nature. [17]

Before Theogiton made his overt sexual advances to Agathon the youth believed it was possible actually and physically to associate with the great spirits of the metaphysical world. Theogiton took advantage of the boy's naiveté to attain his perverse goal by posing as Apollo. After his disillusionment, after Agathon discovered the true nature of his "theophany, " he does not lose faith in his spirits. He is not even fazed when the rejected and embarrassed priest claims that religion is nothing more than a great hoax to deceive the people (X, 21). Agathon continues in his conviction that the gods are real. But now he conjectures that union with the gods is possible only in the realm of ideals. If he could purify and beautify his soul to the extent that he would be as one in thought and desire with the godhead, then he would be worthy to associate with the lofty spirits.

In order to ascertain how to attain beauty and purity of soul, Agathon turned again to Nature. Through the observation of the mysterious workings and astounding unity of Nature -- which he considered to be a mirror of the eternal and the unfathomable -- Agathon felt he could discover the path to perfection. He resolves (in accord with the dictates of eighteenth-century Enlightenment) to imitate Nature: "Ich überredete mich, dass die unverrückte Beschauung der Weisheit und Güte, welche sowohl aus der besondern Natur eines jeden Theils der Schöpfung, als aus dem Plan und der allgemeinen Oekonomie des Ganzen hervorleuchte, das unfehlbare Mittel sey, selbst weise und gut zu werden" (X, 23-24).

Thus Agathon's initial ontological view of the world is primarily a result of his religious upbringing. He is little concerned with phenomena per se but only with the unifying source from which they spring. He is, however, apparently aware of a distinction between sensation and judgment. His idealistic philosophy comes into repeated conflict with material reality the more he comes into contact with men and their world.

The first genuinely serious threat to Agathon's idealism is presented by Hippias' sophism and sensualism. To be sure, the youth has seen his view of the world contradicted by Theogiton, Pythia, and his Athenian compatriots. But these disappointments did not represent a threat to his philosophical principles. The individuals involved were for him merely evidence that they had not attained the same insight into life as he had. Hippias, on the other hand, is apparently able to demonstrate rationally that man's nature is basically materialistic.

It is informative to note that Hippias begins his discourse by referring Agathon to Nature. Both men, therefore, base their theories of life on Nature, although they arrive at opposite conclusions. Only by following the dictates of Nature, Hippias asserts, can man know and realize his true destiny. Hippias asks whom else can man consult "in order to determine how we should live in order to live well" (IX, 102). As for the gods, the sophist asserts that they are either Nature herself or the source of Nature. In either case, "the voice of Nature [is] the voice of the divinity" (IX, 102). Man needs only to be attentive to Nature's voice to know what proper behavior is. But what does the voice of Nature prescribe? According to Hippias, Nature commands each man to pursue his own welfare: "Suche dein eigenes Bestes" (IX, 139). This is the universal law of Nature. There is however a stipulation for man as a social being: Do not infringe upon the rights of others while pursuing your own personal interest (IX, 139-140). By obeying this command man can achieve felicity and self-fulfillment in this world. Furthermore, happiness on earth should be man's chief objective because man knows no other existence.

Hippias arrived at this inference after considering the nature of the Good and the Beautiful. Both are undeniably relative to and dependent upon the social norms of the respective cultures. Yet there is a universal standard for the morally Good and Beautiful. This universal standard is the example given by the "most ingenious, best educated, most vivacious, most sociable, and most pleasant" nation (IX, 138). Hippias maintains that "Das Muster der aufgeklärtesten und geselligsten Nazion scheint also die wahre Regel des sittlichen Schönen, oder des Anständigen zu seyn" (IX, 138). Here the reader is perhaps given an explanation why Athens and Smyrna were chosen for theaters of action in the novel. The sophist concludes: "und Athen und Smyrna sind die Schulen, worin man seinen Geschmack und seine Sitten bilden muss" (IX, 138).

In this discourse Hippias attacks the foundation of Agathon's idealism by endeavoring to demonstrate that all universals are immanently a part of the material world. The morally Good and Beautiful are viewed in a strictly utilitarian and mundane manner. The divine voice of Nature is reduced to the lowly dictate of pleasure-seeking. He recognizes salubrious reason (gesunde Vernunft) as the only valid guide in this world. Imagination, he says, has its place in poetry but not in a philosophy of life (IX, 101).

Agathon's response to Hippias' convincing argument is reminiscent of Don Sylvio's reply to the dilemma of his "twofold" love. Agathon does not attempt to refute Hippias' arguments; instead, he calmly declares he is not convinced that the sophist's view is correct. The only reason which he offers to substantiate his position is completely subjective: "Weil meine Erfahrungen und Empfindungen deinen Schlüssen widersprechen" (IX, 149). Even if the whole world held the opposite view, Agathon states, he would still be convinced of the truth of that which he has intrinsically and intensely felt. Thus the same motif of subjectivity and relativity in the perception of Truth, which was so pronounced in Don Sylvio, plays an important role in Agathon.

For Agathon the heart fulfills a vastly more important function than the mind in the pursuit of Truth. Agathon declares that even if Hippias were able to demonstrate the fallacy of his experiences and sentiments, the sophist would only be able to prove that he is Hippias and not Agathon. But he would not have proven Agathon wrong. Who is to judge objectively the validity of subjective experiences and sentiments, Agathon queries? (IX, 150).

In an earlier discourse between the two men Agathon is more explicit in defining his theory of knowledge and explicating his ontological view. He asserts that the intellect is not the only means of perceiving the godhead but that the heart is more direct and more reliable in perceiving ultimate Truth. Nature, he claims, adresses itself primarily to the sensitivity of the heart, not to the perspicacity of the intellect. The unmitigated effect of Nature on man is more important than a detailed understanding of its intricate workings. The effect of Nature is of chief importance because it directs man's attention to the causes, the source, the divinity. In Agathon's opinion Hippias' heart is awry, not his head. [18] "... und wenn es dein Ernst wäre, die Wahrheit zu suchen, wie wär' es möglich, sie zu verfehlen? sie, die sich dem allgemeinen Gefühl der Menschheit aufdringt? Was ist dieses grosse Ganze, welches wir die Welt nennen, anders als ein Inbegriff von Wirkungen? Wo ist die Ursache davon? ... O Hippias, glaube mir, nicht dein Kopf ... dein Herz ist ein Gottesläugner" (IX, 81).

Agathon goes on to stress the function of the heart in the perception of ultimate reality. "Ein gerades Herz, eine unverfälschte Seele hat nicht vonnöthen, die erste, die augenscheinlichste und liebenswürdigste aller Wahrheiten durch alle diese Irrgänge metafysischer Begriffe zu verfolgen. Ich brauche nur die Augen zu öffnen, nur mich selbst zu empfinden, um in der ganzen Natur, um in dem Innersten meines eigenen Wesens den Urheber derselben, diesen höchsten wohlthätigen Geist, zu erblicken. Ich erkenne sein Daseyn nicht bloss durch Vernunftschlüsse; ich fühle es, wie ich fühle dass eine Sonne ist, wie ich fühle dass ich selbst bin" (IX, 81-82). The concluding remark is a piquant variation of Descartes' "cogito, ergo sum." It stresses the importance of feeling in Wieland's philosophic as well as poetic works. Agathon pities Hippias because Nature has denied the sophist this sixth sense, this sensitivity to the transcendental effect of Nature (IX, 89). [19]

Thus, in effect, Hippias' rhetoric and intellectual agility have been of no avail. He cannot hope to convince Agathon through argumentation that his fanaticism is illfounded and foolish. The only way he will succeed in influencing the youth is by sentiment, by appealing to his heart. To this end the shrewd sophist enlists the aid of the talented hetaera, Danae. Hippias intends to prove to the youth that his notion of rigid virtue is a sham. The sophist believes Agathon will be cured of his "peculiar fanaticism" once he has tasted the pleasures of the flesh, and will then be won over to the materialistic point of view.

Unfortunately, Hippias is disappointed. Danae and Agathon fall in love. Their love is not merely physical, as Hippias had schemed, but also spiritual and therefore enduring and purifying. Normally, Agathon considered the body and the soul as belonging to two different worlds, but in his love for Danae these two worlds seemed to unite (IX, 218). Later, in the discourse with Archytas, Agathon admits in retrospect that he felt he had actually found in Danae those supreme attributes of which he had had only a presentiment at Delphi.

> Die mannigfaltigen Vollkommenheiten der liebenswürdigen Danae, die Feinheit der Bande, womit sie mein ganzes Wesen umwickelte, die Natur meiner Liebe selbst, die ... selbst an die edelsten Triebe und Gesinnungen des Herzens, an alles sittlich Schöne und Gute, so sanft und gefällig sich anschmiegte, -- alles diess gab unvermerkt der Einbildung immer mehr Wahrscheinlichkeit, in Danae das wirklich gefunden zu haben, was ich in den Hainen von Delphi nur geahnet, und aus Unerfahrenheit in die überirdischen Formen und Bilder, die durch die Orphischen Mysterien in meine Seele gekommen wären, gekleidet hätte. (XI, 349-350)

However, Agathon does attribute his view of Danae (as the embodiment of his metaphysical ideals) to the workings of the imagination. He refers to his view of Danae as Einbildung, not as Empfindung. Yet there is more to Danae's significance for Agathon, since he had admitted earlier that when he thinks of his love for Danae he is compelled by some inner power to believe that this love was natural and good (cf. XI, 346). Thus there is an air of ambiguity surrounding Danae's significance. Or does there only appear to be? Once again man's ability to distinguish between Empfindung and Einbildung is evinced. Agathon's love for Danae was genuine, was intensely felt. Thus his heart tells him it was natural and morally good to act as he did. As far as his conception of Danae as the embodiment of spiritual ideals is concerned, Agathon did not rest easy. He was so overcome with his love that he began to think it senseless to seek to know the innermost secrets of Nature. Eventually he began to consider questions of man's origin and destiny to be irrelevant (XI, 351). Still he was not completely satisfied with the conclusions drawn under Danae's influence. An inner voice seemed to say it was improper to so restrict the use of reason. Agathon confesses to Archytas: "Diess ... waren die Resultate der Vorstellungsart, die sich ... meines Kopfes bemächtigte, ohne jedoch mein Herz gänzlich zu befriedigen, noch verhindern zu können, dass nicht von Zeit zu Zeit eine geheime Stimme in mir sich gegen die Gleichgültigkeit erhob, mit welcher meine Vernunft dem Gebrauch ihrer wesentlichsten Kräfte so enge Gränzen setzte" (XI, 351).

Agathon became aware that his head and his heart were no longer in harmony as they had been prior to his love for Danae. The reason for his disquiet was not the love itself but his false conclusion that Danae embodied everything he sought. His mind deceived him, told him to look no further for ethereal ideals, for they do exist embodied in this woman. There is no need any longer for metaphysical concerns. However, Agathon's heart spoke the truth: search further; you have not reached your goal! There are overtones of this sentiment in the admission Agathon shyly makes to Danae during the narration of his experiences in Delphi. Agathon seems to say that he was foolish as a youth to indulge in fantastic Platonic dreams, and excuses himself for having acted so childishly. Still, whether it be justification for his former behavior or a sudden burst of enthusiasm because he believes his dreams of Virtue, Beauty, and Goodness are harmoniously realized in Danae, the hero exclaims that there is definitely truth in the noble inclinations of the soul.

> Und, soll ich dir's gestehen, schöne Danae? selbst, itzt nachdem glückliche Erfahrungen mich von dieser hoch fliegenden Art zu denken zurück gebracht haben, glaube ich mit einer innerlichen Gewalt, die sich gegen jeden Zweifel empört, zu fühlen, dass diese Uebereinstimmung mit unsern edelsten Neigungen, die ihr das Wort redet, der echte Stempel der Wahrheit sey, und dass selbst in diesen Träumen, welche den sinnlichen Menschen so ausschweifend scheinen, für unsern Geist mehr Realität, mehr Unterhaltung und Aufmunterung, eine reichere Quelle von ruhiger Freude, und ein festerer Grund der Selbstzufriedenheit liege, als in allem was uns die Sinne Angenehmes und Gutes anzubieten haben. [20] (X, 11-12)

The cause of disquiet in Agathon's soul is symptomatic of his delusion. While he is in Danae's presence the Platonic ideals seem less immediate. A parallel to Don Sylvio's predicament can be drawn here. In Donna Felicia's presence Don Sylvio finds it difficult to believe that his imaginary princess is the true object of his love. In his case it was demonstrated that his innermost feeling had not deceived him. His love for the imaginary princess was but a foreshadowing of the real thing. So too in Agathon's case. His love for Danae is real, but so is his presentiment of Orphic theosophy. [21] Agathon tried to resolve the conflict by making the two identical (X, 145). The attempt was of course erroneous and it led to disillusionment. Agathon overlooked the fact that it is natural for present sentiment to overshadow even vivid memories of past sentiment. Because he neglected this fact, Agathon concluded that his previous sentiments had merely been beautiful dreams and enchanting delusions (XI, 349).

Through this oversight a stalemate developed between his heart and his head. The truce would possibly have continued indefinitely had not Agathon been so crassly awakened. The awakening served a double purpose: it forced him to continue his quest for the Highest Good, and it made him better acquainted with his own disposition. Hippias reveals to Agathon that Danae is (was) a hetaera by profession; furthermore, he himself had once enjoyed her favors. Shocked, hurt, and disillusioned, Agathon leaves Smyrna eventually; but the author leaves no doubt as to the motivations for his departure. Agathon does not depart because Danae is not the person he considered her to be; neither reason nor love for virtue motivated him. The genuine motivations are jealousy and slighted ego (X, 183-184). The thought that most disturbed Agathon was that he was not Danae's first lover and that Hippias had enjoyed the favors of her bed (X, 177).

Wieland points out (X, 214-220) that although it is theoretically possible for a Greek to unite his concept of virtue with genuine love for a woman, it was impossible in Agathon's case. Although it was acceptable to spend a night with a hetaera, it was socially taboo in Agathon's time to fall in love with one (X, 215-216). In addition, the Greeks did not know the passionate, distracting kind of love; a man must always be in full control of his intellectual powers (X, 219-220). Agathon transgressed by loving a hetaera to distraction; hence he became unmanly in the eyes of his compatriots.

One aspect of Agathon's love for Danae warrants further elucidation. Because he did not know Danae was a hetaera he could judge her impartially. The high esteem in which he came to hold her is justified by her inner disposition, as is evinced in the account of her early experiences and sentiments. Danae is in fact <u>eine schöne Seele</u>, who unfortunately was exposed to wrong influences. Until she met Agathon she had worn the garb and make-up of a hetaera without being one at heart. Agathon's genuine love for her enabled her true nature to emerge from the inner recesses of her soul to which it had been relegated by fate. Agathon saw Danae as she really was and in so doing freed her from her past, for she too began to view herself through his eyes. Out of their union of souls a new person arose, Chariklea. Danae, in effect, died.

The point to be stressed here is the fact that this tremendous change was wrought by the irrational powers of the soul. It is the heart which is best able to "know" the ultimate truth of the matter, not the mind. When Agathon learns that Danae is a courtesan his intellect assumes command of his actions, stilling the voice of sentiment (cf. X, 193). Agathon's mind does not judge Danae according to the same standards as does his heart. He places more trust (erroneously) in rational conclusions than in intensely felt sentiment. In rejecting Danae, Agathon allows himself to be deceived by appearances and by his own self-love. In this respect we must distinguish between noble and base sentiment. Noble sentiment is genuine human love, and only it has the peculiar power of acute perspicacity. Base sentiment, such as jealousy or vanity, impairs and prevents rational clarity, causing man to draw false conclusions.

Another reason for Agathon's departure from Smyrna was his uneasiness at having been idle for so long. He is irritated at himself for indulging in leisure and for having done nothing useful or creative. One of the tenets of the Enlightenment is evident in this belief that man must be constantly engaged in useful activity if he is to fulfill his destiny. Agathon's personal concept of virtue is inherent in this view. With respect to his relationship to Danae, therefore, Agathon reproaches himself primarily for his idleness. The author writes: "Was wollte er denn nun antworten, da er sich selbst anklagen musste, eine so lange Zeit, ohne irgend eine lobenswürdige That, verloren für seinen Geist, verloren für die Tugend, verloren für sein eigenes und das allgemeine Beste, in unthätigem Müssiggang ... unrühmlich verschwendet zu haben?" (X, 178).

The drive to improve oneself, to be useful, and to better social conditions for the benefit of all men is characteristic of Die Geschichte des Agathon. It is the accepted standard against which all characters in the novel are measured explicitly or implicitly. It is the harmonious balance which the Schwärmer Agathon consciously endeavors to achieve between his heart and mind, and which he repeatedly misses because of excessive idealism (Delphi, Athens, Syracuse) or intense personal involvement (Smyrna). Schwärmerei is interpreted in this novel, as in Don Sylvio, as a deviation from this norm. The relation between Agathon's absolute idealism and beneficial social integration must be scrupulously observed in order to detect any change in Wieland's attitude toward this phenomenon. It will become evident that the author ultimately evaluates Agathon's extremism not as Schwärmerei but as Enthusiasmus.

The negative factors in Agathon's decision to leave Smyrna have been mentioned. But what about the positive motivations? Why did he decide to go to Syracuse? Agathon learned that Dionysius, the ruler of Syracuse, had discarded his dissolute way of life to become a disciple of Plato. The bacchanalian court was transformed into a temple of wisdom and virtue. Agathon could not resist the temptation "to assist in the completion of the glorious undertaking of transforming a licentious tyrant into a benevolent prince" (X, 197).

The thought of participating in such a laudable effort revived his waning self-respect and filled him with new zeal and a reaffirmation of the Platonic idealism which had been all but forgotten in his preoccupation with Danae (X, 211). When Agathon arrives in Syracuse, he learns that Dion has been banished and that Plato has returned to Athens, having been unsuccessful in reforming Dionysius. Agathon flatters himself that he may succeed where Plato has failed (XI, 9). Once again Agathon begins to lose himself in dreams which embellish his role in the transformation to take place in Syracuse. The positive motivating factor, then, which led to Agathon's departure from Smyrna was the renewed desire to realize Platonic ideals as governing principles in daily life.

In a sense, Agathon's departure for Syracuse is a relapse into his celestial Schwärmerei. However, Wieland now calls it a "kosmopolitischer Enthusiasmus" (XI, 124), and, as we have seen, enthusiasm is a positive value as opposed to asocial Schwärmerei. [22] This aspect is seen in the fervor with which Agathon entertains the thought of a state governed according to Platonic principles, as well as in the absolute nature of his world view. Agathon is not willing to compromise his principles, is not ready to recognize the hard facts of reality. His type of Schwärmerei becomes most intense when he is most oblivious to the undeniable facts of social and political life. Wieland indicates to the reader even before Agathon arrives in Syracuse that the hero's undertaking is doomed from the outset. Wieland writes that Agathon is traveling to Dionysius' court in order to learn "dass auf dieser schlüpfrigen Höhe die Tugend entweder der Klugheit aufgeopfert werden muss, oder die behutsamste Klugheit nicht hinreichend ist den Sturz des Tugendhaften zu verhindern" (X, 212). Wieland seems to say that absolute virtue in Agathon's sense is impossible in this world (cf. X, 208). To disregard the demands

of mundane existence will result in disappointment and failure. Only with respect
to this tendency does Agathon's enthusiasm degenerate into <u>Schwärmerei</u>.

Agathon favorably impresses Dionysius and quickly advances to an influential position in the republic. Agathon was aware of the difficulties to be encountered in
turning Dionysius into a benevolent despot. Agathon was no longer the youthful
dreamer of Athens who imagined it would be as easy to execute a plan as to conceive one (XI, 51). His naiveté in this respect had been cured. Furthermore, he
no longer held human nature in high esteem, since the Athens affair had demonstrated that a laudable plan and personal integrity would not necessarily gain his
colleagues' support (XI, 51). In any case, circumstances inherent in a given situation may impede or counteract the soundest theoretical plan.

It is actually unfair to say that Agathon no longer esteemed human nature; it would
be more accurate to state that Agathon had learned through his experiences to make
a distinction between the metaphysical, the natural, and the affected man (XI, 50).
The metaphysical man passes his time in dreaming or meditating in solitude. The
natural man is characterized, in Rousseauean terms, by the simplicity and innocence of Nature. The affected man is a product of the civilizing process. The laws,
customs, opinions, and demands of society force man to conceal his true intentions
by pretense and hypocrisy in order to achieve his goal. The affected man is depicted
as "verfälscht, gedrückt, verzerrt, verschroben, und in unzählige unnatürliche und
betrügliche Gestalten umgeformt oder verkleidet" (XI, 51).

As a result of this insight into human nature Agathon realizes that he will be unable
to make a model prince of Dionysius. He therefore sets himself a modest, attainable
goal: he will try to make Dionysius' rough edges less abrasive. In addition, he plans
to reform Dionysius' deeds from within; that is to say, he will make use of
Dionysius' good moods, passions, even his weaknesses, to achieve whatever good
is possible (XI, 52).

Despite his caution, Agathon did not correctly assess the situation. For example,
Agathon intimated to Dionysius that rulers should be less stringently judged in
their private lives because of the public burden they bear. Agathon's intention was
commendable: he proposed to encourage the relationship between Dionysius and his
harmless mistress, Bacchidion. Agathon concluded that since Dionysius could not
forego his extramarital affairs it would be well if the mistress were not scheming
and ambitious. Thus Agathon hoped to avoid harm to the state, but he miscalculated.
Dionysius had restrained himself out of respect for his virtuous friend. When he
heard Agathon speak approvingly of his licentiousness he dropped all pretense of
virtue. At the same time, Agathon was lowered in Dionysius' esteem. Dionysius
was suspicious of a man who praised a virtuous and chaste life but who openly con-
doned carnal escapades. As Wieland says, Dionysius was inclined "to consider
virtue as either fanaticism or hypocrisy" (XI, 57).

There is a double deception here. Agathon misjudged Dionysius' character and the
ruler misunderstood his minister's intention. This ironic deception of appearances

recurs time and again in Syracuse. Agathon thought Philistus and Timokrates were well disposed toward him, and they were not. Kleonissa appeared to be chaste, but she was not. Here, then, is repeated Wieland's conviction that all appearances are deceptive. We are reminded again of the chameleon motif.

Agathon was ultimately toppled from his powerful position by his eagerness to prevent an intimate relationship between Dionysius and Kleonissa. The matter was aggravated by the fact that Agathon had spurned Kleonissa's advances and thereby incurred her spite. Because of his personal moral rigidity and his equally intense desire to retain his influence over Dionysius -- both directly related to the absolute norm of his idealism -- Agathon fell (XI, 123). When there was no longer doubt that Dionysius was returning to his old ways and that Agathon had no more influence on the prince, Agathon became involved in a conspiracy to overthrow Dionysius. The plot was discovered and Agathon imprisoned.

While languishing in jail Agathon begins to lend credence to Hippias' materialistic view of man. He failed because he remained true to his idealistic absolute principles, whereas Philistus embraced sophist political maxims and succeeded. Agathon laments: "O gewiss Hippias, deine Begriffe, deine Maximen, deine Moral, deine Staatskunst, gründen sich auf die Erfahrung aller Zeiten! Wenn haben die Menschen jemals die Tugend hochgeschätzt, als wenn sie ihrer Dienste benöthigt waren?" (XI, 123). Agathon begins to despair of the validity of his idealistic view of man as destined to a life of virtue. He wonders whether his noble concept of man is perhaps mere delusion: "Wie, Agathon, wenn Hippias auch hierin am Ende Recht behielte, und diese idealische Tugend, der du schon so viel Opfer brachtest, selbst die grösste, wenn auch die schönste, aller Schimären wäre?" (XI, 128).

Dejected, Agathon recognizes that he has misjudged his fellow man. He has judged them subjectively by allowing his personal Platonic bias to color his evaluation of man and society. He committed this error although he was aware of the disparity between the metaphysical, the natural, and the affected man. These distinctions are perhaps valid, but Agathon failed to observe in addition that all men do not have the same exalted view of mankind as he himself. Agathon projected erroneously his own basic desires and convictions into other men. Thus he failed to recognize the subjective validity of his view by taking for granted that his metaphysical view was universally binding. Furthermore, he failed to distinguish between the world of ideals and the world of social reality.

> Nein ... die Menschen sind das nicht, wofür ich sie hielt, da ich sie nach mir selbst, und mich selbst nach den jugendlichen Empfindungen eines gefühlvollen wohlmeinenden Herzens und nach einer noch ungeprüften Unschuld beurtheilte. ... An mir lag der Fehler, der sie zu etwas besserm machen wollte, als sie seyn können! der sie glücklicher machen wollte, als sie selbst zu seyn wünschen. (XI, 122)

The hero is forced to recognize the subjectivity of his view and its dependence upon the unique circumstances of his upbringing. Thus both the subjectivity and relativity of his philosophy are indicated here.

A decisive aspect of Agathon's disillusionment in Syracuse, as contrasted to his deception in Smyrna, concerns the number of people involved. Agathon never trusted Hippias and therefore could not be disappointed by the latter's sophism. He considered the sophists to be opportunists and pragmatists; therefore (in his absolute view) they did not warrant serious attention. Thus Danae -- or more accurately Agathon's opinion of their relationship -- was the only source of delusion in Smyrna. In contrast to this single person, everyone in Syracuse was a disappointment to Agathon. And there is strength in numbers. Syracuse represents a serious danger to Agathon's idealistic view of mankind's destiny because all the facts seem to substantiate Hippias' Weltanschauung.

Agathon is on the point of becoming Hippias' disciple when the sophist unexpectedly visits him in prison. Hippias has come to make an offer which would relieve Agathon of material concerns for the rest of his life. All Agathon need do is accompany Hippias to Smyrna. Before making this generous offer, Hippias rebukes Agathon for neither remaining true to his principles nor completely embracing the sophist principle of shrewdness. In his eyes, Agathon is wavering between sophistic wisdom and seraphic idealism (XI, 141). "Dass du den Muth nicht hattest, entweder deinen Grundsätzen ganz treu zu bleiben, oder, wenn Erfahrung und zunehmende Menschenkenntniss dich von der Richtigkeit der meinigen überführte, dich gänzlich von diesen führen zu lassen: das ist es was dich hierher gebracht hat" (XI, 141).

This explanation of Agathon's error -- logical according to reason -- suddenly clarifies the situation in Agathon's mind and heart. It is paradoxical that the sophist's presence afforded Agathon the insight which prevented the final embracing of Hippias' philosophy. Hippias causes Agathon to perceive the real reason for his disenchantment with Platonic ideals. Agathon had been deceived by his vanity, not by his philosophy.

> Nur zu wohl erkenne ich itzt, dass es thöricht war, mit der Cither in der Hand der Mentor eines Dionysius werden zu wollen ... ich kannte die Menschen zu wenig, und traute mir selbst zu viel. Ich wurde nicht gewahr, wie viel Antheil eine zu lebhafte Empfindung meines eignen Werths an der eiteln Hoffnung hatte, höchst verderbte Menschen entweder durch meine Talente, meine Beredsamkeit, mein Beispiel, zu gewinnen, oder -- warum sollt' ich dir nicht die reine Wahrheit bekennen? -- durch die Ueberlegenheit meines Genius zu überwältigen. (XI, 152-153)

His despondency was occasioned by his dependence on and his pride in his accomplishments in Syracuse. Agathon admits that he was vexed at seeing his work undone by court intriguers, and he was offended by Dionysius' estranged attitude (XI, 155-156). He realizes that his growing reliance on the by-products of his good deeds contaminated his reasoning and led to his despair in his philosophy.

Hippias' intervention also alerted Agathon to the fact that, actually, he felt no reproach from within his own heart. He had a clear conscience as to the uprightness and irreproachability of his intentions (XI, 147). He had not compromised his ideals concerning himself but had only been less strict with others when it seemed necessary (XI, 149). Agathon sums up the change that Hippias had wrought in his disposition:

> Deine Gegenwart stellte plötzlich unser wahres Verhältniss wieder her. Ich fühlte mich wieder denselben, der ich war. ... Er [dein Tadel] weckte das volle Bewusstsein in mir auf, dass mein Wille immer redlich, und mein Zweck rein gewesen war: aber mitten unter der Bestrebung, das Ganze meines Lebens in Syrakus gegen deine Anklagen zu rechtfertigen, öffneten sich meine Augen für die feinen unsichtbaren Schlingen der Eitelkeit, des zu sichern Vertrauens auf meine eigene Stärke, und der übermässigen Selbstschätzung, worin meine Lauterkeit sich ungewahrsam verstrickte; und, indem mir mein Gewissen Zeugniss gab, dass ich so schwach gewe[sen] sey als du mich beschuldigtest, sagte mir eben diese innerliche Stimme, dass ich auch so untadelhaft nicht gewesen sey, als die Eigenliebe mir geschmeichelt hatte. (XI, 157-158)

The first impulse to a proper evaluation of his situation came from the irrational side of human nature: "Ich fühlte mich wieder denselben" (italics mine). Agathon's heart clarified his cloudy and erroneous reasoning so that he was able to perceive the truth with his mind as well. Once Agathon again enjoyed a harmonious balance of head and heart, he was also able to apprehend "this inner voice" with the intellect. Here, then, is another example of the leading role played by the heart in Wieland's epistemology. [23]

Hippias' visit, therefore, is an integral part of the novel. The sophist must reappear so that Agathon can once again consider his exalted ideals as universally binding. Hippias' visit is structurally and philosophically a necessary prelude to the normative significance of Archytas' Lebensphilosophie. [24]

The sophist's reintroduction can also be interpreted as Wieland's effort to dissociate himself from Hippias' skepticism. After the novel was published in 1766-67, even Wieland's admirers felt that Agathon fared badly in the philosophical argument with Hippias. Jacobi correctly perceived that Agathon could answer the sophist in no other way than by appealing to his instinct. Yet the impression was given that Wieland advocated the latter's materialism. On Jacobi's advice, Wieland included two additional footnotes in the second edition which were intended to leave no doubt that Wieland and Hippias had nothing in common (cf. IX, 298-299n, 301). Evidently Jacobi felt that Wieland's denial of any affinity between himself and Hippias, included in the preface to the first edition, was insufficient (A, 3-5). [25]

Thus, in order to underscore Agathon's moral integrity and continuing quest of the Highest Good, Hippias had to be brought back into the novel. The importance of this addition and its integral relationship to the rest of the work is attested to in a letter to Göschen on January 30, 1794:

> Ich bin in voller Arbeit am letzten Theil des Agathon. Ausser dem ganz neuen Dialog und Diskurs des Archytas, wovon ich Ihnen schon ehemals

schrieb, habe ich aber noch eine beträchtliche Umarbeitung einer ganzen
Suite von Kapiteln vorzunehmen, welche, ausserdem, dass die <u>Komposizion</u>
des Ganzen dadurch merklich gewinnt, durch einen Besuch, den ich den
Hippias dem Agathon während seines Verhafts zu Syrakus abstatten lasse,
unumgänglich nothwendig gemacht wurde. Durch diese beiden <u>resp.</u> Verände-
rungen und Zusätze erhält unsre neue Ausgabe einen <u>wesentlichen</u> Vorzug. [26]

At the conclusion of Book XI the author pauses to reflect on the various experiences
Agathon has undergone. He points out that in each instance the hero is seen in a
slightly different light. Agathon's behavior was influenced to a greater or lesser
extent by contingent circumstances. In Delphi the youth appeared as a speculative
enthusiast, in Athens as a zealous politician, in Smyrna as an enraptured lover.
Yet these designations -- either individually or combined -- do not exhaust a description of Agathon's character. They are not completely accurate and are not
really true. "Agathon schien in verschiedenen Zeitpunkten seines Lebens, nach der
Reihe ein Platonischer und ein patriotischer Schwärmer, ein Held, ein Stoiker, ein
Wollüstling; und er war keines von allen, wiewohl er nach und nach durch alle diese Klassen ging, und in jeder etwas von der eignen Farbe derselben bekam" (XI,
43).

This passage is a striking echo of the chameleon motif we have encountered several
times already. Wieland once likened himself to a chameleon, intimating that he was
not what people thought he was, just as Agathon appeared to be something other than
what he actually was. Wieland indicates here the deceptive nature of appearances
and the necessity for the observer to penetrate the surface. One should not judge
hastily because appearances are not necessarily reliable. The author points out
that there is a common immutable factor underlying each of these character masks.
It alone is a true and valid expression of Agathon's character. But, Wieland continues, it would be premature to reveal Agathon's basic nature at this time, since
Agathon's distilled essence is properly the product of the experiences he undergoes and the hero has not yet completed the refining stages (XI, 43-44).

Wieland is, of course, begging the question here. The author made no secret of
the fact that Agathon was to be representative of his own experiences. [27] The third
version of the novel could not possibly depict Agathon's distilled essence because
Wieland was not yet conscious of what that essence was. Wieland does not become
fully aware of his true nature until he has struggled with the problems of
<u>Agathodämon</u> (1799). Yet in each of his novels -- beginning earnestly in the evolu-
tion of <u>Agathon</u> and becoming more pronounced in <u>Peregrinus Proteus</u> -- there is
evidence of Agathon's (Wieland's) true nature. For example, in chapter 10, Book
XII, Hippias unwittingly suggests what Agathon's immutable essence is when he
describes the fallen minister as "Arm an Weltkenntniss, aber desto reicher an
Idealen" (XI, 139). At this point in his development Agathon stands in marked contrast to Don Sylvio after his disenchantment, since Agathon is not without "idealistic self-confidence." Agathon's desire to realize his Platonic ideals is his
distinctive character trait.

Agathon's sojourn in Tarentum occasions a detailed explanation of his distilled character. His conversations with Archytas gradually clarify what Agathon really was; they elucidate the underlying essence "which remained the same despite the [changing] external forms" (XI, 43).

What is Archytas' significance for Agathon? Archytas is irrefutable evidence that Agathon's subjective ontological view is universally valid. In Archytas, Agathon finds the mature expression of Orphic and Pythagorean philosophy. In a certain sense Agathon's character development begins with his acquaintance with Archytas. All else has been a mere prelude to the recognition that he has been suffering from a captivating excess of idealism. Although he shares the same basic philosophy with Archytas, he designates the latter's version as wisdom; whereas he labels his own view Schwärmerei. The distinction is between maturity and inexperience. Agathon's view "was based more on feeling and intuition than on firm conviction and clearly conceived concepts" (XI, 353). The novel's point lies in this recognition. This aspect of the work parallels the import of Don Sylvio. There is an ultimate recognition of the inescapable and legitimate demands of practicality, sense experience, and reason.

The object of both novels is to depict the liberation of their respective heroes from their Einbildungen. The expression "liberation" is deliberately chosen to show that the initial and primary stimulus comes from without. Donna Felicia was the immediate cause for Don Sylvio's cure from Schwärmerei; Archytas is proof that the practical application of Platonic principles is possible. There is, however, a significant difference between the types of Schwärmerei in the two novels. In one sense, Don Sylvio's fairy-tale world is not only inane but deleterious. It impairs the fulfillment of his social destiny. The world of Platonic ideals merely lacks a convincing foundation in reason for the youthful hero. Strictly speaking, Agathon's extremism cannot be called Schwärmerei. It is more accurate to term his state "enthusiasm," since he -- unlike Don Sylvio -- is "inspired by a god, not a fetish." The hero's varied experiences supply him with rational arguments for his intuitive "knowledge."

The rational basis for Agathon's exalted idealism is elucidated in the chapter "Darstellung der Lebensweisheit des Archytas." Archytas prefaces his philosophy with the remark that, although no mortal is able to penetrate the mysteries of Nature, the sophist's conclusion that the metaphysical world is therefore inconsequential for man is fallacious (XI, 354). The reduction of the intellect to a state of sensual slavery is inexcusable. "Aber wenn ihm gleich verborgen ist und bleiben soll, woher er kam, und wohin er geht, ... so steht es doch in seiner Macht, zu wissen, wie und wodurch er mit dem grossen Ganzen, dessen Theil er ist, zusammenhängt, und wie er handeln muss, um seiner Natur gemäss zu handeln, und seine Bestimmung im Weltall zu erfüllen" (XI, 355).

In his view, the intellect, which knows no bounds, complements the senses, which are limited to the perception of phenomena. The mind is capable of judgements that are denied the senses. "Seine Sinne begränzen sich ... selbst, und scheinen ihn in den engen Kreis der Thierheit einzuschliessen: aber wo sind die Grenzen der Kraft und Thätigkeit jenes <u>Geistes</u> . . ., der ihm Mittel entdeckt hat, in tausend Fällen die Unzulänglichkeit des äussern Sinnes zu ersetzen, die Irrtümer desselben zu berichtigen, und selbst im Umfang der sichtbaren Natur, der durch ihn unermesslich erscheint, der wirklichen Beschaffenheit der Dinge viel näher zu kommen, als der blosse Sinn vermögend ist?" (XI, 355-356). Here is a definite expression of the ultimate epistemological view in the novel. It is of no consequence that the phenomenal world is mostly deceptive. One should not look for ultimate Truth and Reality in the visible world (as Agathon has done heretofore). Man must turn his glance inward to the invisible world which exists in his soul. Man must look to his own "feelings, thoughts, presentiments, instincts, and aspirations" for Truth (XI, 356). For it is within us that our spiritual egos sort and shift the multitudinous inputs, reducing the many to one, forming the universal from the particular, separating the necessary from the accidental. Archytas exclaims: "Hier, in diesem heiligen Kreise, Agathon, liegt unser wahres, höchstes, ja, genau zu reden, einziges Interesse; diess ist der Kreis unsrer edelsten und freiesten Thätigkeit; hier, oder nirgends müssen wir die <u>Wahrheit</u> suchen, die uns zum sichern Leitfaden durch diese Sinnenwelt dienen soll; und hier ist für den, der sie redlich sucht, keine Täuschung möglich!" (XI, 357). Ultimate Truth can be best realized through introspection, not through observation of phenomena. Here too is expressed one of the important reservations in Wieland's epistemological view: honesty. Candid self-appraisal coupled with salubrious reason will unerringly lead to perception of the Highest Good.

Archytas' basic character traits are integrity and a loathing of hypocrisy and falsehood. He always felt repugnance for injustice (XI, 358). All virtuous acts were performed from a sense of duty, not for personal reward or public approval (XI, 362). Archytas was also antipathetic toward sophistry and all speculation that did not lend itself to practical application or that only led to endless labyrinths of doubt and skepticism (XI, 363-364). On the other hand, the exalted notion of the harmonious unity and existence of all things in God had always been dear to the philosopher. He recognized the deep rift in man caused by the spiritual and animal sides of human nature. Man as animal is limited, his actions determined by external circumstances. Only in the spiritual realm is man boundless and free to determine his destiny.

The highest goal for which man should strive is complete harmony of the spiritual and the animal. In Archytas' opinion this lofty end is attainable only when man's higher nature dominates his lower nature (XI, 368). Such harmony can be attained through "a restless struggle of reason with sensuality, or of the spiritual side of man with the animal . . . until the animal born to obedience has recognized and learned docilely to accept the wise and just rule of reason" (XI, 369). This is the ultimate Truth concerning man's earthly existence and destiny. It can be acquired only through introspection, by hearkening to the rumblings of the human spirit (XI, 369-370). Only through ignorance of his own nature and majesty is man enslaved by his animal desires.

Two faculties of the human spirit are necessary for the recognition of this ultimate Truth: the mind and the heart. Reason can discern causal relationships in the phenomenal world and can apprehend the multitudinous as a totality. Through his mind man perceives the unity, harmony, and order of Nature which superficially appears to be fortuitous. The intellect can guide man to the brink of recognizing that the phenomenal world is nothing more than a reflection of the noumenal one and that the physical world is in the process of perfecting itself, of approaching the perfection of the metaphysical world (XI, 374-375). But here are prescribed the limits of reason; at this crucial point the heart must be implemented to make the leap beyond the limits of reason. The mind is by its very nature incapable of taking this final step. For example, Archytas says:

> Je mehr ich diesen grossen, alles umfassenden Gedanken durchzudenken strebe, je völliger fühle ich mich überzeugt, dass sich die ganze Kraft meines Geistes in ihm erschöpft, dass er alle seine wesentlichen Triebe befriedigt, dass ich mit aller möglichen Anstrengung nichts höheres, besseres, vollkommneres denken kann, und -- dass eben diess der stärkste Beweis seiner Wahrheit ist. Von dem Augenblick an ... fühle ich, dass ich mehr als ein sterbliches Erdenwesen, unendlich mehr als der blosse Thiermensch bin. (XI, 375-376)

Note that the key word is fühle. The final affirmation is an irrational act based as far as possible on a rational substructure.

Archytas also maintains that the completely sensual and dissolute person is, despite contrary influences, not unaware of another facet of his nature which cannot be placated by mere sensuality. Even in a wanton and spiritually apathetic state a nondescript feeling warns man that his true destiny lies elsewhere. "Aber selbst in diesem schmählichen Zustande dringt sich ihm ein geheimes Gefühl seiner höhern Natur wider Willen auf" (XI, 371). Through this feeling man recognizes his oneness with God and the universe. Consequently he knows it is his personal obligation to strive for self-perfection as well as for the spiritual advancement of all men. The individual knows no higher goal than to duplicate in his own divided nature the harmony, order, and perfection of Nature. Truth and uprightness are the means in this process of "re-ligio" (XI, 377). We have here an expression of the humanitas concept which played so important a role in eighteenth-century thought.

Archytas is not oblivious to the accusations concerning his metaphysical philosophy. He is unperturbed by the charge that the belief in a bond between the human soul and the metempirical world is conducive to one of the most dangerous human afflictions: religious Schwärmerei. There is no danger of this development, Archytas claims, as long as the individual possesses salubrious reason. As long as man is aware of the true nature of the marvelous he will not be susceptible to Schwärmerei.

> Denn es hängt ja bloss von uns selbst ab, dem Hange zum Wunderbaren die Vernunft zur Grenze zu setzen, Spielen der Fantasie und Gefühlen des Augenblicks keinen zu hohen Werth beizulegen, und die Bilder, unter welchen die

alten <u>Dichter der Morgenländer</u> ihre Ahnungen vom Unsichtbaren und Zukünftigen sich und andern zu <u>versinnlichen</u> gesucht haben, für nichts mehr
als das was sie sind, für Bilder <u>übersinnlicher</u> und also <u>unbildlicher</u> Dinge
anzusehen. (XI, 382-383)

<u>Schwärmerei</u> results from lack of rational control. The <u>Schwärmer</u> misunderstands
the nature of "fantastic" images; he takes them for <u>das Ding an sich</u>. In so doing
he confuses the icon with the deity. We need only think of Agathon's expectations of
a theophany for a blatant example of this phenomenon. His subsequent <u>Schwärmerei</u>
is less obvious. He attempts more than is humanly, politically, or socially possible.
He does so because he has lost contact with empirical reality. Because of his
overwrought enthusiasm for his "religious" ideals he has failed to understand that
their realization is not possible on a broad basis. They are the result of "Ahnungen
vom Unsichtbaren und Zukünftigen." His idealistic visions apparently belong to the
future, not to the present.

Throughout the novel Agathon attempts to remake the world according to his celestial ideals. When he arrives at the same view of man's limitations as Archytas, his
<u>Schwärmerei</u> vanishes and his <u>Weltanschauung</u> attains maturation. The grown man
is no longer dependent upon graphic explanations, dark mysteries, and blind faith.
He has learned to conceive of his world and his role in it in rational terms. This is
the transition Archytas had undergone, and this is the transmutation Agathon com-
mences. Archytas expresses this important change as follows:

> Aber uns, deren Geisteskräfte unter einem gemässigtern Himmel und unter
> dem Einfluss der bürgerlichen Freiheit entwickelt, und durch keine Hiero-
> glyphen, heilige Bücher und vorgeschriebene Glaubensformeln gefesselt wer-
> den ... liegt es ob, unsre Begriffe immer mehr zu reinigen, und Uberhaupt
> von allem, was ausserhalb des Kreises unsrer Sinne liegt, nicht mehr wissen
> zu wollen, als was die Vernunft selbst davon zu glauben lehrt, und als für
> unser moralisches Bedürfniss zureicht. (XI, 383)

The parallel to the transformation in Wieland's own attitude during the years 1756-
1760 is unmistakable. Agathon-Wieland acknowledges the legitimate demands of this
imperfect world ("von allem was ausserhalb des Kreises unsrer Sinne liegt, nicht
mehr wissen zu wollen," etc.) while not totally relinquishing his Platonic idealism
("und als für unser moralisches Bedürfniss zureicht"). His absolute norms have
been modified, not renounced. In both instances the change was effected by disillusioning experience.

Man guards himself against high flights of fancy and simultaneously realizes his
moral and ultimate destiny by fulfilling the common obligations of daily life. The
conscientious discharge of one's duties is also rich in practical benefit for society
because the individual becomes an influential part of the whole (XI, 386-387).

Reference was made earlier to the immutable factor which underlies the various
roles Agathon assumes. This constant element is the hero's belief in man's lofty

destiny as foreshadowed in Archytas' worldly wisdom. Archytas is the mature re-flection of Agathon's distilled character. At the novel's conclusion the hero has be-come so like his mentor that the citizens of Tarentum "felt that they had lost nothing by Archytas' having passed into a better world" (XI, 396).

Although Archytas is ostensibly the ideal man in Die Geschichte des Agathon, there is good reason to believe that his philosophy is not the conclusive statement of Wie-land's ontological and epistemological views. [28] In a letter dated November 26, 1796, the author assured his daughter Sophie that Archytas' philosophy was not his own. He would like to think like the Pythagorean philosopher but he cannot. For Wieland belief has become dependent upon external influence over which he has no control. He confesses that the true representative of his own beliefs is Agathodä-mon.

> Wie ich mir am Ende aus diesem Gedankenlabyrinth wieder heraushelfe,
> bleibt für diesmahl noch ein Geheimniss und soll es so lange bleiben, bis
> dir das letzte Buch vom Agathodämon -- zu seiner Zeit -- das Allerheiligste
> meiner eigenen Haus Philosophie (wenn ich so sagen kann) aufgeschlossen ha-
> ben wird, welche leider! nicht die Philosophie des Archytas im Agathon ist.
> Ich sage, leider! weil ich in der That, um meines innern Vergnügens und Ge-
> winns an Zufriedenheit u. Seelenruhe willen, wünschen möchte, wie Archytas
> zu glauben. Aber auch glauben hängt nicht mehr von meiner Willkühr ab, als
> die Einrichtung meiner äusserlichen Umstände -- und ich muss glauben was
> ich glaube, wie ich mir gefallen lassen muss was ich nicht ändern kann. [29]

We cannot affirm conclusively that Wieland is referring to the difference between the accepted norm of behavior for the enlightened man (who sees his destiny and fulfillment in the service of mankind) and the "abnormal," estranged behavior of the Schwärmer (who alienates himself from society to enjoy the beatific vision). We have no decisive evidence that Wieland is speaking of this distinction between practi-cal, exoteric activity and idealistic, esoteric meditation. But Archytas' worldly wisdom does stand in contrast to the naive and childlike belief of the Schwärmer. The fantast is not willing to subjugate the irrational forces of the passions to the sober restrictions of reason and empirical reality. He needs mysterious signs and emotional involvement as does the child. Archytas contrasts the enlightened citizen to the Schwärmer (XI, 383), who is not satisfied with a diet of sensations alone.

The enlightened individual constantly refers to the realities of the empirical world, whereas the Schwärmer interprets phenomena according to his "philosophical" bias. Furthermore, it is characteristic of the dreamer to withdraw from society.[30] Perhaps Wieland was referring to the social emphasis of Archytas' worldly wisdom when he disavowed Archytas' philosophy and acknowledged Agathodämon's beliefs as his own. The author's identification with this thinker indicates a break with strict Enlightenment thinking and a re-emphasis of the irrational forces in man. Thus Wieland apparently insinuates that happiness and personal spiritual fulfill-ment -- through harmonious cooperation of the head and heart -- are not actually possible in this world. It would seem that he gradually comes to the conclusion that man can realize his true destiny only in the next world.

In this evaluation of Wieland's attitude toward Archytas we must also consider the author's statement to Zimmermann in December 1762. He announces that a philosopher even more dangerous than Hippias will appear in the novel. This other philosopher is more dangerous because more honest with himself and others. [31] This second philosopher can be none other than Archytas. Why did Wieland consider his philosophy so dangerous? Was it because of Archytas' (the Enlightenment's) almost total subjugation of man's animal and irrational nature (XI, 368)? We have seen that Wieland shied away from over-emphasizing either the rational or the irrational side of human nature. He desires to achieve harmony between man's head and heart not through the tyranny of one side but through a delicate balancing of the respective forces.

There is also doubt as to whether Archytas' philosophy is really feasible, considering man's nature. Archytas admits that only a very few men regulate their lives according to the insight he himself has gained (XI, 365). Agathon reiterates this observation at the end of the novel (XI, 391). But, above all, it is stated that Archytas is not a normal man; he is an exceptional product of Nature, for he has never personally experienced the power of the passions (XI, 177). It is due to the circumstances of Nature alone that Archytas is possible. "Die Natur schien sich vorgesetzt zu haben, in ihm zu beweisen, dass die Weisheit [d.h. Archytas' Philosophie] nicht weniger ein Geschenk von ihr sey als der Genie; und dass ... es dennoch der Natur allein zukomme, diese glückliche Temperatur der Elemente der Menschheit hervorzubringen, welche ... endlich zu dieser vollkommenen Harmonie aller Kräfte und Bewegungen des Menschen ... erhöht werden kann" (XI, 176-177).

We might also consider in this connection Archytas' statement about himself: "Wohl mir ... dass ein Zusammenfluss günstiger Umstände, Erziehung, Unterricht, frühzeitige Anstrengung des Geistes, und Aufmerksamkeit auf die Stimme meines guten Dämons mich davor bewahrt haben, diese unglücklichen Erfahrungen an mir selbst zumachen!" (XI, 372).

If man is so dependent upon the caprice of Nature for the attainment of his ideals, what remains for him to determine? The weakness of Archytas' philosophy becomes evident here, and Wieland sensed the flaw. Perhaps the author considered Archytas more dangerous than Hippias because Archytas was in line with popular Enlightenment thought. For example, his philosophical system is described as one "which ennobles human nature without inflating it and opens up vistas into better worlds without alienating man from or making him useless in the present world" (XI, 378). On the other hand, Hippias' epicurean philosophy was not as widely accepted in enlightened circles in eighteenth-century Germany. Archytas would then be more dangerous than Hippias because the fallacy (the one-sidedness of his system) is more evident. Why? Because one is more apt to find fault with a philosophical system with which one does not agree. An enlightener concurs with Archytas in his view of the world. For this reason he is unlikely to consider the latter philosopher's view to be a mixture of truth and fallacy.

Despite their antipodal relationship (egoism versus altruism) and diametric conclusions, both Hippias' and Archytas' philosophies suffer from the same basic fault:
one-sidedness. Although Hippias does not deny the existence of a metaphysical
world, he says we cannot really know its existence, and therefore it is of no concern to us (see IX, 298, 78n, 120; XI, 354). We are born into the material world
and have to make the best of it.

It is also worthy of note in considering his position relative to Hippias that Wieland
does not always consider Hippias a sophist, and that Hippias' philosophy really
warrants serious study. Wieland confided to Riedel in October 1768: "Entre nous,
der Discours dieses nämlichen Hippias ist nicht unwürdig, ein wenig studiert zu
werden; ... es ist gar viel Wahres darin, das unsere guten Deutschen noch nicht
recht verstehen." [32] Thus Wieland neither entirely rejects Hippias nor uncondi-
tionally accepts Archytas.

The goal of both thinkers -- happiness in life -- is the same; but their methods are
diametrically opposed. Hippias turns the human intellect into a slave of the passions.
Archytas, on the other hand, calls for complete hegemony of the intellect (XI, cf.
368). He stresses the noumenal world and its importance for man because the
visible world is for the most part deceptive and accidental (XI, 356). The passions
must never become violent and must be as completely as possible regulated by the
mind. Although Archytas also recognizes man's dual nature, he denies fulfillment
of one side of man's being. Thus, in stressing man's participation in a greater
unity with mankind and God, Archytas too becomes one sided in his philosophical
view.

The addition of the Archytas episode in the third version of the novel is significant
for the attempt to round out Agathon's character and follow his development to the
originally intended end. From the novel's very inception Wieland had intended to
include both "Die geheime Geschichte der Danae" and "Die Lebensweisheiten des
Archytas." [33] However, external circumstances and the incomplete development
of Wieland's own character prevented the execution of the plan. Yet it was always
Wieland's desire and intention to complete Agathon to his own satisfaction. That it
was not easy for him to carry out the plan is obvious from the letter to Göschen
written in February 1794. "Ich schicke Ihnen, lieber Göschen, hier ein Stück Ma-
nuskript vom Agathon, welches ganz neu ist, und mir mehr Mühe gekostet hat, als
ich Ihnen sagen möchte. Aber der moralische Werth des ganzen Agathon hieng davon ab, und nun erst bin ich mit mir selbst und meinem Werke zufrieden." [34] In
a communication of April 14, 1794, he asserts that the Archytas episode is "die
Krone" of the entire work. [35]

These assertions do not refute the fact that Archytas' philosophy was not Wieland's
last word about ontological questions. Rather, these statements are significant
from an historical point of view. Even as Wieland recognized the historical significance of his early work, such as "Die Natur der Dinge," [36] so too can the third
version of Agathon be considered an historical document of Wieland's intellectual
evolution.

Although Wieland no longer advocated Archytas' particular type of asceticism in 1794, that specific formulation of Archytas' thought was necessary to complete the novel as originally conceived in the 1760's. Wieland's own philosophic position had changed, but Agathon had started on a path which had to lead to Archytas' court if the hero were to remain morally and psychologically consistent. [37] We are therefore compelled to conclude that all three versions of Agathon are bascially emanations of the same epistemological position. The only noteworthy difference between the first and later versions is a mollification of the strident appeal to the heart. We have seen that Agathon invokes his intuition of the deity's existence in reply to Hippias' objection. In the second version Wieland uses rational arguments to supplement the hero's naive response. Finally, in the third version the dialogue between Archytas and Agathon is introduced to explain more articulately the basic moral and philosophical view of the novel. The distinction therefore involves a shift from a naive emphasis of the heart to a sophisticated synthesis of the heart with the head in the quest for the Highest Good. Nevertheless, it remains clear that the clairvoyance of the heart takes precedence over rational explanations in the perception of Truth. All concessions to the Enlightenment's demand for supremacy of the understanding cannot obfuscate this fact. It can for this reason be asserted with Hans M. Wolff that "Die Vernunft erweist sich also als vom Gefühl abhängig, und Wieland bemüht sich, diese Abhängigkeit so deutlich wie möglich zu machen." [38] The three versions of Agathon reflect accurately Wieland's fundamental epistemological view, which underwent no change with respect to the functions of intuition and reason.

Other aspects of the novel warrant closer inspection, for they reveal important characteristics of Wieland's epistemological view. The following pages will be concerned with the functions of Danae and Psyche and with the poetic aspect of reality. Danae's ostensible function is to acquaint Agathon with sensuality, which is as much a part of his nature as ideality. Danae has already been discussed from this perspective. Here we are concerned with a subtle aspect of her character. Wieland makes the point that one's innermost conviction and subjective feeling of what is true of false -- even though one is predisposed to a particular interpretation -- is more valid and more true than the opinion of other men. An example of this belief occurs in Danae's first narration of her experiences. Her intention is to please Agathon and to retain his respect and love. To this end she describes her errors and feelings in a manner which makes them understandable and excusable. Danae is selective in relating her experiences. Wieland says that her biased account of her early life is truer than other versions which stress her weaknesses and shortcomings.

> Sie sah natürlicher Weise ihre Aufführung, ihre Schwachheiten, ihre Fehltritte selbst, in einem mildern, und (lasset uns die Wahrheit sagen) in einem wahrern Licht als die Welt; welche auf der einen Seite von allen den kleinen Umständen, die uns rechtfertigen, oder wenigstens unsre Schuld vermindern, nicht unterrichtet, und auf der andern boshaft genug ist, um ihres grössern Vergnügens willen das Gemälde unsrer Thorheiten mit tausend Zügen zu überladen, um welche es zwar weniger wahr aber desto komischer wird. (X, 165)

Danae thus avoided extremes, depicting herself as neither free from fault nor burdened with guilt. This passage also seems to substantiate the earlier statement that Wieland shied away from extremes.

Danae's experiences demonstrate the innate, irrational instinct for truth. There is an obvious parallel between Danae and Donna Jacinte in Don Sylvio. Both were exposed at an early age to the art of coquetry. Danae too feels that the life of a prostitute is not her destiny. "Aber ein mir selbst unbekanntes innerliches Wider-streben machte mich ungelehrig für ihren Unterricht. Mein Herz schien mir zu sa-gen, dass ich für einen edlern Zweck gemacht sey" (XI, 239). Furthermore, Danae feels particularly attracted to the Beautiful. In Danae, Shaftesbury's influence is pronounced, for there seems to be identification of the Good, Beautiful, True, and Virtuous. "... denn ich fand etwas in mir -- ohne zu wissen oder mich zu beküm-mern was es war -- das mich weder mit dem, was ich um mich her sah, noch mit mir selbst und mit dem Beifall, den ich erhielt, zufrieden seyn liess. Die Natur hatte die Idee des Schönen in meine Seele gezeichnet; noch sah ich sie bloss durch einen Nebel; aber das Wenige, was ich davon erblickte, that seine Wirkung" (XI, 235). Subsequently, Danae -- then called Myris -- swore an oath to follow the Graces in everything.

A further parallel can be drawn between Psyche and Danae. Their differences were only superficial. This is emphasized by the fact that the two women are fast friends at the novel's conclusion. Danae's history is prefaced by the remark that a schöne Seele will ever remain one even though she may err and go astray intermittently (XI, 227). Danae refers to this fact when she draws a comparison between herself and Psyche. Both women are basically the same. Circumstances -- over which we have no control -- made the difference and caused each woman to develop in her unique manner. "Wie du siehest, Agathon, hatte die junge Myris einen feinen An-satz zu eben dieser schönen Schwärmerei, welche in den Hallen und Lorbeerhainen von Delphi deiner Seele die erste Bildung gab. Die Umstände machten den ganzen Unterschied. Zu Delphi erzogen, würde sie eine Psyche geworden sein" (XI, 237-238). [39]

The relationship between Agathon and Psyche is especially indicative of the relia-bility of the heart in the perception of Truth. The couple loved one another as brother and sister. They are in fact brother and sister, but they had no way of knowing it. For this reason the role which the heart plays is vitally important. There is a charming irony in their self-delusion that they are close blood relatives because their minds try to approximate the truth of the heart. Since there is no rational proof of their relationship, they do not believe the undeniable impulse of their hearts. It is important to note that their hearts tell them to love as brother and sister, not as man and woman. [40] The irony lies in the fact that the voice of the heart, which says "you are brother and sister," is interpreted as meaning "in spirit." Certain facial features lend credibility to their inner voices, but the mind misconstrues the physical evidence.

Oft waren wir enthusiastisch genug, die Vermuthung, oder vielmehr die blosse Möglichkeit, einander vielleicht so nahe verwandt zu seyn, als wir es
wünschten, für die Stimme der Natur zu halten; zumal da eine wirkliche oder
eingebildete Aehnlichkeit unserer Gesichtszüge diesen Wahn zu rechtfertigen
schien. Da wir uns aber die Betrüglichkeit dieser vermeinten Sprache des
Blutes nicht immer verbergen konnten: so fanden wir desto mehr Vergnügen
darin, den Vorstellungen von einer natürlichen <u>Verschwisterung der Seelen</u>,
und von einer schon in einem vorhergehenden Zustande in bessern Welten an-
gefangenen Bekanntschaft, nachzuhängen. (X, 52; see also IX, 282)

Even with regard to the spiritual aspect of their relationship the heart spoke the
truth. They did think and feel alike; they shared the same ideals. Agathon says
that everything he expressed appeared to be an echo of Psyche's own sentiments.
His ideas existed in an embryonic stage in Psyche's soul (X, 48).

The relationship between Agathon and Psyche emphasizes anew the <u>Sympathie</u>
aspect of Wieland's epistemological view. In <u>Agathon</u> like is also unerringly drawn
to like. In addition, Agathon expresses the total spiritual harmony between himself
and Danae as <u>Sympathie</u> (X, 163). This irresistible and irrational force also
explains the attraction between Danae and Psyche. Furthermore, <u>Sympathie</u> is the
unifying bond in Archytas' group of relatives and friends (XI, 389).

Psyche's function in the development of Agathon's character was to nurture the
sensibility of his heart (IX, 281). Her very name indicates her significance for
him. In Greek and Roman mythology Psyche was a maiden beloved by Eros. After
many tribulations caused by the jealousy of Venus she is united with Eros and
accorded a place among the gods as a personification of the human soul. The parallel to our hero is obvious: Agathon, Psyche's natural and spiritual brother, aspires
to a higher state.

The poetic reality (<u>Romanwirklichkeit</u>) of <u>Agathon</u> is indicative of the epistemological
view expressed in the content of the novel. <u>Das Natürliche</u> of empirical reality is
fused with <u>das Wunderbare</u>, the heart of poetic reality. [41] From this union emerges
a concise statement of Wieland's attitude toward ultimate reality. Only poetry and
the arts can be considered expressions of ultimate Truth because they -- paradoxically -- <u>expose</u> the essence of being while disguising phenomenal reality. True
art addresses itself directly to sentiment and aspiration. Its effect on man is all-
important, [42] not the syllogisms and other rational evidence it might bring to bear.
Man <u>senses</u> the truth and beauty of art first. Only subsequent to this irrational
reaction does man attempt to explain the irrational in rational terms. This is
precisely the statement Wieland seems to be making about man's ability to know
Truth. Man is incapable of penetrating the mysteries of Nature with his mind;
therefore he must ultimately let the heart be his primary guide.

It will be recalled that the unifying bonds of fictional reality and empirical reality
are similarity and possibility. To be probable -- and therefore credible -- events
of fictional reality must resemble events in the phenomenal world, though these

events might not actually occur in the physical realm. These are the principles upon which Wieland based the novel. Only if the two worlds are related in this manner can poetic reality lay claim to probability. And only through this probability can poetry achieve its intended effect. These principles of similarity, possibility, and probability are the factors that impart the aspect of truth to Die Geschichte des Agathon. [43] In the preface to the first edition (1766-67), Wieland wrote:

> Die Wahrheit, welche von einem Werke, wie dasjenige ist, so wir den Liebhabern hiermit vorlegen, gefordert werden kann, bestehet darin: dass alles mit dem Laufe der Welt übereinstimme; dass die Karakter nicht bloss willkührlich nach der Fantasie oder den Absichten des Verfassers gebildet, sondern aus dem unerschöpflichen Vorrathe der Natur selbst hergenommen seyen; dass in der Entwickelung derselben sowohl die innere als die relative Möglichkeit, die Beschaffenheit des menschlichen Herzens, die Natur einer jeden Leidenschaft, mit allen den besonderen Farben und Schattierungen, welche sie durch den Individualkarakter und die Umstände jeder Person bekommen, aufs genaueste beibehalten, das Eigene des Landes, des Ortes, der Zeit, in welche die Geschichte gesetzt wird, niemals aus den Augen verloren, und, kurz, dass alles so gedichtet sey, dass sich kein hinlänglicher Grund angeben lasse, warum es nicht gerade so, wie es erzählt wird, hätte geschehen können. Diese Wahrheit allein kann ein Buch, das den Menschen schildert, nützlich machen, und diese Wahrheit getrauet sich der Herausgeber den Lesern der Geschichte des Agathon zu versprechen. (IX, iv-v)

Despite the concession made to the demands of the Enlightenment (utility) in the last sentence, the overwhelming emphasis on the intricate balance of the rational and irrational powers in man necessary for the creation of authentic art is evident. Poetry is the result of a combined effort by both the heart and the mind. Yet the heart plays the essential role as visionary, while the mind plays the also essential -- but supporting -- role of architect.

An analogy may clarify the relation between the head and the heart in Wieland's poetic and epistemological view of Truth. The heart is comparable to a man standing on the top rung of a ladder. Because of his position he enjoys a distinct and unhampered view of his surroundings. The intellect, on the other hand, is like a man standing on the bottom rung of the same ladder. His view of his surroundings is inadequate and indistinct because sorely limited. Only by tediously climbing the ladder rung by rung can he attain the same view as the man above. So too can the mind approximate the insight which the heart enjoys, but only by properly assessing the data known to it at any given level on the ladder of knowledge. Only by correctly evaluating empirical facts can the mind advance to the next rung. The heart has no need of this tedious process. A further distinction between the two faculties is the irrational act of faith which only the heart is capable of. This act of faith is the assumption that ultimate reality lies in a non-material world.

Wieland added "Ueber das Historische im Agathon" in later versions, ostensibly to stress the innate and necessary connection between poetic and empirical reality. [44]

"The polarity of poetry and truth" is not only characteristic of Agathon (and Don Sylvio) but also "belongs to the enduring, fundamental elements of Wieland's [entire] poetic work." [45] In the course of the novel Wieland repeatedly refers to this relationship. He states, for example, that events in the phenomenal world often seem strange or wondrous. The reason for this effect is ignorance of the contingency of things. So too do the events in a novel appear strange when the causal relationships are unknown (IX, 23). At another point in the novel, Wieland stresses the need for regulating the imagination by reason (XI, 383). Just as unrestrained fantasy leads to Schwärmerei or ineffectualness (in the eyes of the Enlightenment), so too no work of art is possible without the restrictions implemented by reason. Elsewhere he indicates that Nature gives rise to the wondrous (X, 10-11).

Wieland also underscores the advantage of art over the intellectual process. He often expresses the wish that he could paint a scene or a thought instead of describing it with words -- the tools of the intellect (XI, 231). The author also compares and contrasts Homer with Heraclitus in order to explain the advantage of poetry over philosophy in attaining a view of ultimate reality (IX, 106). Poetry uses images, colors, and emotional vividness and is more effective because these attributes entertain and activate the entire man. "The sober treatises of philosophers," on the other hand, depict nothing other than "a series of words, which are not images but mere symbols of abstract concepts" (IX, 106).

On the basis of this exegesis we must consider that interpretations of Wieland's human ideal as "the sociable man" [46] or "urbanity"[47] are short-sighted undertakings resulting from an overemphasis of the author's relationship to the Enlightenment. In fact, such conclusions could be considered superficial. To be sure, it is true that Wieland is concerned to a great extent with man's role within a certain society, "which influences him and which he influences." [48] The author's exhortation to the reciprocally beneficial social integration of the individual is manifest above all in the person of Archytas. However, if the critic penetrates the cloak of the Enlightenment which covers Die Geschichte des Agathon, he will be able to approach a fuller appreciation of Wieland's personal philosophy. He must then take cognizance of the fact that Archytas, as the normative individual, is an unrealizable ideal, since ordinary men are incapable of such perfection and such harmony of the head and the heart. [49] The study of Peregrinus Proteus should better substantiate the insights gained from the analysis of Agathon.

NOTES

1. Martini ed., I, "Nachwort," 939. See also "Ueber das Historische im Agathon," Gruber ed., IX, 17.
2. Cf. Wieland's appraisal of Aristipp in "Ueber das Historische im Agathon," Gruber ed., IX, 17-18. The latter's philosophy acts as a regulator against the extravagances of the mind which are implicitly detrimental.
3. Cf. Otto Freise, Die drei Fassungen von Wielands Agathon (Göttingen: Kaestner, 1910), p. 11.
4. AB, II, 197; "Ueber das Historische im Agathon," Gruber ed., IX, 17; Jacobis auserlesener Briefwechsel (1825-27; rpt. Bern: Herbert Lang, 1970), I, 28 (Wieland to Jacobi, April 11, 1771).
5. DB, I, 7 (11. 7. 1763).
6. Cf. Lange, "Zur Gestalt des Schwärmers," p. 159.
7. For a detailed account of the inception and execution of Die Geschichte des Agathon, see Freise, pp. 3-27. Martini aptly describes the novel as "das geistesgeschichtliche Dokument einer Krisensituation." "Nachwort," I, 941.
8. AB, II, 164.
9. Robert Keil, ed., Wieland und Reinhold (Leipzig & Berlin: W. Friedrich, 1885), p. 178.
10. See Heinrich Vormweg, "Die Romane Chr. M. Wielands," Diss. Bonn 1956, for a more thorough consideration of style and structure than can be offered in this study. Cf. esp. pp. 382 ff. et passim. See also Jacobs, passim, and Buddecke, pp. 169-237.
11. The periodic sentence still occurs in Agathon, but is prominent only in those sections which date back to the earliest version.
12. In the first version of Agathon (A) the roles of editor, omniscient author, and interested reader are much more pronounced than in the third version (C). Cf., e.g., the chapter "Moralischer Zustand unsers Helden" (A, pp. 364-376), which is essentially a dialogue between author and reader. The chapters "Nachricht an den Leser" (A, pp. 362-364) and "Apologie des griechischen Authors" (A, pp. 377-381) clearly underscore the separate roles of author and editor. In C, "Moralischer Zustand" is drastically reduced in size and less intimate in tone (cf. XI, 119-129). "Nachricht an den Leser" and "Apologie" have been deleted in C. This radical shift in the roles Wieland plays (accompanied by a reduced reliance on irony) in the conclusive version indicates more concern with the phenomenon of Schwärmerei. Wieland is no longer "merely" engaging in a charming pastime.
13. In this and the following instances I cite the wording of the third version (C) for consistency's sake. I have included references to both A (first version) and C to enable the reader to compare the phraseology. When changes in wording have seemed particularly significant, I note them. In general, the alterations in C result in a less intimate style. E.g., the form of address in A of the passage cited reads "meine zärtlichen Leserinnen."
14. Cf. Jacobs, p. 31.

15. It will be recalled that Wieland used this same method in <u>Don Sylvio</u> in elucidating Donna Jacinte's character. She, by the way, is a close spiritual relative of Danae.

16. Cf. with the passage from "Ueber den Hang der Menschen, an Magie und Geisteserscheinungen zu glauben" (1781): "<u>Die Natur</u> (gleich als ob sie eifersüchtig sey, sich über ihren verborgenen Mysterien von sterblichen Augen überschleichen zu lassen) erscheint immer wundervoller, geheimnissreicher, unerforschlicher, je mehr sie gekannt, erforscht, berechnet, gemessen und gewogen wird. Die unendliche Mannigfaltigkeit und der grenzenlose Schauplatz ihrer Wirkungen verschlingt unsern Geist; er verliert sich in einem Ocean von Wundern, an welchen, wie viel wir auch erklären und begreifen zu können meinen, doch noch immer unerklärbares und unbegreifliches genug übrig bleibt, um die verlegene Imaginazion in ihre alte Lage zurück zu werfen." Gruber ed., XXXII, 131-132.

17. "Ueber den Hang der Menschen," Gruber ed., XXXII, 123-142. The influence of the Swiss theoreticians on Wieland in this respect is apparent when we read in Breitinger's <u>Critische Dichtkunst</u> (1740; rpt. Stuttgart: Metzler, 1966), I, 61: "Der Mensch hat von Natur eine angebohrne unersättliche Wissens-Begierde, diese erstrecket sich so wohl auf das Mögliche als auf das Würckliche, ja die Erfahrung lehrt, dass der Mensch noch viel begieriger ist, das Mögliche und Zukünftige zu erforschen, als sich das Würckliche und Gegenwärtige bekannt zu machen."

18. See also Michel, p. 295.

19. It is especially enlightening to compare the first version with the third (the second is basically the same as the third) in connection with this confrontation between Hippias and Agathon. In the first version Agathon's reply to Hippias' logical demonstration of the sole legitimacy of empiricism is purely emotional. He appeals to his feelings, his intuition: "Ich sehe die Sonne, sie ist also; ich empfinde mich selbst, ich bin also; ich empfinde, ich sehe diesen obersten Geist, er ist also" (A, 40). In the second and third versions, however, Wieland feels compelled to revert to rational explanations: "Ich erkenne sein Dasein nicht bloss durch Vernunftschlüsse" (IX, 81). Although Agathon's argument remains basically "irrational," an attempt is made in the later versions to concede to the empirical method. It is therefore significant that Wieland endeavors to unite the heart and the head in harmonious cooperation at this stage in the evolution of his epistemological view. Cf. Freise, pp. 32-33, 90-91.

20. In the first version Wieland wrote: "Selbst izt, da mich glükliche Erfahrungen das Schwärmende und Unzuverlässige dieser Art von Philosophie gelehrt haben" (A, 150). It is indicative of a reassessed attitude that "Unzuverlässige" has been deleted and that "das Schwärmende" has been expressed less disparagingly. The general tone of the passage tends to substantiate my claim that Wieland's "grosse Wandlung" in the mid-1750's was not as drastic as some critics suggest. Cf. chap. 1.

21. Vormweg, p. 405, has apparently not comprehended the true function of love in Wieland's view.

22. This positive appreciation of Agathon's idealism was not necessarily the result of a changed attitude toward the hero which was introduced in the second and third versions. It is possible that Wieland considered Agathon an enthusiast

(positive sense) from the work's inception. This assumption is suggested by the author's reference to Agathon's extremism in the preface to the 1767 edition as "liebenswürdiger Enthusiasmus." IX, x. Yet we have seen that Wieland did not then strictly distinguish between the two terms.

23. Cf. also XI, 132. The irrationality of the reaction is stressed: "Die Theorie des Sophisten verlor im unmittelbaren Anblick seiner verhassten Gestalt alles Täuschende, was ihr Agathons eigne verstimmte Fantasie geliehen hatte; und sobald er in dem Manne, den er vor sich sah, den ganzen lebhaften Hippias, wie er ihn zu Smyrna verlassen hatte, wieder fand, fühlte er auch in sich den ganzen Agathon." The adjective "ganz" indicates the re-established harmony of Agathon's head and heart.

24. Jan-Dirk Müller, Wielands Späte Romane (München: Fink, 1971), p. 89.

25. Cf. Jacobi, I, 79-89 (to Wieland, 10.27.1772) and 92-94 (to Wieland, 10.30. 1772). Freise discusses this misunderstanding concerning Wieland's personal appraisal of Hippias' skepticism and epicureanism. Cf. pp. 33-35 and 91-92.

26. Cited in Gruber ed., LIII, 56-57.

27. AB, II, 162 (to Zimmermann, 1.5.1762); Freise, pp. 7, 17; Gruber ed., LIII, 58.

28. For a discussion of Wieland's attitude toward Archytas' philosophical system, see Freise, pp. 100-101; and Herbert W. Reichert, "The Philosophy of Archytas," Germanic Review, XXIV (1949), 8-17.

29. Keil, p. 226.

30. Lange, "Zur Gestalt des Schwärmers," pp. 152-154.

31. AB, II, 202-203.

32. DB, I, 220. Perhaps Müller, p. 90, has discovered the aspect of Hippias' thinking which prompted this remark. He states that the sophist is the only one who recognizes "the individual conditionality of Agathon's ideals." Both Agathon and Archytas see them as absolute and universally binding. See also Buddecke, p. 205.

33. See A, 409; AB, II, 304 (to Zimmermann, 5.12.1768); preface to third version, IX, xvi; Freise, pp. 18, 23, 88-89, 92-93.

34. Cited in Gruber ed., LIII, 59.

35. Ibid., p. 60.

36. Gruber's preface to Wielands Sämmtliche Werke, p. x; Wieland's preface to the collected works, p. 5. Cited in Göschen ed., XXV; DB, I, 82 (to Gessner, 2.16.1769).

37. Freise maintains that the Archytas episode disrupts the unity of the final version (p. 105); but Reichert seems to agree with Erich Gross in contending that the unity is not impaired (Reichert, p. 8).

38. Wolff, p. 208.

39. It should be noted that this comparison and contrast -- which underscores the nature of the schöne Seele -- is possible only in versions two and three, since the first did not contain Danae's life history. The philosophic content and the artistic structure (Danae's narration balances Agathon's) are thereby improved in the later versions. Jacobs, p. 103, has correctly pointed out an important distinction between the Donna Jacinte and Danae episodes. In the latter the decisively important narrator has disappeared, and with him the

possibly ironic and alienating commentaries. Thus the atmosphere created is more serious in comparison to Donna Jacinte's adventures.

40. Regine Schindler-Hürlimann, <u>Wielands Menschenbild. Eine Interpretation des Agathon</u> (Zürich: Atlantis, 1964), p. 120, argues that the love between Agathon and Psyche is unnatural whether it be Platonic or sensual. Kluckhohn, p. 170, states that their "metaphysical" and "intellectual" love is improper as heterosexual love but fitting as love between siblings.

41. Paul Böckmann, <u>Formgeschichte der deutschen Dichtung</u>, I, 3rd ed. (Hamburg: Hoffmann & Campe, 1967), esp. 567-578, demonstrates the importance of the marvelous in the evolution of poetic theory in the eighteenth century. Through this concept the imagination was freed from the demands of good sense, and poetry gained in symbolic worth (p. 573). I might add that in the second half of the century poetry grew also in religious value; for example, among the Romantics. Of course, shortly after mid-century Hamann and Herder were proclaiming the religious nature of language and literature.

42. Cf. Müller-Solger, p. 311. He sees effect as the distinctive principle of Wieland's work after 1758.

43. Oettinger examines Wieland's poetics. Wieland's dependence upon Bodmer and Breitinger is especially well explicated (pp. 34-51). However, Oettinger contends that <u>Don Sylvio</u> and <u>Agathon</u> demonstrate the author's break with the fundamental principle of <u>das Wunderbare</u> expounded by the Swiss theoreticians (pp. 49-51) and his identification with the empirical theory of poetics as advanced by d'Alembert and Diderot (pp. 57-119). I cannot agree entirely with Oettinger's conclusions, but his study is worthwhile for a consideration of the poetic theories that influenced Wieland.

44. Wieland was influenced by Breitinger (esp. pp. 52-64, 129-142) in this respect.

45. Müller-Solger, p. 312.

46. Schindler-Hürlimann, pp. 22-23, 39, 131.

47. Jacobs, pp. 24, 42, 46, 88; Vormweg, p. 404.

48. Schindler-Hürlimann, p. 86.

49. Michelsen, pp. 179-180, states: "Die Norm selbst, die Vorstellung des vollkommenen Menschen wird als Idee noch aufrechterhalten, aber dass sie nicht zu erreichen ist: ihre Nichtrealisierbarkeit wird jetzt das schärfste Opprobrium wider sie. Nichts vermag diese Tatsache besser zu illustrieren als die dreimalige Umarbeitung, die Wieland mit seinem Roman -- vor allem mit dessen Ende -- vornahm, und das Unbefriedigende gerade dieses Endes in allen Fassungen."

Chapter 4

PEREGRINUS PROTEUS: ENTHUSIASM AND GNOSIS

... ein guter Mensch, in seinem dunklen Drange,
ist sich des rechten Weges wohl bewusst.
-- Goethe, Faust I, Prolog im Himmel, 328-329

Peregrins geheime Geschichte in Gesprächen im Elysium (1791) is Wieland's
vindication of the enthusiast. It is a product of that final period in Wieland's life
in which he wearied of believing in nothing. [1] He had come to recognize the inadequacy of the intellect in comprehending man and his world. The positive appraisal
of the Schwärmer parallels the distinction the author made in 1775 between
Schwärmerei and enthusiasm under the influence of the Storm and Stress movement
with its emphasis on irrationality and inspiration. Wieland was convinced that not
all fantasts were quacks or deceivers. Those he regarded as insincere, as hypo-
crites and impostors (e.g., Cagliostro, Nikolas Flamel, St. Germain, Swedenborg), he dealt with unmercifully. But those fantasts whom he considered to be
sincere (e.g., Lavater, Mesmer) he defended and urged understanding for them. [2]
In this sense, Johann Kaspar Lavater supplied the immediate impulse to Peregrinus
Proteus. [3] Yet it was not really a matter of justifying Lavater (or Peregrinus) but
an attempt to come to grips with irrationality per se. [4] The theme of the novel is
not, as Strich writes, "the war against the literal conception of mythology," [5] but
Wieland's struggle for inner clarity concerning the phenomenon of Schwärmerei.

It is evident that the novel is not merely a rehash of Agathon. The fact that Wieland
again takes up the motif of Schwärmerei attests to the significance the phenomenon
had for him. Sengle writes that "Die 'Schwärmerei' -- das hat Wieland im Lauf seines Lebens erkannt -- ist ein Urphänomen, ein Stück der Menschennatur. Man
schafft sie damit, dass man über sie lacht, nicht aus der Welt. Vielleicht -- das
beginnt der alte Dichter zu ahnen -- fehlt dem Menschen, der keinen Anteil an ihr
hat, etwas zum Menschsein, jedenfalls zur Grösse." [6] The disappointment Wieland
expressed to Gleim at the novel's poor reception further evinces his intense concern for the problem of Schwärmerei. [7]

From 1786 to 1788 Wieland worked on his translation of Lucian's writings. It was
through these endeavors that the Swabian became acquainted with and intrigued by
the historical figure of Peregrinus Proteus. The first fruit of this interest in
Peregrinus was the essay "Ueber die Glaubwürdigkeit Lucians, in seinen Nachrich-
ten von Peregrinus" which Wieland appended to the translations. [8] This essay
forms the embryonic stage of the novel, which is not only a vindication of the
Schwärmer but an apology for Lucian's unfair treatment of the fantast. Since Wieland does not condemn and revile Peregrinus as does his favorite author, Lucian,

one must conclude that Wieland also knew Aulus Gellius' comment on the religious fanatic: "Philosophum nomine Peregrinum, cui postea cognomentum Proteus factum est, <u>virum gravem atque constantem</u>." [9] It is obvious from a letter to the classical scholar, Heyne, that Wieland knew precious little about Peregrinus and his circumstances. [10] Yet what he lacked in historical information was more than compensated for by his <u>Menschenkenntnis</u>.

Before turning to the novel, a few words about its historical characters, Peregrinus and Lucian, are in order. Peregrinus was a Greek Cynic philosopher who lived in the second century A.D. He is most remembered for his spectacular suicide by fire following the observance of the 236th Olympic games (A.D. 165). The primary source for Peregrinus' life is Lucian's satiric letter "On the Death of Peregrinus." Peregrinus was born to a well-situated merchant in Parium, in Mysia. He later associated with the Christian community in Syria, where he played an important role until his estrangement from it. Thereafter he traveled to Alexandria in order to learn from the Cynic philosopher Agathobulus, whose views he combined with his own concept of Christianity. Peregrinus next journeyed to Rome, but was expelled for insulting Emperor Antonius Pius. After his return to Greece his popularity gradually declined. Finally, he announced his cremation, which took place before many spectators, including Lucian.

Lucian (c. 125-190) was born at Samosata in Syria. His parents being of limited means, Lucian was apprenticed to an uncle who was a sculptor. However, the youth soon abandoned the position in favor of rhetoric. Several years were spent in Ionia perfecting his Greek and his knowledge of the classical authors. Adopting the profession of a rhetorician, he traveled widely in Greece, Italy, and Gaul where he met with his greatest success. At the age of about forty he abandoned rhetoric for dialogue and made Athens his permanent home. In old age he accepted a well-paid clerical post in Egypt in the service of the emperor. Lucian is best remembered as a satirist, excelling in wit and elegance of style.

The sparse information concerning Peregrinus presented Wieland with an ideal situation (as was the case with <u>Agathon</u>). By implementing his knowledge of psychology he was able to accomplish the aim about which he had written to Heyne: "to place Peregrinus in the proper light." [11] It has been aptly pointed out that the historian would be sorely disappointed in the work as an historical document, for it is permeated with poetry (e.g., the episodes involving Mamilia, Dioklea, Faustina). [12]

The principal theme of the novel is the same as that of its two predecessors. Many of the predominant motifs are also encountered: the relativity and subjectivity of perception, the deceptiveness of appearances, the influence and source of the wondrous, the functions of reason and intuition in the pursuit of knowledge. There is also the same inherent relationship between form and epistemologic view. The social by-product of this work, however, is different. The hero is not cured of his extremism nor of his asocial attitude. Peregrinus begins and concludes his life as an untempered enthusiast. In a very definite sense this work questions the efficacy of salubrious reason and bourgeois society.

One of the first things to strike the reader of this novel is the hero's exotic name. In fact, his name is significant for the epistemologic view expressed. "Peregrinus" means "exotic," or "coming from foreign regions," or "upon a pilgrimage." Thus the protagonist's given name reflects his characterization as a misfit in this world. Indeed, the fantast himself considers the world a form of exile; his true home lies beyond the confines of experiential reality.

The surname "Proteus" is also symptomatic of the work's philosophic statement. Proteus was a prophetic sea god who had the ability to assume various forms when threatened. Peregrinus was considered by some to be a quack, by others to be a deluded and naive dreamer, and by yet others to be a salutary demigod. This aspect of the Protean hero is reminiscent of the chameleon motif. The mythical Proteus would impart his prophecies only under duress. Peregrinus might be likened to the sea god in this respect also. During his lifetime the visionary was frequently deluded. However, whenever he was "forced" to recognize the deception he immediately reaffirmed the reality of his ideals. Thus each disappointment served as a means of impelling the dreamer to a "prophecy" of his true beliefs. The nuances of the term "prophecy" are also significant for Wieland's view of Peregrinus. "Prophecy" can signify a foretelling, a premonition of truth by one who is inspired by God. Surely the echo of Wieland's interpretation of the enthusiast as a God-inspired man is unmistakable. One is tempted to equate the enthusiast with the prophet.

In Greek "Proteus" is derived from "protos" which means "first." This connotation of being first, coupled with the sea god's ability to change his form and combined with his prophetic powers, induced the ancients to designate him a symbol of the primeval substance. [13] He became, as it were, a paragon of ultimate Truth reflected in Nature. An Orphic priest sang of him:

Proteus tönt mein Gesang, der Meeresschlüssel Besitzer,
Welcher, zuerst erzeugt, der Natur Anfänge geordnet,
Wandelnd den heiligen Stoff in vielgestaltiger Bildung,
Allgeehrt, vielrathig, ein Kundiger dessen was da ist,
Oder was vormals war, und was Zukünftiges seyn wird;
Denn die erste Natur hat in Proteus alles geleget. (XXVII, 401)

In this one term many leitmotifs encountered in this study are incorporated: the chameleon, the enthusiast, the symbolic and hieroglyphic aspects of Nature. The hero's very name, therefore, is of immeasurable consequence.

Since Wieland was undeniably well versed in Greek mythology, literature, philosophy, and history, it can be assumed that he was aware of the full import of the connotations. For example, in the fairy tale, "Der Stein der Weisen" (1786), the elusive quintessence of Nature is designated "Proteus" (XXVII, 53-54). The nuance of the word is particularly significant for the present novel, for Peregrinus is on a quest for ultimate Truth, the final possession of which eludes him repeatedly.

Peregrinus Proteus was born and raised in Parium, a Roman colony on the eastern shore of the Dardanelles. Because his mother had died while he was quite young and his father was often away on business, Peregrinus lived with his maternal grandfather, who saw to his education. Like Don Sylvio the youth possessed a hyperactive imagination which flourished in his physical isolation from the world. The grandfather, Proteus, can be likened to Donna Mencia, since he endeavored to impart to the youth the values he had collated from Pythagoras, Hermes, Zoroaster, Buddha, Abaris, and Orpheus (XXXIII, 46, 49). However, Peregrinus did not view these men and their teachings in the same light as did his grandfather. Whereas his mentor considered the various theories merely as a source of amusement, Peregrinus took them seriously. It will be remembered that Donna Mencia also failed to influence her protégé as she intended. Thus, in each case the "pupil" did not accept the identical view of life of his mentor, although he retained a predisposition for metempirical realms.

Like Don Sylvio, Peregrinus accidentally discovered the writings which influenced him most. Among them were Empedocles' work on Nature, several of Plato's dialogues, and a number of works by Heraclitus. Plato's Symposium, particularly Diotima's theory of love, made the profoundest impression on the youth (XXXIII, 53).

When Peregrinus was eighteen he was confronted with human sensuality for the first time. The unsuspecting youth entered into a Platonic relationship with his enamored cousin, Kallippe, who was unhappily married. The young woman's attempted seduction ended in failure when her aged husband intervened and Peregrinus narrowly escaped discovery by leaping through a window. Despite this exposure to sexuality, Peregrinus remained naive and undaunted in the pursuit of Platonic ideals.

He next traveled to Athens in search of philosophers who could advance him in his noble efforts at spiritual perfection (XXXIII, 89). However, his sojourn in Athens ended in delusion and disappointment (as did Agathon's). He is blackmailed for allegedly seducing a handsome youth named Gabrias. In actuality Peregrinus had desired to mold the young man into a neo-Xenophon (XXXIII, 79). This experience jolted Peregrinus out of his exalted reveries and opened his eyes to his real situation and the ruthless nature of people (XXXIII, 82-83). It will be remembered that Agathon's attempt to better the Athenians also ended in disappointment. In the motif of homosexual seduction there is an echo of Theogiton's unsuccessful debauchery. The earlier attempt by Kallippe to seduce the unsuspecting Peregrinus is paralleled by Pythia's onslaught against Agathon's virtue.

After his disappointing experience in Athens, Peregrinus departed for Smyrna. It is here that he learned of the holy priestess Dioklea, who resided in a remote area of Halicarnassus. She reputedly associated with the gods and enjoyed powers of divination. Aroused by the wondrous reports about this woman, Peregrinus resolved to go to her and request instruction in the sacred mysteries.

Halicarnassus fulfills for Peregrinus a function similar to that of Delphi and Smyrna for Agathon. The religious devotee experienced an apparent theophany. However, the goddess Venus Urania ultimately revealed herself as the wealthy Roman, Mamilia Quintilla, and Dioklea exposed herself as the noted pantomimic dancer, Anagallis. The two women feigned their respective roles of goddess and priestess in order to ensnare the Platonic youth in their web of carnal wantonness.

Peregrinus' disappointed belief in theophany is reminiscent of Agathon's disillusionment in Delphi. Peregrinus' mental state at this time is described in terms that echo strongly Don Sylvio's dreamy state in which fantasy and reality were mixed.

> Die damalige Jahrszeit, (es war im Anfang des Sommers) der reine Himmel dieses schönen Landes, dem wenige in der Welt zu vergleichen sind, die durch die lieblichste Kühlung gemilderte Wärme, alles trug das seinige bei, einen Jüngling von zwanzig Jahren, der so sonderbar gestimmt war, in diese Art von wachenden Träumen zu versetzen, wo, unter einem Schlummer der Sinne den das Flattern eines Schmetterlings erwecken kann, das Zauberspiel der begeisterten Einbildung zum Anschauen und die leiseste Ahndung der Seele zur Empfindung wird. (XXXIII, 102-103)

The tone of this passage recalls the fairy-tale atmosphere of Don Sylvio. It is the same season, the lulling effect of Nature is noted, the youths are approximately the same age, there is the unnoticed blending of Empfindung and Einbildung in which a butterfly plays a role. The similarity between the two novels in this passage seems to underscore the interplay of fantasy and reality in Peregrinus Proteus.

In addition to his disillusionment with respect to his theophany, Peregrinus was also disappointed in his own nature. He was forced to recognize his frailty after having allowed himself to become intoxicated with the orgiastic carnality of his seducers. (His seduction by Faustina and Dioklea is reminiscent of Danae's success with Agathon. Yet Peregrinus' relationship was not marked by any spirituality.) His first disappointment can be described as his Entgötterung (XXXIII, 164), his second as cognizance of his bestiality (XXXIII, 181). This twofold recognition of his nature was a necessary prelude to his further "development." [14]

Dejected -- but not despairing -- Peregrinus secretly fled Mamilia's villa. [15] While aimlessly wandering in Syria, he made the acquaintance of Kerinthus, the charismatic leader of a clandestine Christian sect. In his characteristically enthusiastic manner, the fantast readily pledged obedience to Kerinthus (Apollonius von Tyana) and the brotherhood. For seven years Peregrinus fulfilled an apostolic mission for the sect, bringing many Christian communities into the impostor's fold.

However, the visionary is once more rudely beguiled in his noble aspirations. He believed that Kerinthus and his followers were sincere in their professed intention of effecting the spiritualization of all human desires and in advancing the moral improvement of mankind. Through Dioklea, who is disclosed as Kerinthus' sister, the enthusiast discovered the religious mesmerist's true goal. Kerinthus was not interested in man's spiritual life. He used his followers to effect a political revolution which would have placed him at the head of the new state. Thus he was actually the antipode of Christ, his professed model. Disillusioned with the practice of Christianity, Peregrinus ceased to associate with Christians but did not reject his exalted ideals.

Peregrinus spent his remaining years as a cynic and misanthrope. Ten of these years he lived in Alexandria as an ascetic. His sole purpose was to master his baser nature, which was obstructing his path to moral perfection. Persuaded by a Roman nobleman to make another attempt at reforming the world, Peregrinus accompanied the nobleman to Rome. Rome, however, proved to be his Syracuse (cf. XXXIII, 133-135). Not only were his anticipations thwarted but he was untrue to himself in succumbing to the irresistible Faustina, spouse of Marcus Aurelius. Peregrinus was banished from Rome after a fiery denunciation not only of Faustina but of the Emperor Antonius Pius. He devoted his last years to preparing himself for his announced self-immolation, which was witnessed by Lucian.

The immediate result of the similarities between the psychogenesis of Peregrinus, Agathon, and Don Sylvio is the demonstration of the spiritual bond that unites them. Yet valuable insights into Wieland's epistemology and his philosophical position can be acquired by observing the disparate effect of the parallel influences on Peregrinus. Both Don Sylvio and Agathon ultimately responded favorably to the forces counteracting their particular biases. Peregrinus, on the other hand, never swerved from his preconceived theosophic conception of Truth. This fact is of the utmost importance for Wieland's final concept of epistemology and the resultant effect on the author's social theory.

The structure and style of Peregrinus Proteus reflect the exoneration of this exotic and bizarre hero. At the same time, these elements highlight the essentially epistemologic world view of the protagonist; that is, the structure and style of the novel stress the interrelationship of fantasy and reality. The work is constructed to afford the handicapped fantast (handicapped because he was not "sensible" like other men) the opportunity to rectify the misconceptions about his sincerity propagated by Lucian. However, the novel is not only a vindication of Peregrinus (and therefore of irrationality) but also an apology for Lucian (and rationality).

Wieland is able to demonstrate that both the romantic and the rationalist were sincere in their endeavors to represent Truth, but that each was deceived by appearances. Thus Lucian's biased portrayal of Peregrinus is psychologically explained; the satirist did not intentionally misrepresent his antipode. Lucian says: "Ich schilderte dich damals wie ich dich sah oder zu sehen glaubte" (XXXIII, 32; see also preface, p. v). The novel, then, is a careful blending of "fact" (Lucian's report) and "fancy" (Peregrinus' vindication). In the end Wieland is able to expose "fact" as fancy and "fancy" as fact. The implication is that the imagination is necessary for the cognition of ultimate Truth. The novel is characterized by this intricate interplay of fantasy and reality, as will be seen.

The various segments of Peregrinus Proteus will each be examined in turn, with an eye to its epistemologic import. The components are: the preface to the first edition of 1791, an excerpt from Lucian's report on Peregrinus, an introductory dialogue between Peregrinus and Lucian, and the first-person narrative of the protagonist's experiences.

The preface is intrinsic to the entire work for a number of reasons: it puts in proper perspective the constituent parts of the novel; it explains who Peregrinus and Lucian were and how the author acquired this new information about them; and, finally, the style and tone of the preface anticipate the overall epistemologic view. The opening sentences of the preface are ironic, an indication of the author's changed attitude toward the Schwärmer. Wieland explains that he has a natural ability to converse with departed spirits (cf. "Lustreise ins Elysium" [1787], XL, 243-254). The satiric element is heightened by the allusion to Swedenborg, generally considered a quack by the enlighteners. [16] Wieland continues in his titillatingly ironic tone but draws a subtle distinction between his use of this ability to overhear the conversations of departed spirits and Swedenborg's use of it. In drawing this distinction he provides the reader with what can be called a statement or purpose.

> Ich gestehe, dass mir diese Gabe Unterredungen verstorbener Menschen zu behorchen zuweilen eine sehr angenehme Unterhaltung verschafft: und da ich sie weder zu Stiftung einer neuen Religion, noch zu Beschleunigung des tausendjährigen Reichs, noch zu irgend einem andern, dem geistlichen oder weltlichen Arme verdächtigen Gebrauch, sondern bloss zur Gemüthsergötzung meiner Freunde, und höchstens zu dem unschuldigen Zweck, Menschenkunde und Menschenliebe zu befördern, anwende; so hoffe ich, für diesen kleinen Vorzug (wenn es einer ist) Verzeihung zu erhalten, und mit dem Titel eines Geistersehers, der in unsern Tagen viel von seiner ehemaligen Würde verloren hat, gütigst verschont zu werden. (XXXIII, i-ii)

In contrast to writers like Swedenborg, Wieland intends to use his extraordinary gift solely to entertain his friends and -- this next statement is extremely important for the positive appraisal of some visionaries -- to advance the understanding and love of man. The formulation "Menschenkunde und Menschenliebe zu befördern" is an allusion to Lavater's Physiognomische Fragmente zur Beförderung der Menschenkenntnis und Menschenliebe (1775-1778). He states his intention ironically ("höchstens zu dem unschuldigen Zweck"), but its actual sincerity is unmistakable (cf. "Verzeihung," "Würde," "verschont").

The reader is confronted with an apparent philosophical paradox in this situation, since he is urged to accept fantasy ("diese Gabe") for reality. However, if we interpret this "gift" in a slightly different light; that is, as poetic inspiration which makes of man a second creator, then we see that what Wieland actually achieves is the establishment of another link between the poetic and the empiric worlds. It has been suggested that artistic truth is a more reliable indication of the Highest Good than is empirical fact. By supplementing the sketchy facts of history with fanciful psychological embellishments, Wieland is better able to get to the truth of the matter. Thus once again the inherent relation between style and epistemologic content in the novel is manifest.

The general tone of the preface is jesting and congenial as in the afterword to Don Sylvio. Thus yet another link to that novel can be established. Wieland relies upon the portrayal of Peregrinus' adventures as plausible and possible as a means of convincing the reader of their authenticity. The principles of verisimilitude, possibility, and probability are the same factors Wieland relied upon in depicting Agathon's metamorphosis. The assumption of probability as evidence of truth is therefore also reminiscent of the foreword to Agathon, in which Wieland offers an apology for "poetic truth." "Poetic truth" (or controlled fantasy) can be considered an accurate foreshadowing of ultimate Truth.

There are other noteworthy aspects of the preface. For instance, the reader is given insights into the author's attitude toward Peregrinus and Lucian. Although Lucian is Wieland's friend, he is not accepted uncritically. The satirist is described as ".... Lucian der Dialogenmacher, der sich ehemals mit seinen Freunden Momus und Menippus über die Thorheiten der Götter und der Menschen lustig machte, übrigens aber (diesen einzigen Fehler ausgenommen) eine so ehrliche und genialische Seele war und noch diese Stunde ist, als jemals eine sich von einem Weibe gebären liess" (XXXIII, iii). Wieland considers Lucian's caustic ridicule of human and divine folly to be improper ("diesen einzigen Fehler"). The obvious allusion is to Peregrinus' inordinate enthusiasm. This observation is important for a just interpretation of the novel and an understanding of Wieland's philosophic position. Too often Wieland has been seen as Lucian's admirer, but not as his critic. [17] Lucian's prejudice against Peregrinus is manifest when he describes the dreamer as "the greatest of all fools" and a "half-crazed charlatan" who "was ruled by sensuality and eccentric fantasies" (XXXIII, v). In retrospect the final statement of the above citation ("eine so ehrliche und genialische Seele ... als jemals eine sich von einem Weibe gebären liess") is seen as a veiled revelation of man's inborn penchant for error. Man is by nature finite and his horizon is restricted. It is for this reason that Wieland criticizes Lucian's caustic denial of that which cannot be comprehended with the intellect (the connotation of "Thorheiten").

In the preface Wieland also casts doubt on the credulity of Lucian's report. He underscores the fact that the letter is composed not only of what Lucian personally witnessed but also of hearsay (XXXIII, v-vi). In addition, two important questions are raised which indicate the dual function of the novel: an apology for Lucian and a vindication of Peregrinus.

> ... ob Lucian in seinem Urtheile von ihm [Peregrinus] so unparteyisch, als man es von einem ächten Kosmopoliten fordern kann, verfahre? und: ob Peregrin wirklich ein so verächtlicher Gaukler und Betrüger und doch (was sich mit diesem Charakter nicht recht vertragen will) zu gleicher Zeit ein so heisser Schwärmer und ausgemachter Fantast gewesen sey, als er ihn ausschreit? (XXXIII, vi)

These are the two questions Wieland endeavors to answer in and through the novel, and he succeeds in demonstrating the deceptions of both while simultaneously evincing their sincerity. He accomplishes both by varying the point of view.

Immediately following the preface is an excerpt from Lucian's eyewitness report of Peregrinus' self-immolation in A.D. 165. [18] Without this inclusion, the author asserts in the preface, "this whole conversation would be incomprehensible and its narration purposeless" (XXXIII, viii). [19] Lucian depicts Peregrinus as a wanton and mischievous charlatan who was caught in adultery, debauched a youth, and committed patricide for the inheritance. The sole motivating factor in his life, according to the satirist, was egoism. He desired the esteem and admiration of the people. Desire for notoriety was also the reason for his suicide. In a word, Peregrinus Proteus is seen through the eyes of one who detests all fantasts as impostors. At best Lucian considers them eccentric fools. The report is a prime example of the blending of subjectivity (fantasy) and objectivity (empirical reality). In light of Lucian's letter and Wieland's preface, the dialogue between Peregrinus and Lucian is readily comprehensible. Seen in relation to the bulk of the novel, the preface and the excerpt stress perceptual relativity, which is thoroughly clarified in the first-person narrative. The preface presents Wieland's view, the excerpt Lucian's. Thus these two elements fulfill a structural and a poetic end.

The structure of Lucian's report of Peregrinus' circumstances is intriguing, for it has apparently served as the model for the structure of the novel proper. In Lucian's letter to Cronius on Peregrinus' death, the fantast is seen from two perspectives. The first is conveyed by Peregrinus' friend and fellow Cynic, Theagenes. His appraisal of the eccentric visionary is of course positive. The other perspective is supplied by an unidentified individual who obviously considers the Cynics to be charlatans and impostors. There is little doubt that the unidentified person is Lucian himself. [20] Thus in Lucian's account two prejudiced views are given, one for and one against. This situation is paralleled in the novel. The reader is aware of the distinction between the opinions of Lucian and Peregrinus. In a later context the structure of the first-person narrative will be analyzed in detail.

The "Einleitung" originally appeared as a dialogue in the Teutsche Merkur (1788), entitled "Peregrin und Lucian, ein Dialog im Elysium." [21] It forms the nucleus of the first-person narrative, sets the stage for Peregrinus' "geheime Geschichte," and continues the dominant theme of perspective. Their encounter in Elysium 1600 years after the fantast's self-immolation is of course in the eighteenth century. Each is surprised to find the other in Elysium. Lucian's presence is pungently ironic, since he did not believe in an afterlife. In a sense, therefore, the outcome of the debate between the romantic and the rationalist is anticipated. The satirist's presence in Elysium reveals the veracity of Peregrinus' world view; the irony of Lucian's presence is stressed through repetition at the conclusion of the novel (XXXIV, 186).

The introductory dialogue continues the leitmotif of perceptual perspective. [22] Peregrinus speaks, for example, of the perennial prejudices and biases to which man is so susceptible. It is in fact almost impossible to be objective.

> Selten ist der Erzähler ein Augenzeuge, noch seltener der Augenzeuge ganz
> unbefangen, ohne alle Parteilichkeit, vorgefasste Meinung oder Nebenabsicht;

fast immer vergrössert oder verkleinert, verschönert oder verunstaltet er,
was er gesehen hat. Du, zum Beispiel, hattest den Willen mir kein Unrecht
zu thun: aber ich war ein Christianer gewesen und du hieltest alle Christianer
für Schwärmer oder Schelme; ich war in den Orden des Diogenes übergangen,
und dein Hass gegen die Cyniker ist bekannt genug, da du keine Gelegenheit
versäumtest, ihm die möglichste Publicität zu geben. Wie hättest du also
den armen Peregrin, mit allem guten Willen ihm kein Unrecht zu thun, in
keinem ungünstigen Lichte sehen sollen? Ihn, auf den der ehemalige
Christianer und der nunmehrige Cyniker einen doppelten Schatten warf?
(XXXIII, 33-34)

Placing the pair in Elysium, however, fulfills a specific function in connection with
the question of perspective, since in the next world falsehoods cannot be told.
Elysium guarantees the veracity of Peregrinus' "confessions." Neither the protagonist nor the antagonist are predisposed any longer (XXXIII, 42). This claim to
impartiality is overtly repeated at the conclusion of the novel to convince the
reader that the reappraisal of Peregrinus is sincere (XXXIV, 186). [23] With regard
to Peregrinus' and Lucian's presence in paradise, the introductory dialogue (more
than the preface) serves the specific structural purpose of assuring the reader that
the disputants avoid all sophistry.

The enthusiast declares himself prepared to narrate his experiences as he himself
sees them. Thus another dominant theme is touched upon when he informs Lucian:
"Wenigstens gewinnest du immer so viel dabei, dass du nichts von mir hören wirst,
als was ich selbst für Wahrheit halte" (XXXIII, 33). The motif implied is of course
that of intrinsic experience. Peregrinus' declaration is reminiscent of Danae's
comment to the same effect. Her "partial" view of her life was more accurate than
the world's. This circumstance suggests that the "geheime Geschichte" (i.e.,
intrinsic experience) is the only solution to the dilemma of man's inability to perceive objectively. [24]

Let us turn to an analysis of the structure and style of the first-person narrative.
In previous works, Wieland assumed the roles of editor and translator in addition
to that of omniscient narrator. His use of the narrator's role occasioned a confi-
dence-inspiring rapport with the reader by means of which he could indicate how
the reader should evaluate the various subjective views presented. In Peregrinus
Proteus Wieland takes a different tack. Only in the foreword does he directly
address the reader. His purpose is to prepare the reader for the ensuing dialogue
and narrative. Other instances of direct intervention by the narrator are insignificant and peripheral. [25]

It has been aptly pointed out that the omission of the omniscient narrator is evidence
of an essentially subjective view of reality. [26] The reader is no longer guided
through the maze of reality (reflected in the Romanwirklichkeit). Rather, the individual must rely on his own subjective evaluation of the aggregate of the polyperspective. Not only is the novel comprised of subjective views of reality (Peregrinus,
Lucian, Dioklea, Kerinthus, Dionysius, etc.), but the reader himself also brings

to the work his own preconceived notions. For this reason the frequently encountered theme of intrinsic experience assumes paramount importance, for it is the guarantee of truth. [27]

The unintentionally prejudiced views in the novel can be considered to be less salient because the reader is not constantly reminded by an author figure that the individual views expressed are subjective. That is to say, in contrast to Don Sylvio and Agathon there is no explicit common norm against which the "aberrant" person is placed. From the stylistic point of view the reader is forced to determine the veracity of Peregrinus' ideals without the benefit of an expressed guide. (Elysium as a structural device guarantees the truth, but it does not explain the author's epistemology.) Subjectivity rather than objectivity is now the major criterion. Even as the use of irony in the previous novels was decisive for an accurate understanding of those works, so too is its use or non-use indicative of the epistemology in Peregrinus Proteus. The difference is that, in this novel, the absence or reduction of irony plays a greater role.

The novel abounds in examples of essentially subjective perception. For instance, Peregrinus is not only viewed by Lucian but also by Kallippe, Gabrias' contriving father, Dioklea, Dionysius, Faustina, etc. Each judges him according to his own particular bias. Kallippe sees him solely as a sex object, Gabrias' father as a money source, Dioklea as a foolish but lovable enthusiast, Kerinthus as an enraptured visionary unworthy of initiation into the inner circle of confidants, Faustina as an entertaining eccentric. [28] Despite the absence of the omniscient author and the presence of the myriad perspectives, the reader is given subtle indications as to which point of view carries the greatest weight. Wieland wants his public to judge Peregrinus as he does, but he does not want to force his opinion on them. Thus he must persuade by viewing his subject from all angles while conveying one distinct impression. The subtle means the author utilizes involve the first-person narrative, the use of dialogue, supportive characters, and irony.

Peregrinus relates his own experiences, which lends his view an authoritarian and dogmatic tone, since he should know best what his real motives were. When Agathon, Danae, and Donna Jacinte related their experiences in retrospect, the effect was justification of themselves and an explanation of their strengths and weaknesses. [29] The intimacy and immediacy of their autobiographies lent greater credence to their respective views. The same is true of Peregrinus. The use of the first person is further necessitated by the structure of the novel, which is basically a protracted dialogue. [30]

Critics have pointed out that dialogue and conversation are fundamental characteristics of Wieland's prose. [31] Wieland's frequent utilization of this technique (in various forms) is seen as evidence of his ideal of urbanity. [32] I have already stated that I believe urbanity was only a stage in the development of Wieland's ideal. Wieland uses dialogue, in my opinion, primarily as a means of presenting more than one view, thereby stressing perceptual relativity. Dialogue naturally involves more than one person, and thus leads the seeker into society. This introduction into society, however, is not an end in itself but rather the means to a higher goal. The "exalted" goal to which all of Wieland's heroes strive can be termed self-recognition. The sincere exchange of views greatly facilitates clarity of thought and must necessarily advance the quester toward his objective. This function of colloquy is most pronounced (aside from the present novel) in Agathon's extensive conversations with Hippias and Archytas, and in Don Sylvio's discussions with Don Gabriel. The hegemony of dialogue in these instances should not be surprising, since Don Gabriel, Hippias, and Archytas are rational philosophers attempting to educate impractical fantasts. Furthermore, Don Sylvio and Agathon were considered aberrant by Wieland at the time of their conception. He thought then that man could best fulfill his destiny (as perceived in social terms) by following the dictates of reason.

The object of Peregrinus Proteus is not identical to that of the other two works. The enthusiast is not seen as an errant individual who must be saved for society. In contrast to Don Sylvio (less so in Agathon's case), Peregrinus is equal to his opponent. The antipodes of the philosophical spectrum are represented in Peregrinus and Lucian: the enthusiast and the Epicurean, the romantic and the skeptic (XXXIII, 39). It should not be expected, therefore, that dialogue in this novel will fulfill exactly the same function as in Don Sylvio and Agathon.

Vormweg has aptly pointed out that "not the dialogue, but Peregrinus' narrative is in the forefront." [33] Yet the integral role of the dialogic "interruptions" in the explication of Peregrinus' narration must not be discounted. Lucian represents the reader and anticipates the questions which the reader formulates as he follows the hero's adventures. The actual exchange between Lucian and Peregrinus serves to draw out the important differences between the Epicurean's world view and that of the enthusiast. The disparities are underscored by the satirist's initially sarcastic comments and by his later serious attempt to understand better the fantast's inimitable position.

The plausibility of Peregrinus' perspective is substantially reinforced by Lucian's objections, queries, and skepticism, which the protagonist can satisfactorily allay each time. The dialogue thus embodies the roles played by Wieland in the previous novels and reflects the dialectic interplay of ideas. The author engages in an inner monologue, as it were, in an effort to determine the respective aptitudes of the head and the heart as purveyors of metempirical and moral goods -- of ultimate Truth. The function of dialogue in the present work is integrative, therefore, but in a philosophic sense, not a social one.

The hybrid composition of the work -- narrative and colloquy -- most appropriately reflects its epistemologic design. The dialogic passages reveal disparities in world views, whereas the narrative and reflective passages psychologically explain how the divergent views came to be held. Sengle states in this respect: "In der Verbindung von Dialog und Roman findet er [Wieland] die gemässe Form für das behutsame, nach allen Seiten ausblickende Erzählertum seines Alters." [34]

Another relevant aspect of the novel's composition which reveals Wieland's philosophic affinities is the function of the secondary figures. For example, one can hardly compare the educative roles of Hippias and Archytas to the contrastive roles of Dioklea and Dionysius. [35] Wieland does not give the latter characters the same care and attention as the former. Of the two minor characters of relative significance in Peregrinus Proteus, only Dionysius is imbued with the author's sympathy. He is in many ways reminiscent of Hippias or Don Gabriel. This resemblance possibly explains the favorable impression he makes. Dioklea, on the other hand, is Peregrinus' counterpart. She too is a protean figure, but she is conscious of the temporariness of her roles and plays them to her greatest advantage. [36] Perhaps she appeals less to the reader precisely because she lacks sincerity. Both Dionysius and Dioklea seem pale alongside Hippias and Danae. One reason for their ineffectuality in controlling the protagonist's extremism is his resistance to change. Hippias and Archytas fared better because Agathon was responsive. Peregrinus is not malleable like Don Sylvio and Agathon. Almost from the beginning Peregrinus' world view was firmly and unalterably set (XXXIV, 129).

The lack of strong supportive characters in Peregrinus Proteus can also be explained by Wieland's attitude toward their philosophies. Hippias and Archytas were able to present convincing arguments because Wieland identified with them to a certain extent. He too was seeking a philosophy of life. In 1791, however, Wieland was more certain of himself. The lack of strong supportive characters reflects the author's opinion that the Schwärmer is not to be condemned or ridiculed. Thus Peregrinus' subjective view is the more persuasive for lack of substantial counterargument.

Another subtle means that Wieland employs to convey his affinities and aversions is irony. Only the views of the two chief figures will be examined in this connection because Lucian more or less incorporates the anti-fantast attitudes of the minor characters. Lucian's ironic comments are most explicit in the first part of Peregrinus' narration. At first they are unmistakably mocking, but they later become increasingly ambiguous until they are not ironic at all but serious. Thereafter, Lucian indulges in witty or humorous observations (aside from sober queries). An example of Lucian's inimical wit is given at the beginning of the second chapter. Peregrinus has finished relating his disappointing experience in Athens and is now trying to explain his concept of eudaemonia, which is derived from Diotima's theory of love. The quester rises through the various stages of corporeal beauty and physical harmony to the contemplation and possession of the spiritual source of all beauty, the Highest Good. To his dismay he found no one in Athens who could have instructed him in this wisdom. Lucian interrupts Peregrinus' explication of the sublime life with the flippant remark: "Und fandest du denn, guter Peregrin, in ganz Athen keine ehrliche Glycerion, die dir die Wohlthat erweisen konnte, dich von allem diesem Unsinn auf einmal und von Grund aus zu entledigen? Denn, so viel ich merken kann, fehlte dir doch nichts als diese Cur" (XXXIII, 89-90).

Lucian's ironic comment jolts the dreamer out of the ethereal spheres of the sublime and makes him aware of the satirist's almost contemptuous opinion of such exalted ideas. The deflating effect of Lucian's remark is, however, scarcely noticeable, since Peregrinus refuses to be deterred from his purpose. He acts as if the remark were spoken in earnest and uses it to his advantage. Latching onto the word "cure" he explains that enthusiasts do not consider their inspired state a malady.

At other times, however, the protagonist cannot so deftly pass over an impertinent comment. For example, on another occasion the enthusiast is speaking of the theopathetic exultation which the Venus Urania icon aroused in him: "Ich fand vor der Thür einen von den Knaben, der mir das feierliche Gewand wieder abnahm, und ich kehrte mit einem neuen Bilde in meiner Seele zurück, das, so zu sagen, ihre ganze Weite ausfüllte, aber, anstatt kalter Marmor zu seyn, von aller der Liebe belebt war, die --" And Lucian completes the sentence with "-- der kalte Marmor in dir angezündet hatte!" (XXXIII, 124). Peregrinus is too absorbed in remembered ecstasy not to be irritated by Lucian's caustic interjection. Thus, before Peregrinus continues, the notation "nach einer kleinen Pause" appears in small print. Wieland uses this means to indicate the hero's disappointment with Lucian's levity. The preceding quotation also evinces the continuity of one of the most telling features of Wieland's style: the periodic sentence. Its infrequent use, in comparison to Don Sylvio, is understandable, since Peregrinus Proteus is not a comic novel even though Müller labels the protagonist a "Don Quijote der Religion." 37

When Peregrinus began his story Lucian was still skeptical. The impression is given that the rationalist does not expect the fantast to be able to place himself in a better light. But as the dreamer progresses, the satirist must admit that Peregrinus' view is unexpectedly convincing. This recognition brings about a changed attitude toward the acceptance of the protagonist's anomalous adventures. His remarks take on an ambivalent undertone. The reader is uncertain whether the observation is meant ironically or seriously. In fact, the statement can be mocking for the person looking for parody and sincere for the individual expecting earnestness. For example, Peregrinus has described the theophany of Venus Urania and now tries to explain his ecstasy. He is aware that words cannot express these sublime emotions, and he apologizes for his failure to express the inexpressible. Since Peregrinus' naive belief in the actuality of theophany is a prime target for sarcasm, we would expect Lucian to reply with acerbity; instead, he says:

> Es ist freilich schwer von unnennbaren Dingen zu sprechen, und von ausserordentlichen Gefühlen einem andern, der in seinem Leben nichts ausserordentliches gefühlt hat, einen Begriff zu geben. Ich entbinde dich also eines vergeblichen Versuchs um so lieber, da du mir bereits genug gesagt hast, um sehr deutlich einzusehen, dass du, mit aller möglichen Bestrebung, dem Blinden, den du vor dir hast, keinen anschaulichern Begriff von den Farben der unsichtbaren Gegenstände, die du ihm schilderst, mittheilen könntest. (XXXIII, 145)

This passage can be taken to mean exactly what it says. Lucian has stated at the beginning of the dialogue that "Nature had equipped him with a cool head" (XXXIII,

23). Thus, if he were now well disposed toward Peregrinus, he would naturally remind him that he had never experienced extraordinary emotions, and that any effort to convey an impression of them would be fruitless. He will nevertheless accept the enthusiast's word for such exceptional sensations. On the other hand, the passage might be expressing the sophist's antipathy for Peregrinus' emotionalism. Lucian could be asking derisively: How can you be so preposterous as to think you can speak accurately of things that do not exist? How can you expect to convey such emotionalism to a staunch rationalist? How can you consider me blind when you yourself cannot see? Both interpretations are justifiable in context. Peregrinus' reply to Lucian seems to indicate that Lucian's remark was straightforward, but the possibility of irony is not ruled out. Peregrinus responds: "Ich verstehe den Wink, und werde in meiner nächsten Beschreibung, wo nicht so deutlich, doch wenigstens so kurz als möglich seyn" (XXXIII, 145). The ambivalence of Lucian's comment is manifest.

Finally, we are presented with a statement which might be expected to be insincere but which is not. Peregrinus has just narrated his erotic adventures in Mamilia Quintilla's villa, which he began in a Platonic fever and ended in a bacchanalian frenzy. The enthusiast is dejected at having become so enmeshed in the web of carnal appetites. During the narration Lucian had remarked several times that Peregrinus in the arms of a voluptuous Mamilia and the embrace of a sensual Dioklea was in an enviable position. Thus it is surprising when the satirist displays so much understanding for Peregrinus' dejection caused by his infidelity to his Platonic ideals. Lucian says:

> Ich muss gestehen, Freund Peregrin, dass du einen reichen Stoff zu Selbstgesprächen aus der Villa Mamilia mitgebracht hattest. Mit aller meiner Kälte kann ich mich doch so ziemlich in deine damalige Lage hinein denken, und ich zweifle sehr, ob sich eine schmerzlichere für einen Jüngling, der mit so hohen Erwartungen dahin gekommen war, erfinden liesse. (XXXIII, 204)

Surely there is no ironic undertone in this declaration! Lucian has progressed from almost total skepticism to complete confidence in Peregrinus' integrity.

In the second part of Peregrinus Proteus Lucian refrains from caustic witticism and engages in punning or in laconic humor. This change in Lucian's humor reflects his altered attitude toward the incurable zealot. There is a more pronounced feeling of congeniality and camaraderie between the two men. Through this circumlocution Wieland expresses his affinity to and sympathy for the extremist Peregrinus. At the same time, Lucian does not lose favor with the author but is now depicted as a true cosmopolite who is tolerant and understanding of all views, no matter how disparate from his own.

Examples of this new congeniality occur relatively frequently. For instance, Peregrinus is explaining the drastic measures he took to gain control over his carnal appetites. One method was to scourge his back with a whip until blood flowed. Lucian makes a pun of the flagellation: "Und was war der Erfolg dieser listigen

Art dem Feind in den Rücken zu fallen?" (XXXIV, 37). Shortly after, Peregrinus relates how Dioklea unexpectedly visited him during his incarceration (reminiscent of Hippias and Agathon, with similar consequences). The religious fanatic can hardly believe his eyes when she appears in Christian garb. When she admits that Kerinthus brought about her enlightenment, Peregrinus exclaims ecstatically: "Ists möglich? Kerinthus? ... Kerinthus, der mich auf eine so wunderbare Weise gerettet hat, Kerinthus hat auch dich aus den Klauen der Dämonen gerissen, und der unermesslichen Seligkeiten des Reichs der Himmel theilhaftig gemacht?" (XXXIV, 41).

Dioklea replies: "Ich habe dir noch weit wundervollere Dinge zu entdecken, mein lieber Proteus; aber vor allen Dingen lass dich bitten, diese seltsame Sprache, die dir, wie ich höre, so geläufig geworden ist als ob du nie eine andere gesprochen hättest, mit einer natürlichern zu vertauschen" (XXXIV, 41). At this point Lucian interrupts Peregrinus' story with the witty remark: "Darum hätte ich dich selbst bitten wollen" (XXXIV, 42).

The above quotations are examples of the evolving good will between the two philosophers. However, they are seen from Lucian's standpoint. One of the best examples of their congeniality is reflected in their mutual banter near the end of the novel. Peregrinus explains his reasons for accompanying the young Roman noble to his home:

> Ich schmeichelte mir, einen jungen Mann von so glücklichen Anlagen nach und nach völlig gewinnen zu können, und ... ihn zum Werkzeuge der grossen Reformation zu machen, von welcher ich mir in meiner Einsamkeit zu Alexandrien einen schönen Plan geträumt hatte, dessen Realisierung lediglich von der einzigen kleinen Bedingung abhing, den regierenden Theil der Welt in Weise und den gehorchenden in Patrioten zu verwandeln. (XXXIV, 135-136)

Peregrinus' conscious irony is manifest in the expressions "lediglich" and "einzige kleine Bedingung." Lucian retorts in the same vein: "Ein artiges kleines Projekt!" (XXXIV, 136). The exchange is light, jovial, and consciously ironic on the part of both participants. Furthermore, Peregrinus continues his tale of the Roman noble in the same light, ironic tone. The enthusiast has come to recognize the folly of his Roman undertaking, and Lucian has come to accept the visionary as honest and sincere. Thus the sophist is no longer acrimonious toward his adversary. The style of the passage demonstrates the equality of the opponents, since only persons who feel they are equals will engage in banter. Of course the fact that this repartee occurs 1600 years post facto also accounts somewhat for the mellowed and tolerant disposition of the two men.

Lucian's use or non-use of irony in the novel is therefore especially helpful in determining Wieland's epistemologic and philosophic view. Another reflection of the philosophic point of view is presented in Peregrinus-Wieland's conscious parody of the fantasy world. For example, on one occasion the hero is apparently lost in a forest. His guide is puzzled as to how he could have lost his way, since he knows the forest well (it was intentional). Peregrinus mockingly inquires whether a woodland spirit could have led them astray (XXXIII, 237). Soon the guide sees a light shining through the trees; Peregrinus comments, "Es ist vielleicht ein Irrwisch, wenn es nicht der Mond ist" (XXXIII, 238). Elsewhere the terminology also reflects the fairy tale motif. The hero speaks of the machinations in Mamilia's villa as "Feerei" (XXXIII, 112), of his passion for Venus Urania as "Bezauberung" (XXXIII, 141-142, 149), of the villa as a "Zauberpalast" (XXXIII, 151), and of his repeated "Entzauberung" (XXXIII, 218). The servant girls in the villa are described as "nymphs," "amorini," or "Zefyretten" (XXXIII, 156, 186). The fairy tale atmosphere is most evident in the section dealing with Peregrinus' experiences in Halicarnassus. The reason is obviously the intention of the two women to maintain the fantast's illusions. Later in the novel Peregrinus speaks of the transformation his dank prison cell undergoes when Dioklea dispenses incense in the vaulted room illuminated by a flickering candle. He describes his cell as a room in a "Feenpalast" (XXXIV, 40).

The fairy tale motif naturally invites the question: Why? Wieland's overt objective is certainly not the same as in Don Sylvio. This satiric element seemingly unites the hero's exalted idealism with Don Sylvio's quixotic delusions. It was indicated with regard to Don Sylvio that fairy tales are basically idealistic. Perfection and fulfillment are possible in the poetic world. For example, it was through his naive belief in the truth of the wondrous that Don Sylvio experienced "wondrous" adventures. Agathon finds his way into a perfect society which bears the distinct mark of a poetic solution. We have also seen that Nature is the source of das Wunderbare and that man is imbued with an incessant longing for perfection. Perhaps the presence of the fairy tale atmosphere is to stress the point that Peregrinus' extreme idealism is fulfillable only in a perfect (fantasy) world, not in the empirical one. In this sense, the function of the wondrous would be figurative -- prefiguring the perfection which is to come. Thus, that which man envisions in this imperfect world of things is a premonition of eternal completion.

Jan-Dirk Müller has indicated Wieland's conscious association of the fairy tale and myth with empirical reality in the author's late works. His conclusion is important for this study: "Im Märchen und im Mythos spiegelt sich die Vollendung der Wirklichkeit; Märchen und Mythos sind Umschreibungen des Ueberschusses über das normal Wirkliche hinaus." [38] Only when we recognize the idealistic content of fantastic visions will we comprehend the significance of enthusiasm for Wieland's epistemology and philosophy. [39] Seen in this light, Don Sylvio, Agathon, and Peregrinus Proteus seem to constitute a trilogy. The fantasies of Don Sylvio are combined with the moral idealism of Agathon to produce the theomorphism of Peregrinus. [40]

A further aspect of irony in the novel involves Peregrinus' ridicule of Kerinthus' reputed miracles. He scoffs at the charlatan's cure of possessed (neurotic) persons by a laying on of hands (accompanied by a protracted massaging motion) (XXXIV, 23). He mocks the "resurrection" of a young girl (XXXIV, 24). Peregrinus treats these feats derisively because he, a former disciple of Kerinthus, had likewise been deceived. Now, however, the blinders are removed from his eyes, and he is also aware of his own sincerity. Thus this aspect of self-irony underscores Kerinthus' fraud and Peregrinus' integrity. It will be seen that Schwärmerei and Enthusiasmus reflect this distinction. [41]

The stylistic and structural elements examined above reflect Wieland's ultimate epistemologic position. That perception is in the author's opinion subjective and relative has been repeatedly stressed. But in this novel the all-pervasiveness of cognitive subjectivity is emphasized even more by the absence of an omniscient author. For a better understanding of the innate relationship between form and content let us turn to an analysis of Wieland's epistemology in Die geheime Geschichte des Peregrinus Proteus.

The author's love of irony is again manifest when two relatively minor characters concisely formulate Wieland's philosophic position. Both the religious impostor Kerinthus and the sagacious, practical Dionysius express the fundamental maxim of Wieland's ontology. At the outset of their acquaintance Kerinthus informs the naive quester: "Nichts ist was es scheint, wiewohl dem Erleuchteten Alles scheint was es ist. Die Natur ist eine Hieroglyfe, wozu wenige den Schlüssel haben, und der Mensch kennet alles andre besser als sich selbst" (XXXIII, 213).

This statement could well be taken as the motto not only of this novel but of Wieland's life as a whole. It contains many of the concepts encountered in this study: the deceptiveness of perception, the perspicacity of the enlightened individual, the symbolism of Nature, and the all-important Delphic adage "Know yourself." Once again the motif of introspection as a necessary prerequisite for enlightenment is promulgated. The latent meaning of Kerinthus' remark is that man must first understand himself -- his desires, appetites, aspirations -- before he can hope truly to discern the mysteries of Nature. This introspection is the key to all knowledge. Dionysius is even less ambiguous in his critical insight. He advises Peregrinus: "Das was du suchest, lieber Peregrin, ist weder hier noch dort, weder bei dieser noch bei jener Partei oder Sekte: es ist in dir selbst oder es ist nirgends" (XXXIV, 108). It is obvious in context that Dionysius refers to Peregrinus' longing to expedite man's moral perfection.

The above passages indicate that knowledge can best be acquired not through observation of empirical phenomena but rather through scrutiny of the human spirit. Müller-Solger has noted the necessary role of introspection in Wieland's pursuit of Truth: "Dieses Bewusstsein, dass die Kenntnis der Seele der Schlüssel für das Verständnis des Weltganzen ist, wird zur tragenden Schicht aller gedanklichen und dichterischen Arbeit Wielands." [42]

Although introspection as the path to knowledge avoids the possibility of perceptual error, it incurs the inherent danger of error in judgment. Lucian addresses himself to this problem, intending to demonstrate to Peregrinus how his "erroneous" ideas arose.

Wie sehr, guter Peregrin, bestätigt dein Beispiel die grosse Wahrheit, dass es nicht die Dinge selbst, sondern unsre durch die Individualität bestimmten Vorstellungen von ihnen sind, was die Wirkung auf uns macht, die wir den Dingen selbst zuschreiben, weil wir sie unaufhörlich mit unsern Vorstellungen verwechseln! (XXXIII, 114)

Lucian feels he is pointing out the deceptiveness of the imagination. What he actually indicates is man's inability to perceive objectively the phenomenal world. How can any individual be completely free of all bias and predisposition? It was manifest in Don Sylvio von Rosalva that reality is twofold: empiric and poetic. The former is independent of man and, in Wieland's opinion, not the valid object of true knowledge. The latter is contingent not only upon each individual's impression of phenomena but also upon the effect of certain innate, vague intuitions. This "zweifache Art von Wirklichkeit" is also evident in Peregrinus Proteus.

Wieland is here concerned with subjective reality as is evident from the work's structure and style. [43] In order to grasp the repercussions of a purely subjective reality, man must know the essence of human nature. In the course of the novel, human nature is illuminated from two major standpoints: that of the empirical rationalist and that of the exalted dreamer. Peregrinus relates his life story in order to convey to Lucian the "genesis of his ego" (XXXIII, 197). In so doing he hopes to convince Lucian of the reality and legitimacy of his "fantasms." The introductory dialogue to the hero's story evinces the disparate views of human nature held by Peregrinus and Lucian. Lucian is amazed to find Peregrinus in Elysium. He was convinced that buffoons and quacks would never be admitted to the happy isles (which Lucian did not believe in!), since experience had taught him to be "somewhat skeptical toward all highflying presumptions of certain people, whose intentions seldom remained long ambiguous" (XXXIII, 29). Lucian thus became prejudiced against all super-terrestrial claims.

To guard against the dangers of the imagination, Lucian advises: "Wer zum Menschen geboren wurde, soll und kann nichts edleres, grösseres und besseres seyn als ein Mensch -- und wohl ihm, wenn er weder mehr noch weniger seyn will!" (XXXIII, 29). Taken out of context this statement could be interpreted as exhorting man to realize the god in him and destroy the animal. Understood in this sense it would echo a leitmotif found in Wieland's works. [44] But in context the connotation is far removed from this meaning. The import is revealed when Peregrinus objects:

Aber, lieber Lucian, gerade um nicht weniger zu werden als ein Mensch, muss er sich bestreben mehr zu seyn. Unläugbar ist etwas Dämonisches in unsrer Natur; wir schweben zwischen Himmel und Erde in der Mitte, von der Vaterseite, so zu sagen, den höhern Naturen, von unsrer Mutter Erde Seite den Thieren des Feldes verwandt. Arbeitet sich der Geist nicht immer empor, so wird der thierische Theil sich bald im Schlamme der Erde verfangen, und der Mensch, der nicht ein Gott zu werden strebt, wird sich am Ende in ein Thier verwandelt finden. [45] (XXXIII, 29-30)

Lucian sees man primarily as an animal, destined to nonexistence at the point of death (cf. XXXIV, 186). Man therefore should not delude himself with notions of immortality and theomorphism. [46] Peregrinus views man primarily as a demigod, who must first go through a purification process before entering eternity. The rest of the novel is a vindication of this concept of human nature and, necessarily, of the means by which it is mediated.

When Wieland-Peregrinus speaks of man's middle position between heaven and earth, he is voicing the notion of the Great Chain of Being postulated by Plato and Aristotle, systematized by the Neoplatonists, and brought to full fruition in the eighteenth century. [47] The tremendous impact that the ancients exerted on the eighteenth century explains the ease with which Wieland was able to depict the concerns of his age in a Hellenistic setting. [48] The battle between the ancients and the moderns is indicative of this influence. The grouping of ideas known as the Chain of Being formed the context of Wieland's philosophy. The author's epistemological concern within this system is also reflected in the quotation above. Peregrinus alludes to an indisputable daemonic element in human nature which underscores an intrinsic affinity between man and God. This daemonic element demands clarification, since Wieland's theory of knowledge hinges upon it. We will see that das Dämonische implies those concepts and nonrational functions of the mind and heart that have been exposed as crucial to Wieland's epistemology. The leitmotifs of imagination and instinct are innately related to the daemonic. The ideals, which played such a decisive role in Agathon and the minor writings, are the objective of this irrational force. The reunification with these ideals (that is, with the deity) constitutes the coveted state of eudaemonia not only for Agathon but also for Peregrinus.

Early in the first-person narrative the reader learns that the daemonic element in man is related to the wondrous. For the hero's grandfather the wondrous was nothing more than an amusing plaything. For himself, however, the wondrous acted as a catalyst; it affected in no small way the development of his personality.

> Ihm war das Wunderbare nichts als eine Puppe, womit seine immer kindisch bleibende Seele spielte; bei mir wurde es der Gegenstand der ganzen Energie meines Wesens. Was bei ihm Träumerei und Mährchen war, füllte mein Gemüth mit schwellenden Ahndungen und helldunkeln Gefühlen grosser Realitäten, deren schwärmerische Verfolgung meine Gedanken Tag und Nacht beschäftigte. (XXXIII, 49-50)

The prime importance of the wondrous in this context is its ability to stimulate vague premonitions of exalted realities. The disparate opinions of grandfather and grandson on the nature of the wondrous is reflected in the antipodal views of Peregrinus and Lucian on the function of the imagination. Lucian used his imagination only to entertain himself and others. But the enthusiast found a more fitting use for the fantasy. Through it he was able to excite a certain latent force within his soul which could divine metaphysical realities (XXXIII, 26). In a definite sense Peregrinus considered the imagination to be a sixth sense (cf. Agathon's claim, p.

81). In order for this force to be reliable, however, the individual involved must fulfill a stipulation: he must be salubrious ("ein unschuldiger und guter Mensch") (cf. XXXIII, 25-27). This condition is of course reminiscent of the "healthy" individual noted earlier. In this context, das Dämonische in man is more clearly defined as the power of divination (XXXIII, 26). Unfortunately, not all men become aware of this force, and most men do not develop it to the extent that Peregrinus did.

Peregrinus refers to the development of this sense as a paring away of superficialities in order to expose the essentials (cf. XXXIII, 31, 53-54). Because of his exceptional and pronounced propensity for the wondrous, Peregrinus was able at an early age to cut through the layers of his humanity and free the daemonic within him. The extrasensory perception which the Abschälungen made possible was fully developed before Peregrinus left his grandfather's house.

The youth was always aware of the daemonic element in him, but he could only conceive of its essence in vague terms. Not until his introduction to Diotima's theory of love did Peregrinus find fitting terminology for and definition of das Dämonische. The intellect clarified the indistinct sensations of the heart. This development parallels the metamorphosis Agathon underwent from his early Schwärmerei to Archytas' wisdom. The indistinct premonitions of his youth found rational clarification in Archytas' philosophy. Peregrinus now envisions this daemon in terms of Diotima's concept of love: "an intermediate thing between mortal and immortal Nature" (XXXIII, 54). The true breakthrough comes with the realization that this daemon is not extraneous to himself as he originally thought, but that he is himself the daemon. He no longer stands in need of external stimulus in order to determine his ultimate destiny; the daemon within him intuitively perceives the Highest Good. To attain the realization of all his aspirations, he need only follow the dictates of das Dämonische.

> Nun fühlte ich mich gleichsam von mir selbst entbunden, fühlte, dass der Dämon der weisen Diotima in mir, oder vielmehr, dass ich selbst der Dämon sey, der keiner Vermittlung eines dritten, sondern bloss des ihm eigenen ewigen Verlangens und Aufstrebens nach dem höchsten Schönen und Vollkommnen nöthig habe, um im Genuss desselben Eudämon, das ist, der reinsten Wonne, deren ein Dämon fähig ist, theilhaftig zu seyn, und im Genuss des Göttlichen sich selbst vergöttert zu fühlen. (XXXIII, 55)

Knowledge for Peregrinus concerns only the attainment of this state of eudaemonia.

The continuity of Wieland's thought, from his earliest essays through the novels of the 1760's and to the works of the 1790's, is transparent in this passage. The Plato-Shaftesbury nexus of ideas still dominates the author's thinking. The eternal longing of the soul for spiritual goods -- for the Beautiful and the Perfect -- is indicative of man's higher calling. Man is destined to rise to the status of a god. It must be stressed -- as in the case of Don Sylvio and Agathon -- that Peregrinus intuits his true nature. He arrives at this conclusion only secondarily via a rational process. It is interesting that conversations concerning Verstand and Vernunft are instigated by Lucian or Dionysius, whereas debates on the nature and function of the imagination, instinct, and the wondrous are prompted primarily by Peregrinus (cf. XXXIII, 21, 25, 44, 75, 83-85; XXXIV, 100).

The relationship of the daemonic to the divine and the nature of the incessant longing of the human soul for fulfillment is further clarified in Peregrinus' explanation of the reasons for his suicide. Through the long years of his abstinent and ascetic life, and through the disappointments occasioned by his contact with his fellow man, Peregrinus had gradually become less animal and more spirit. He looked upon his body and the physical world as obstacles to the fulfillment of his deepest desires (XXXIV, 179). He no longer considered his life to be of benefit to mankind and now flattered himself (Schwärmerei) with the notion that his death might serve as a source of edification (XXXIV, 180). Above all, his self-immolation was prompted by his longing to return to his original element, of which the daemonic was a vestige (enthusiasm). Basically, Peregrinus considered earthly existence a form of enforced exile. Suicide was for him a release. It was the quickest means to effect the return to his original state. "In Rücksicht auf mich selbst war es die kürzeste, edelste, der ursprünglichen Natur des Dämons in mir, der mein wahres Ich ausmachte, angemessenste Art, nach einer schon zu lange dauernden Verbannung auf dieses verhasste Land der Täuschungen, der Leidenschaften und der Bedürfnisse in mein ursprüngliches Element zurückzukehren" (XXXIV, 181).

The concept of death as a release from banishment is also indicative of the continuity of Wieland's philosophy. It is very striking that this interpretation of death was espoused by Wieland forty years prior to the composition of Peregrinus Proteus. In his first literary effort, [49] the didactic poem "Die Natur der Dinge" (1754), the young author wrote:

O Tod! du süsser Tod! dich scheuet nur ein Thor!
Du hebest das Geschöpf zu seinem Ziel empor;
Du trägst der Gottheit uns und unserm Glück entgegen,
Wie froh will ich mich einst in deine Arme legen!
(Göschen, XXV, 119)

These verses could have been uttered by Peregrinus himself! In light of this observation I cannot comprehend how a critic can refer to Peregrinus' departure from the world as a tragedy. [50] It is also puzzling how a critic can overlook the positive aspect of the enthusiast's suicide. To say that his death is "marked by an apparent element of defeat," [51] is incontestable -- from the world's point of view. To understand the significance death held for the protagonist, we must think like him. Certainly Peregrinus does not consider his death fanatical. He describes his impatient yearning for death as "die letzte Leidenschaft, die ich der Weisheit noch aufzuopfern hätte" (XXXIV, 182). Peregrinus' self-immolation is thus very similar to Empedocles' death in Hölderlin's dramatic fragment. By throwing himself into the Aetna the prophet-philosopher exerted his right to return prematurely to the gods;

death assumes here mystic proportions as a reunification with the One. [52] The parallel to Novalis' view of death as expressed in "Lehrlinge zu Sais" and "Hymnen an die Nacht" is obvious as well.

It seems strange, therefore, that Peregrinus' motives should be impugned by critics whereas Empedocles is admired. The widespread disparagement of the Schwärmer is apparently the cause of such derogatory interpretations. [53] Unfortunately, the critics have not taken sufficient note of the distinction Wieland made between Schwärmerei and enthusiasm. Although Wieland refers to Peregrinus as a Schwärmer, the epithet ehrlich clearly indicates that the author considers him to be an enthusiast. This interpretation is further underscored by the fact that Peregrinus is truly inspired by God, not by a fetish. Enthusiasm is not an evil and, even if taken to an extreme, will not impair the individual's recognition of Truth. After all, God is Truth. And the Wahrheitssucher is -- like Peregrinus -- on a pilgrimage that leads him through this world into the next. Whether one considers the enthusiast a quack or a savior is totally dependent upon the viewer's perspective. This observation brings us back to the central epistemological question of the study. We are immediately reminded of Wieland's essay "Was ist Wahrheit?" or Goethe's epigram on Truth: "Eine nur ist sie für alle, doch siehet sie jeder verschieden, / Dass es Eines doch bleibt, macht das Verschiedene wahr." [54]

The positive aspect of the hero's self-immolation is apparent in his conception of eudaemonia. The protagonist gives an explicit definition of his notion of eudaemonia relatively early in the narrative. It is of course intrinsically bound to the daemon in his breast.

> Seitdem mich der Dämon der Liebe, den die Wahrsagerin Diotima dem Sokrates offenbarte, auf die Entdeckung gebracht hatte, dass ich ein eingekörperter Dämon dieser Art sey, schien mir nichts natürlicher, als das Verlangen, mich selbst und die Wesen meiner Gattung sowohl, als die höhern, mit denen meine Natur verwandt war, besser kennen zu lernen. Diese Kenntniss war die einzige, die ich meiner würdig hielt, da sie mich geraden Weges zur Eudämonie führte, jener erhabenen Geisterwonne, die mir nichts Irdisches weder geben noch rauben konnte, und nach welcher zu streben mein angebornes Vorrecht war. Und was konnte diese Eudämonie anders seyn, als das Leben eines Dämons zu leben, mit Dämonen und Göttern umzugehen, und von einer Stufe des Schönen zur andern bis zum Anschauen und Genuss jener höchsten Urschönheit, jener himmlischen Venus zu gelangen, welche die Quelle und der Inbegriff alles Schönen und Vollkommnen ist? (XXXIII, 88)

Peregrinus' notion of eudaemonia has nothing to do with the material world. How can his death then be tragic or fanatical? Only through death could he attain "the contemplation and enjoyment of that highest Beauty which is the source and quintessence of all beauty and perfection." Advancement through progressive stages of the beautiful in order to secure the ultimate metaphysical source is reminiscent of Diotima's concept of spiritualized love.

Peregrinus' whole life is seen as a quest for this eudaemonia. His experiences and delusions were the result of his attempt to find the correct and shortest path to this state of fulfillment (XXXIII, 89, 205). Lucian is of course skeptical, and wonders how the enthusiast could persist in his quest after experiencing so many disappointments. The satirist inquires whether Peregrinus ever doubted the existence of the ideal, perfect world. Peregrinus' reply is an emphatic no. Just as his physical eyes convinced him of the existence of the sun, so too did his spiritual eye (instinct) convince him of metempirical realities (XXXIII, 90) (note echo of Agathon). The presence of the ideals in his soul imparted a sense of inner peace and freedom that caused him to look with disdain on the never-satisfying sensual pleasures of this world (XXXIII, 91).

The most stringent test of the actuality of these ideals was the animal stupefaction Peregrinus experienced in Mamilia's villa. Reigning like Dionysius over a protracted bacchanalia, he indulged in every carnal delight. Yet an indistinct feeling and presentiment made him aware of how deceived he was in looking for the sublime in the arms of Mamilia and Dioklea. This vague feeling reassured him that his infidelity was not irreversible, that all was not lost (cf. XXXIII, 181-182, 184-185). The intrinsic experience of the divine in his soul was the cause of his quick recuperation after this and every relapse. It was his infallible lodestar (XXXIV, 129-130). Peregrinus cites this moral instinct as evidence of the existence of his ideals. He states that if his former disposition and exalted manner of thinking had been chimerical, if his lofty conceptions had been merely artificial substitutes for real delights, then the genuine pleasures of Halicarnassus should have cured him of his "immature" delusions. This, however, was not the case.

> Aber jene Ideen und Gesinnungen, wie viel oder wenig sie auch mit Wahnbegriffen in meinem Kopfe verschlungen seyn mochten, waren meinem Gemüthe natürlich und wesentlich; die moralische Venus, die meinem Geiste vorschwebte, war kein Fantom, sondern ewige unwandelbare Wahrheit; nicht dieses Ideal, sondern meine durch erwachende Naturtriebe überraschte Fantasie, hatte mich in das künstliche Netz gelockt, das meiner erfahrungslosen Jugend von sinnlicher Liebe und Wollust gestellt wurde. Diess, däucht mich, macht einen grossen Unterschied. (XXXIII, 197-198)

The allusion to the "moral Venus" is concrete evidence that real knowledge in Wieland's epistemology can only be of moral Truth. [55] All other forms of knowledge are basically unreliable because man is subject to perceptual and judicial error. Examples of such errors are provided in Peregrinus' twofold deception in Halicarnassus. First, the hero is misled by his theurgic bias (the Wahnbegriffe mentioned above) to expect a theophany (see also XXXIII, 204-205). In this instance, he erred in judgment. Second, he was beguiled by his aroused sensuality. In this case, his senses deceived him. To be sure, Peregrinus perceived correctly. Thus he did not err in sense perception; rather -- and this is important for the moral nature of Truth in Wieland's view -- the hero was led astray by sense pleasure. Because sensual pleasures are the result of the animal in man and not the daemonic, Peregrinus was aberrant. Absolute Truth, in Wieland's view, can only be spiritual or moral in nature. Gnosis is the single reliable and worthwhile type of knowledge.

The hegemony of (moral) intuition in Wieland's epistemology is further stressed by the many references to the deceptive nature of appearances in the novel. The first words of the dialogue are "Täuschen mich meine Augen" (XXXIII, 23). At the conclusion of the novel, Peregrinus refers to the material world as "dieses verhasste Land der Täuschungen, der Leidenschaften und der Bedürfnisse" (XXXIV, 181). The mention of passion in this connection necessarily infers that it too is a cause of beguilement.

The deceptive nature of man's material existence is a leitmotif which has been traced in the preceding chapters. It has been observed that the heart is man's most reliable guide through this labyrinthine world because it is not susceptible to the errors of <u>Verstand</u> and <u>Vernunft</u>. In <u>Peregrinus Proteus</u> the heart plays a similar role. The hero's notions of the daemonic and of instinct are functions of this irrational force. The wondrous is the result of the heart's effect on the imagination. Since Kerinthus and Dionysius have given concise expression to Wieland's philosophic view in this work, it is certainly more than coincidence that Dioklea should give a fitting statement of the heart's unimpeachability. She tells Peregrinus:

> Das sicherste Mittel dich vor den Blendwerken der Einbildung zu verwahren, ist ihrer Geschäftigkeit Einhalt zu thun, und dich gänzlich den Gefühlen deines Herzens zu überlassen. Durch diese allein kannst du hoffen, die Göttin dir günstig zu machen. Das <u>Herz</u>, nicht die Einbildungskraft, ist das <u>Organ</u>, das ihrer Mittheilungen empfänglich ist. (XXXIII, 127)

Dioklea's motive in urging Peregrinus to heed the sentiments of his heart is quite mundane. It is a ruse to debauch the Platonic lover. The covert purpose of Dioklea's advice is gradually to lure him away from his theopathy and prepare him for the sybaritic Mamilia. Nevertheless, Dioklea's counsel is a succinct statement of the heart's function in Wieland's epistemology. If man would harken to the moral dictates of the heart and restrain his passions, he would not be led astray.

It is characteristic of the nexus of form and content and of Wieland's irony that Peregrinus' opponents express his point of view. Lucian, Dionysius, and Dioklea do not intentionally formulate Peregrinus' philosophy. In fact, they intend to countermand it (especially in Lucian's case). Yet from Peregrinus' perspective their formulations are clearly "enthusiastic." Thus Wieland is able to lend the protagonist's extreme position greater argumentative support. Because the novel is recognized as a vindication of the <u>ehrlicher Schwärmer</u>, the reader schooled in Wieland's prose style rapidly becomes aware of additional and sometimes latent points of view. I have also tried to demonstrate how the reader comes to identify with Peregrinus and to interpret the world through his eyes. Hippias was Agathon's opponent to the end. Lucian, Dionysius, and Dioklea see themselves as the hero's antagonists, but they unwittingly become his mouthpiece.

The danger an overwrought imagination poses for man is recognized by Dioklea. She knows that Peregrinus is deceived by his theopathetic visions. One of his other antipodes in the novel, Dionysius, also recognizes that the imagination is the source of the hero's disappointment. Dionysius rightly warns Peregrinus that his plan to join a Johannite family will end in disillusionment. Because Peregrinus' imagination paints life in unrealistic colors (XXXIV, 107-108), Peregrinus will never find what he seeks in this world. Thus his situation parallels Agathon's dilemma, for both are forced to recognize that men are not as they pictured them (XXXIII, 173). Dionysius sees that the only way Peregrinus can live at peace with himself and in harmony with his exalted ideals is to quit the company of men. He advises the enthusiast to become a Cynic; only as a hermit (!) can he hope to avoid deception (XXXIII, 110-111).

Peregrinus' abandonment of human society is significant for both the concept of enthusiasm and Wieland's reputed ideal of urbanity. Man is liable to Schwärmerei as long as he expects to encounter the sublime in the mundane, or as long as he thinks he can reshape society according to certain ideals. Second, it is utterly impossible for some men to live in society because of the perennial conflict between individual idealism and general practicality. Man must compromise himself in order to function in society. An exceptional individual like Peregrinus, "who loves Truth so passionately," is incapable of compromise (XXXIV, 110). For him an asocial life is his only assurance of attaining his lofty goal.

Lucian had pointed out that, from the rationalist's point of view, Peregrinus' greatest character fault was his lack of shrewdness (Klugheit) (XXXIII, 85-86). Had he possessed this social virtue (reminiscent of "Theagenes"), he would not have been so deluded in life. The enthusiast replied that had he possessed this virtue his life would have been radically different. In a word, he would not have been Peregrinus (XXXIII, 86). This assertion strikes a theme encountered in Don Sylvio and Agathon. In each novel the protagonist affirms that he is unique. His singularity is the result of his subjective reality. Although the heroes affirmed their right to their uniqueness, Peregrinus is the first to adhere to his right to be different. The absence of a recognized norm (reflected in the want of an omniscient author) only serves to underscore the singularity of all views and therefore the subjective validity of the Schwärmer's. This right to a subjective reality further stresses the nonconformist characteristic of Wieland's ultimate humanistic ideal. 56

Certain aspects of the novel's epistemological view still need elucidation. There is a parallel to the daydreaming tendencies of Don Sylvio and Agathon. Peregrinus states that he has enjoyed indescribable visions in such "dreams" which have left an indelible mark on his soul. The visions can be so deeply etched into one's being that the individual would never believe that they might be delusions (cf. XXXIII, 103). On another occasion the enthusiast tells Lucian that his seraphic view of life is understandable if one has experienced the ecstasy that such a view of life can impart. There are visions, he says, which make man happier than the most fortunate circumstances. Peregrinus is surprised that Lucian is apparently unaware of this fact. "Aber solltest du nicht wenigstens diess erfahren haben: dass es Träume giebt, die uns glücklicher machen, als wir wachend je gewesen sind, und deren wir uns, selbst nach dem Erwachen, noch immer mit Vergnügen erinnern?" (XXXIII, 92). That Peregrinus is in Elysium proves that his "dreams" were not misleading. The presentiments they provided (obviously induced by the daemonic) are genuine. Wieland uses the dream motif to express the divine in human terms. [57]

Little has been said about the functions of reason with respect to Peregrinus. The explanation is simple: the enthusiast is guided by his heart alone. The role of the head in the quest for Truth is expounded by his adversaries, Lucian and Dionysius. The reader must keep in mind that neither of these men believed in an afterlife, nor did they believe in the reality of the ideals espoused by the fantast. They considered the ideals laudable but impractical.

Lucian tells Peregrinus that man should strive to be neither more nor less than human. Peregrinus answers that man must strive to be more than human to avoid degenerating into a beast. Lucian counters by saying that salubrious reason is sufficient to prevent this deterioration (XXXIII, 30-31). It would seem that Lucian's stand only serves to maintain the status quo without actively striving for improvement. The ironic fact that Lucian is in a heaven in which he did not believe seems to underscore the inadequacy of reason as man's sole guide.

Dionysius also attempts to persuade the incurable fantast that reason is sufficient for a felicitous life. According to the rationalist, Peregrinus has committed the regrettable mistake of choosing emotion and imagination as his guides. Experience should have proven by now that these guides continually lead man from the path of Truth. He urges Peregrinus to try the only infallible guide: reason. "Die Vernunft, glaube mir lieber Peregrin, die Vernunft ist der gute Dämon des Menschen, und die Eudämonie, nach welcher du strebest, ist die Frucht eines nach ihrer Vorschrift geführten Lebens, oder es giebt gar nichts, das diesen Namen verdient, diesseits des Mondes" (XXXIV, 100). In Dionysius' strident appeal for reason as master guide and architect, we hear the voice of the eighteenth-century Enlightenment. The wording of his assertion is in conscious contrast to Peregrinus' claim that intuition is man's benevolent spirit.

The conclusion of the novel, as well as its setting, demonstrates beyond a doubt Wieland's affinity for Peregrinus. Peregrinus remained faithful to the dictates of his heart; never did he have recourse to the intellect as his primary guide. It has been maintained that the conflict between the head and the heart is unresolved in the novel. [58] Yet the very fact that Lucian learns to accept the enthusiast as his equal indicates that something has been won. The Schwärmer is no longer decried as a buffoon; rather, he is viewed positively. [59] Peregrinus even seems to fare better than Lucian. Whereas the latter was limited to empirical reality, the enthusiast divined the ultimate realities. Peregrinus represents the logical continuation of the Schwärmer-motif that has been traced from Don Sylvio and Agathon. What Peregrinus says of himself can also be said in defense of these two extremists as well. "Alles Missverständniss hört nun auf, und Peregrinus Proteus steht nun, als ein Schwärmer, wenn du willst, aber wenigstens als ein ehrlicher Schwärmer vor dir da" (XXXIV, 185).

This assertion should preclude a false interpretation of "ehrlicher Schwärmer." Wieland has legitimized Peregrinus Proteus, and with him the irrational in man. Peregrinus' life was the correct way -- for him. Lucian's way of life was appropriate to himself but inappropriate for Peregrinus. [60] This seems to be the import of Sengle's apparently paradoxical statement: "Es kann sich nicht darum handeln, Peregrins Leben als richtig zu erweisen: es bleibt ein Schwärmerleben; aber darum, das weiss Wieland jetzt, ist es noch kein schlechteres Leben als das der Vernünftigen." [61]

The mutual acceptance of romantic and rationalist belies, perhaps, the observation that Wieland advocated harmonious cooperation of the head and heart. We must remember, however, that a delicate balance of the two forces was the author's ideal. Peregrinus and Lucian represent the extremes, not the norm. Sincerity is the salutary factor for both men. Neither intended to deceive either himself or his fellow man. Thus they encounter one another as equals.

To summarize, the continuity of the dominant epistemologic leitmotifs has been demonstrated. Yet there has been a subtle shift in emphasis concerning perception. The implications of Don Sylvio and Agathon come to full fruition in this work and are explicit. The absence of the omniscient narrator (and his irony) indicates the rejection of a universally binding norm; the daemonic has been introduced to underscore man's basically divine nature; the conception of "inner form" has been cited to stress the singularity of each individual. The structure of the novel reflects the basic epistemologic view by indicating the various subjective, prejudiced perspectives, which are nevertheless valid -- for the individual concerned. In general there is a de-emphasis of the social and the rational in man's life and an increased recognition of the irrational side of human nature. These are the primary ontologic innovations of Peregrinus Proteus.

NOTES

1. Sengle, p. 479.
2. Cf. Wieland's essays: "Gedanken über Lavaters Magnetismus," "Nikolas Flamel, Paul Lukas, und der Derwisch von Brussa," "Swedenborgs Offenbarungen und der tierische Magnetismus und Somnambulismus," "Ueber den Hang der Menschen, an Magie und Geistererscheinungen zu glauben," etc. Strich, I, 200, apparently has not noted the distinction Wieland makes between the sincere and the insincere fantast.
3. Sengle, p. 482.
4. Ibid.; Wulff, p. 13.
5. Strich, I, 201.
6. Sengle, p. 481. Müller-Solger, pp. 35, 52-61, sees the continuity of the novel with Wieland's earlier work in the Platonic and pietistic motifs.
7. AB, IV, 29-30.
8. See Lukians Sämtliche Werke, trans. C. M. Wieland, ed. Dr. Hans Floerke (München & Leipzig: Georg Müller, 1911), II, 394-404.
9. The Attic Nights of Aulus Gellius, trans. John C. Rolfe (1927; rpt. Cambridge: Harvard University Press, 1960), II, 392; see also Wulff, pp. 1-25, for Wieland's acquaintance with the sources.
10. AB, III, 397 (1.10.1788).
11. Ibid.
12. Sengle, p. 483.
13. Gruber ed., XXVII, 400-401. Cf. also Pauly/Wissowa, Realencyclopädie der classischen Altertumswissenschaft XXIII, 1 (Stuttgart: A. Druckenmüller, 1957) columns 942, 969.
14. Müller, p. 117, recognizes that Peregrinus does not undergo progressive development as do Don Sylvio and Agathon.
15. Reimer, p. 98, points out that Peregrinus fled, not to avoid temptation, but out of disgust for himself.
16. Wulff, pp. 120-167.
17. Müller, p. 24, n. 34, speaks of the narrator's Akribie in the preface, and cites the quoted passage as an example of the roles played by Wieland. In Müller's opinion Wieland merely engages in arabesque repartee. In his interpretation of the passage he exposes Wieland's critical attitude toward Lucian -- but does not recognize it as such. He does not accept the parenthetical remark ("diesen einzigen Fehler ausgenommen") as spoken in earnest. Müller notes the (apparent) incongruity of the epithet, "ehrliche und genialische Seele," but overlooks the implication of perennial human error ("von einem Weibe"). For him the narrative "is only a pretense for the game which the narrator introduces."
18. Gruber cites the date as A.D. 168 (XXXIV, 217), but recent research places it three years earlier. Cf. A. M. Harmon, trans., Lucian (1936; rpt. Cambridge: Harvard University Press, 1955), V, 24, n. 1. Hereafter cited as Harmon.
19. Vormweg, p. 194, feels it belongs "only with reservation" to the novel proper.

20. Harmon, pp. 8-9, n. 2, presents the arguments for this assertion. See also the "Einleitung," XXXIII, 35-37.

21. Sengle, p. 480.

22. Eugene E. Reed, "Leibnitz, Wieland and the Combinatory Principle," Modern Language Review, 56 (1961), 529-537, examines the connection between Leibnitz' mathematical principle and Wieland's structural point of view.

23. It is no accident that Lucian is the one who recalls this unique condition. He seems to be addressing the reader, not Peregrinus. The latter, after all, does not need to be reminded. The style itself reflects the seriousness of the remark, since there is a pronounced pause before Lucian continues: "Dieses reinere Element, das wir nun bewohnen, macht es uns glücklicher Weise eben so unmöglich uns selbst als andere mit Parteilichkeit anzusehen" (XXXIV, 186).

24. Cf. Buddecke, p. 238: "Der Terminus 'geheim,' der in den Titeln zahlreicher Aufsätze auftaucht und im 'Agathon' vor allem auch den in Tarent verfassten Rechenschaftsbericht des Helden ... ist keine leere, verbale Dekoration. Hinter ihm verbirgt sich sowohl der Anspruch wie die Fähigkeit, verborgene innere Vorgänge und Wirkungszusammenhänge aufdecken und erklären zu können." One can therefore establish a connection between Wieland's knowledge of psychology and his epistemologic view. The "Gabe" to which Wieland refers in the preface is an echo of his ability to expose inner processes and nexuses.

25. See, for example, the parenthetical comment (XXXIII, 17) and "acting instructions" (XXXIII, 23, 91, 123, 124, 236, 258; XXIV, 3, 14, 36, 75, 118, 158). It is significant for Lucian's changing opinion of Peregrinus that his initial skepticism ("den Kopf ein wenig schüttelnd") becomes congeniality ("lachend," "lächelnd"). The smiles and laughter are not derisive but sympathetic. Müller, p. 29, n. 54, also points out that Peregrinus' mention of the Greek term "Aporrheta" in explanation of "the name of inexpressible things" (XXXIII, 277) is actually an intervention by the narrator (Müller says "editor"), since Lucian and Peregrinus are supposedly conversing in Greek, and thus the term would need no clarification.

26. Müller, pp. 29, 35.

27. Cf., for example, Lucian's remark: "Wir sind zwar sogar im Elysium nicht gänzlich von den geheimen Einflüssen der Eigenliebe frei; aber da es unmöglich ist, dass wir vorsetzlich gegen unser Gefühl und Bewusstsein reden sollten, so bin ich gewiss, dass ich über alles, was du selbst am besten wissen kannst, die reine Wahrheit von dir erfahren werde" (XXXIII, 33). It is a salient aspect of Wieland's irony that Peregrinus' adversaries often formulate the principles of his philosophy.

28. Dioklea too is illuminated from various perspectives. From Menippus' standpoint (XXXIII, 98), Myrto's (XXXIII, 187-191), from her own (XXXIV, 49-69), and from Peregrinus' (XXXIV, 170-172). See Müller, p. 36. Müller also indicates the polyperspectives of the preface and of Lucian's report, pp. 26, 36.

29. It is interesting that portions of Danae's and Jacinte's early histories are related in the third person -- an obvious shift in perspective. Danae alternates constantly between first and third person as she tells of her early days in Athens (XI, 237-248). Don Eugenio concludes Jacinte's story after she has told of the harrowing temptations she withstood (VI, 98-114). His perspective

reinforces her evaluation of herself, and we are forced to recognize her veracity.

30. Vormweg, p. 316, indicates the allotment of dialogue in the three novels: Don Sylvio, 38 percent (with the Biribinker episode, 58 percent); Agathon (3rd version), 20 percent (with Hippias' excurse and the autobiographical inclusions, 49 percent); Peregrinus, 100 percent. In the last instance Vormweg does not consider the preface and Lucian excerpt as part of the novel.

31. Jacobs, p. 38, passim. Marga Barthel, Das "Gespräch" bei Wieland. Untersuchungen über Wesen und Form seiner Dichtung (Frankfurt, 1939), passim.

32. Jacobs, pp. 42, 89, passim.

33. Vormweg, p. 193.

34. Sengle, p. 480.

35. Reimer, pp. 106-107.

36. Müller, p. 188.

37. Müller, p. 103.

38. Müller, p. 185. For his consideration of the interrelationship of myth, fairy tale, and reality, see pp. 96-105. Cf. Sengle, "Von Wielands Epenfragmenten," p. 68. Strich's judgment of Wieland's attitude toward mythology (see p. 105) has been outdated by Müller's reassessment and by Müller-Solger's examination of the dream motif in Wieland's work.

39. Sengle, p. 352, indicates Wieland's changed attitude toward the fairy tale after about 1780: "Aber man muss auch sehen, dass das Märchen unter den neuen Voraussetzungen eine wesentlich veränderte Bedeutung gewinnt. Es ist nicht mehr blosses Kostüm, Allegorie der Illusion, sondern Symbole des Idealen, d.h. einer geistigen Wirklichkeit."

40. Cf. Michelsen's comment, p. 202: "Der Enthusiasmus, der ihn [Wieland] in seiner Jugend ergriff, und der zeitweise unter dem Einfluss Bodmers alle Merkmale religiöser Schwärmerei annahm, wird, indem der zur Welt Bekehrte im selben Augenblick mit sichtbarer Vorliebe, wenn auch mit skeptischer Pose in phantastische poetische Bezirke flieht, im Grunde nicht verraten, sondern konserviert."

41. In the light of these findings, one concludes that the Xenian author was unjustly harsh on Wieland when he had Peregrinus say to Lucian: "Siehest du Wieland, so sag' ihm: ich lasse mich schönstens bedanken, / Aber er that mir zuviel Ehr' an, ich war doch ein Lump." Johann Wolfgang von Goethe, Goethes Werke (Weimar: Hermann Bühlau, 1893), V, 257.

42. Müller-Solger, p. 318.

43. Cf. Müller, p. 195.

44. A, p. 378; Agathodämon, XXXV, 46, 411.

45. Compare this assertion with the question the narrator poses in Agathon (A, p. 369): "Was ist die Tugend ohne dieses schöne Feuer, ohne diese erhabene Begeisterung, welche den Menschen über die übrigen seiner Gattung, welche ihn über sich selbst erhöht, und zu einem allgemeinen Wolthäther, zu einem Genius, zu einer subalternen Gottheit macht?" -- "Wir gestehen es, sie ist ohne diese ätherische Flamme ein sehr unansehnliches, sehr wenig glänzendes Ding."

46. Müller, p. 167, claims that Peregrinus "becomes an animal because he attempts to be complete spirit." Unfortunately, he does not define "animal" nor does he cite examples from the novel. If Müller is referring to Peregrinus' submission to lust -- and I think he is -- then he has overlooked the fantast's repeated efforts to rid himself of all bestial desires after each relapse. One should not criticize Peregrinus for being human just because he endeavors to be more than human. Müller's argument is based on the uncritical assumption that empirical reality, in Wieland's view, is and should be the determining factor in man's life (cf. p. 120).

47. Arthur O. Lovejoy, The Great Chain of Being (New York: Harper & Row, 1960), p. 183.

48. Cf. E.M. Butler, The Tyranny of Greece over Germany (Boston: Beacon Press, 1958); Müller, pp. 123-125; and Wulff, pp. 80-88, indicate the intellectual parallels between the first and second centuries A.D. and the eighteenth century.

49. See also editor's footnote to "Sympathien," Gruber ed., XXXIII, 208.

50. Jacobs, p. 40; Müller, pp. 104, 119; Sengle, p. 484. Müller insinuates that Peregrinus erred in believing there was but one exemplary way of life. Müller apparently overlooked the enthusiast's own admission that there are other ways of life but only one for himself, determined by his peculiar makeup (cf. XXXIII, 86). Peregrinus is condemned along with Don Sylvio for holding "false ideals" (Müller, p. 104). It is an enigma how Müller can claim that Peregrinus' ideals are false and question the viability of any norm -- all in the same breath. Müller-Solger, p. 184, esp. n. 4, has correctly interpreted Peregrinus' suicide; that is, as not being tragic.

51. Reimer, p. 105. Apparently Sengle, p. 484, is the only critic to differentiate between Peregrinus' decision to immolate himself and to do it publicly for the edification of his fellows. Sengle speaks only of the latter decision as Schwärmerei.

52. H.O. Burger, ed., Annalen der deutschen Literatur (Stuttgart: Metzler, 1971), p. 533.

53. Influenced by the English empiricists, many enlighteners rejected the notion of innate ideas. They felt justified in decrying all concepts which transcended the empirical world as Schwärmerei and Wahnsinn. Could they have had things their way, they would have liked to free man from the influence of imagination (cf. Oettinger, p. 123). That not only the Romanticists (as Oettinger indicates) but also Wieland attempted to demonstrate the efficaciousness of fantasy in the search for Truth has become clear. For a consideration of Wieland as fore-runner of the Romanticists, see Ermatinger, "Das Romantische;" and Ludwig Hirzel, Wielands Beziehungen zu den deutschen Romantikern (Bern: A. Francke, 1904).

54. Goethe, Werke, V, 308.

55. Cf. Alfred E. Ratz, "C.M. Wieland: Toleranz, Kompromiss und Inkonsequenz," Deutsche Vierteljahresschrift, 42 (1968), 497. Ratz speaks of the "singularly practical and moral worth of Truth" for Wieland. I agree with the moral aspect of Truth, but I cannot agree when he contends that the value of Truth is neces-sarily practical. Peregrinus belies this assertion. Furthermore, Ratz does

not consider Wieland an idealist (p. 501). He only sees the author's attempt to adjust to life without considering the source of moral dictates in Wieland's opinion.

56. In Musarion, Wieland went so far as to assert that men are born to certain roles. Cf. XII, 56. This concept of singularity -- later designated "innere Form" -- will be examined in more detail later.

57. Müller-Solger, p. 305.

58. Jacobs, p. 79.

59. Jacobs, p. 8; Müller, p. 167; Oettinger, p. 124; Reimer, p. 106; Wulff, pp. i, 92, seem to have missed the point here.

60. Peregrinus confesses to Lucian: "Bei mir ging, vermöge der individuellen Form meines Wesens, alles über die Aristotelische Linie der Mässigung hinaus. Wen ich nicht mit Schwärmerei lieben, mit Entzückung loben konnte, den musste ich mit Abscheu fliehen, mit Bitterkeit tadeln. Wie hätte sich die Welt mit einem solchen Menschen, oder er sich mit ihr, vertragen können?" (XXXIV, 175-176).

61. Sengle, p. 484.

Chapter 5

AGATHODAEMON: "DEUS IN NOBIS"

La vérité ne sauroit nous venir de dehors, elle est en nous.
-- F.H. Jacobi, Werke, IV/1, 139

On February 28, 1799, Wieland sent the last book of Agathodämon to his publisher, Göschen. Wieland called the novel "the most important and the best of his works in more than one respect." The value he placed on it is evident in the many revisions that Book 7, the heart of the work, underwent. In the end he was able to affirm that he "had done his best and thus fulfilled his duty as a man, a popular educator, and a poet." [1]

Two years earlier, in a letter to his daughter, Sophie Reinhold, Wieland had asserted that not Archytas but Apollonius of Tyana was the expression of his "house philosophy." [2] This comment primarily concerns the disavowal of the rational basis and realizability in this world of Archytas' harmonious synthesis of man's antithetic nature. The subtle distinction between Archytas' and Apollonius' views will be of secondary importance in this consideration. More pertinent for us is the significance of Agathodämon for Wieland's theory of knowledge. In light of the foregoing comments, and because the novel was published in 1799 (eight years after Peregrinus Proteus and five years after the conclusive version of Agathon), this work should better serve to confirm or disprove our findings.

According to K.A. Böttiger, Wieland looked upon Agathodämon as a counterpart to Agathon and Peregrinus Proteus. [3] It too is a vindication of an unappreciated historical figure in the second century A.D., who had been decried as an impostor and a charlatan. Wieland's reassessed evaluation of the Schwärmer is manifest in the fact that he did not execute his plan as originally conceived. In the plan of 1774 Wieland called Apollonius a Don Quixote and Damis his Sancho Panza. But in the novel of 1799 Apollonius is free of all derogatory connotations. [4] Strich, on the other hand, sees the novel as a "justification of mythology" per se, and is less concerned with the role of the Schwärmer. [5] Wieland seems to have been influenced by Herder's essays, "Vom Erlöser der Menschen" and "Von Gottes Sohn." [6] The close thematic similarity of this novel to Agathon, and especially to Peregrinus Proteus, is evident in the line quoted from Ovid's Fasti which appeared in the first edition: "Est Deus in nobis, agitante calescimus illo." Finally, by delineating certain parallels between the two men, Sengle has also noted that Apollonius is apparently symbolic of Wieland himself. [7] When we consider that Agathon has strong autobiographical overtones, the bond between it and Agathodämon appears even stronger.

<u>Agathodämon</u> is actually a letter written by Hegesias of Cydonia to his friend Tima-
genes which contains an account of Apollonius' life and philosophy. On his travels
Hegesias had heard of a "good spirit" who was attended by a "nymph." Determined
to learn the truth of the matter, he ventured into the hills where he discovered
Apollonius' abode. The epistolary form of the work is further marked by conversation and dialogue. The different types of writing [8] (epistolary: intimacy, authenticity: conversation/dialogue: objectivity, dialectics) are used to bring out more
emphatically the basic dialectic nature of the content and to persuade the reader
that Apollonius' mystical view is correct. Conversation gravitates to the more
profound topics: for example, the existence of daemons, man's penchant for the
marvelous, ultimate reality, and the nature of Christianity. The discussions also
serve to rectify misconceptions concerning the prophet's integrity.

It is indicative of the novel's import that the conversations are accompanied by the
enjoyment of seemingly endless vistas in which sea and air merge (XXXV, 329-330),
or which are pleasantly interrupted by soaring and ennobling song of man and bird
(XXXV, 182-185, 326). These stylistic aspects are symptomatic because they
affect Hegesias <u>emotionally</u> and <u>irrationally</u>. The movement in the novel is both
literally and figuratively upward. For example, Hegesias must climb a plateau to
reach Apollonius; both ascend a rise overlooking the sea; frequently their eyes
are directed upward to follow the flight of a bird or to gaze at the stars. At other
times the eye is directed at the expansiveness of the sea. This physical and optical
movement is complemented by the emotional uplifting of the soul through the effects
of song and vista and by the spiritual stimulation resultant of their conversations
on religion. The unmistakable tendency of all this (e)motion is toward the "Romantic" sense of the boundless and infinite; in short, the human soul is transported in
contemplation of the Infinite One.

We encounter a symbolism in Wieland's use of numbers as well which affirms and
expands this connotation. Hegesias spends three days with the master after which
he emerges from the rocky abode as a man reborn. The number three is not only
reminiscent of the days Christ spent in the sepulchre to prove the veracity of his
word but also of the Trinity. The novel consists of seven books. Seven is of course
the mystical number which is reducible to the theological number three and the
number four designating either the four corners of the earth or the four elements.
In mythology they are often identified with gods. In the context of <u>Agathodämon</u>,
the sum of the divine three and the terrestrial four represents the interrelationship
of empirical and metempirical reality which forms the philosophical basis of the
novel. This interpretation is further heightened when we consider that the culminating seventh book is devoted entirely to Christ and his legacy. As the Son of God
and the son of man Christ encorporates within his person both the infinite Three
and the finite four. Taken together, these various stylistics features point the way
to the message of Pythagorean Christianity.

Apollonius was born to wealthy parents in the town of Tyana in Asia and received a
better than average education. His father sent him first to Tarsus in Cilicia to complete his studies and then to the neighboring town of Aegä. During these years he

studied various philosophies and established an organization which operated clandestinely for the rejuvenation of the Pythagorean order. Next he traveled to Samothrace and Thessaly to be initiated into the Orphic arcana of the first and the occult magic of the second. Equipped with this knowledge, Apollonius set out to improve his fellow man spiritually by intentionally deceiving them when necessary. Religion was a tool he used to lead men to humanitas. His crowning achievement was the "resurrection" of a "deceased" woman. The renowned magician has now withdrawn to the solitude of the mountains in order to spend his remaining days in peaceful contemplation.

In Agathodämon Wieland again avoids the extremes of enthusiasm (Peregrinus) and skepticism (Lucian). He is more concerned with the truth of Christianity. [9] Apollonius (graceful beauty?) takes Pythagoras and Diogenes as his models. He feels that if he can combine Diogenes' independence and contentedness with Pythagoras' deeper insights, dignity, and charisma, he will reach heights never before attained by man (XXXV, 59). Christ also exerted a powerful influence, albeit belatedly, on Apollonius.

Agathodämon manifests all the essential elements of Wieland's epistemology as they have been traced through Peregrinus Proteus. In this connection, we will consider Wieland's estimation of man and Nature, which necessarily entails the concepts of the daemonic, intuition, the imagination, introspection, the wondrous, and infinity.

The important questions for Agathodämon (the good spirit) concern his earthly existence. Man should ask himself: What am I in my present form? What are my abilities and aptitudes? How can I best use them and to what end? What is my destiny? (XXXV, 287). Questions concerning the nature of things are inane because we are incapable of knowing their essences (XXXV, 287). The true object of study and knowledge is man himself. The sage asks rhetorically:

> Und was könntest du denn mehr verlangen? ... In das Geheimniss der Natur
> selbst einzudringen, ist uns verwehrt. Der Kreis der Menschheit ist nun einmal unser Antheil, und der Umfang, worin alle unsre Ansprüche eingeschlossen sind. Sobald wir uns über ihn versteigen wollen, finden wir uns mit einem undurchdringlichen Dunkel umgeben; oder das Licht selbst, das uns dann entgegen strömt, ist so blendend, dass es für Augen wie die unsrigen zur dichtesten Finsterniss wird. Aber o dass wir die Würde unsrer eigenen Natur erkennen möchten! es ganz durchschauen und immer gegenwärtig haben möchten, dass der Mensch nichts grösseres kennt noch kennen soll als sich selbst; dass er alles, was er zu seiner Vollständigkeit bedarf, in sich finden kann, und dass seinem ewigen Wachsthum an Kraft und Vollkommenheit keine andere Grenze gesetzt ist, als die wesentliche Form seiner eigenen Natur, über welche er sich eben so wenig hinaus denken als hinaus dehnen kann, er müsste sich denn nur ins unendliche -- Nichts ausdehnen wollen! (XXXV, 29-30)

The exhortation to introspection, the Orphic adage "gnothi seauton," is the corner-stone of Wieland's philosophy (Enlightenment tradition). In Agathodämon's view man is composed of two diametrically opposed forces: body and spirit. It is erroneous to think that these two forces are or can be united harmoniously into one (Christian tradition). Nature herself will never undertake to synthesize two antithetic elements. Such harmonious unions are possible only in poetic creations and are artificial at best (XXXV, 61-62).

Man is a paragon of opposites. On the one hand he has an innate drive to transcend the visible world, to breach the confines of creation. On the other, his finiteness sets limits to his yearning for infinity ("über welche er sich eben so wenig hinaus denken als hinaus dehnen kann, er müsste sich denn nur ins unendliche -- Nichts ausdehnen wollen!"). [10] The empirical world, "the realm of appearances and deceptions which man has erroneously grown accustomed to consider the real world," is insufficient to still man's incessant longing (XXXV, 18). There is al-ways something lacking, and our anticipations are always betrayed. As a result, philosophers and poets have created ideal worlds "which, as often as man has seriously endeavored to actualize them, have caused so much disaster" (XXXV, 18-19). There is an irrational force in man which induces him to consider the external world as mere building blocks from which he can construct worlds accor-ding to his own liking. Nevertheless, after his vain and ruinous efforts, man must recognize "the divine in Nature." This discovery only awakens the impertinent desire to fathom the arcana of Nature. The attempt to uncover the true nexus of phenomena, the primeval causes, and the quintessence of Nature leads the quester irresistibly back to himself. The study of Nature ultimately directs man to the scrutiny of his own nature (cf. XXXV, 19). Man is thus forced to take himself as the model and standard of the unknown (cf. XXXV, 19, 30). [11]

The interrelationship of Nature and human nature becomes for Agathodämon the basis of his philosophy: "Die Natur war nun meine einzige Gesetzgeberin, und, meiner Natur gemäss zu leben, mein letzter Zweck. Diese beiden Formeln ... nahm ich in dem hohen Sinne der Pythagorischen Grundbegriffe" (XXXV, 61). [12] The wise man considered his spiritual ego to be his true nature; consequently, for him to live according to his nature, the animal in him must be subordinated to the spirit (XXXV, 62). The more spiritualized he became, the more he lived in har-mony with the divine design. Like Peregrinus, Agathodämon also looked upon his body as a burden (XXXV, 62). He conceived of the relationship between body and spirit as analogous to the connection between the hand and the will. The body is to be attuned to the melodic harmonies of the spirit (XXXV, 62). [13] This analogy is of course reminiscent of the Platonic and Shaftesburean concepts of kalokagathia and the virtuoso which so greatly impressed Wieland.

Man's spiritual nature is referred to as "the god in us," and this is the meaning of das Dämonische for Agathodämon (XXXV, 63). He was often misunderstood when he spoke of his daemon. Simple people thought that daemons actually existed in Nature as separate entities (Don Sylvio's naive belief). Such conceptions are the result of ignorance, since many people have not learned to distinguish the con-

sciousness of themselves from the sensations received from the external world
(XXXV, 159). The unsophisticated also confuse their dreams with empirical reality,
wantonly intermingling them (XXXV, 163). Man must be taught to differentiate between his inner, subjective world and external things. Until he recognizes the true
nature and origin of the daemonic man is susceptible to Schwärmerei. If man has
not achieved this insight, the imagination can play havoc with his thinking. But
after this recognition, the interplay of fantasy and reality can be a welcome asset
to man's pursuit of eudaemonia. For example, Agathodämon states that eternity is
a proper concern of man. However, man can have no definite knowledge of what
the afterlife will bring. Man is capable only of premonitions of his future state.
In this respect, the fantasy can make up for the inadequacy of the mind, which is
limited to experiential reality.

> Indessen, warum sollt' es der Einbildungskraft, deren eigenthümliches Ge-
> biet das unendliche Reich der Vermuthungen und vermeinten Möglichkeiten
> ist, nicht erlaubt seyn weiter zu gehen, und mit harmlosen Träumen, aus
> helldunkeln Aufblitzungen und Vorgefühlen der künftigen Welt gewebt, die Un-
> geduld der Erwartungen einzuwiegen? (XXXV, 290)

Hegesias' reply to this explanation of the role of fantasy has importance for the
interpretation of the role of the dream in this study. He states: "für mich würde
ein Traum, an welchem Apollonius etwas anmuthendes findet, beinahe das Ansehen
einer Urkunde haben" (XXXV, 290). For the exceptional man, for a man with a
highly developed consciousness of the Dämonisches (Peregrinus, Apollonius),
dreams and the imagination assume an almost prophetic function. [14] Wieland underscored the repercussions of these dreams for mankind when he remarked to
Böttiger: "Freilich habe ich immer in meiner Ideenwelt geträumt, aber in diesen
Träumen war doch nicht blosse Phantasie. Sie waren aus der Blüte menschlicher
Betrachtungen aller Jahrhunderte zusammengesetzt." [15] These dreams are thus
the cumulative result of mankind's religious and philosophic yearnings through the
ages.

It is man's fate ever to strive to reach an unattainable goal (XXXV, 293); striving
for perfection is a fundamental characteristic of human nature. Agathodämon uses
a discussion of this character trait to demonstrate man's basic irrationality. Man
is incapable of conceiving of infinity because he must think in finite terms; his
imagination can transcend physical reality but is still compelled to assume a
starting point. Kymon, Apollonius' faithful servant, correctly interprets the Her-
metic circle as symbolic of infinity. Man can continue to conceive of the constantly
expanding circle until his exhausted fantasy can no longer function; then he loses
himself "in infinity like a drop of water in the ocean" (XXXV, 286). Apollonius is
very pleased with his "disciple" and exclaims:

> Diess war es, guter Kymon, und war alles, was Hermes mit seinem Zirkel
> ohne Umkreis wollte. Dein gerader Sinn hat ihn sogleich gefasst, und wehe
> dem Sofisten, der dich mit seiner Logik darüber schikaniren wollte! Diess
> angestrengte vergebliche Streben, und zuletzt diess Verlieren unser selbst

in dem alles hervorbringenden und alles verschlingenden Unendlichen, --
diess ist die einzige Art, wie Wesen unserer Gattung -- nicht zum Begriff,
aber zu einem dunkeln, die ganze Seele ausfüllenden Gefühl desselben sich
erheben können; einem Gefühl, das mehr werth ist, als die subtilste Wort-
erklärung des trocknen Dialektikers, der uns Rechenpfennige für Münze,
und Worte für Sachen giebt. [16] (XXXV, 286)

In light of this reply we can scarcely doubt the irrational and emotive -- yes Romantic -- character of Apollonius' knowledge. [17] This is especially true when we consider that in an earlier conversation Apollonius referred to sentiment (Gefühl) as
"an organ attuned to all of Nature and the key to the language of all creatures"
(XXXV, 183).

The importance of the illogical forces in man as the primary perceivers of Truth
is also evident in the respect and awe he feels for Christ and his teachings. In
comparing himself to Christ, Apollonius asserts that, despite superficial similarities, the difference between them was considerable. [18] Agathodämon only
appeared to be what Christ actually was (XXXV, 334). Christ, who carried his
God in his heart and was animated by Him, did not deceive the people, whereas
Apollonius feigned belief in and worship of the gods. Apollonius refers to Christ's
divine inspiration as enthusiasm. "Nenn' es immerhin Enthusiasm; genug, es war
kein geheuchelter: sein Gott lebte und webte in ihm, sprach aus ihm, wirkte durch
ihn, war der herrschende Gedanke seiner Seele, der Gegenstand seiner innigsten
Anhänglichkeit, seines lebendigsten Zutrauens, sein Bewegungsgrund, sein Zweck,
sein Mittel" (XXXV, 335).

This description of Christ could easily be applied to Peregrinus Proteus for he too
lived only for the realization of the daemonic in him. Christ was an extremely
sincere man who never doubted his mission. His sole purpose was to advance the
moral perfection of mankind. His concept of belief was an irrational one. It was
based on an intense feeling rooted in his very nature. All of the foregoing can also
be asserted about Peregrinus Proteus. Christ's belief cannot be expressed in
rational terms because if is an emotional experience. "Was Er glauben nennt, ist
eine auf inniges Gefühl gegründete Gesinnung des Gemüths, mit einer geistigen
sinnlichen Vorstellung verbunden, welche ehe Anschauung als räsonnirter Begriff
zu nennen ist; mit Einem Worte, nicht Begreifen, sondern Ergreifen dessen, was
nicht begriffen werden kann noch soll" (XXXV, 340).

The affinity between Apollonius' basic views and Christ's is evident in Agathodämon's
allusion to the similarity between Christ's teachings and the theories of Pythagoras
and Plato or even of Socrates and Epictetus (XXXV, 338). At the same time, Christ's
philosophy is "ten times more personal" than Pythagoras' (XXXV, 339). This personal touch has influenced Agathodämon's own Lebensphilosophie. Christ conceived
of God as his father and of all men as his brothers. In the end, Apollonius also
thinks in these terms (cf. XXXV, 61, 411).

At the conclusion of Apollonius' and Hegesias' protracted discussion, Apollonius directs his attention to three major questions: man's delight in the wondrous, his theory of religion, his concept of God. Agathodämon basically rejects the use of the miraculous to induce men to live better lives. There are, he concedes, times in everyone's life when one needs a crutch in order to progress. But as one matures and becomes sophisticated in the use of reason, the wondrous is to be discarded in favor of the aids innate in human nature (XXXV, 406-408; see also 156-169). Agathodämon's concept of religion as it relates to everyday life is similar to Christ's teachings. However, there is one major reservation. Apollonius makes allowances for the individual, subjective limitations in each person. This qualification adds a new dimension to the phenomenon of Schwärmerei. Apollonius asserts that every man has an innere Form which makes him quite distinct from other men. Christ also had his distinct "inner form." Thus any man who loses his distinctiveness in servile imitation of Christ will be much less like the Master than the man who does not disregard his singularity. The first man could be labeled a Schwärmer (XXXV, 409).

The reservation that Wieland puts in Agathodämon's mouth has already been depicted by our author in Peregrinus Proteus. Both fantast and skeptic have been admitted into Elysium because each has remained faithful to his inborn limitations, his specific innere Form. The importance that inner form had for Wieland's thinking is underscored in the dialogue, "Agathon und Hippias, ein Gespräch im Elysium," which appeared in the Attisches Museum a year after the publication of Agathodämon. The following exchange on perfection occurs:

> "Agathon: ... 'Oder, was nennst Du Vollkommenheit?' Hippias: 'Das, was wir von Natur sind, ganz zu sein, und es in einem so hohen Grade, in so reicher Uebereinstimmung mit uns selbst zu sein als möglich...' 'Denn, wofern wir anders etwas mehr als ein blosses Aggregat von Zufälligkeiten sind, so muss den Bestimmungen, die wir von aussen her erhalten, und denen, die uns unsre eigne Willkür gibt, etwas eigentümliches und beständiges zum Grunde liegen, und was könnte das anders sein als die individuelle Form, von welcher sich niemand trennen kann? Die reinste Uebereinstimmung mit dieser Form ist unsre Vollkommenheit, unser letztes Ziel; denn aus sich selbst kann niemand herausgehen, um ein anderes zu suchen.' '... Der inneren Form selbst, welche sich wohl verbilden, verzerren und verstümmeln, aber nicht anders ausbilden lässt als durch Entwicklung; nicht wie der Künstler aus demselben Marmorblock einen Apollo oder Marsyas bilden kann, sondern wie der Keim einer Pflanze, Stiel, Blätter, Blume usw. aus sich selbst herausbildet ...'" [19]

Perfection, therefore, is the realization of one's individuality. And this perfection of man is likened to the metamorphosis of a plant which obeys its own botanical laws. It is particularly significant for our investigation that Hippias has the last word and not Archytas. No longer is there a universal norm which is to serve as the binding standard of human behavior, because man is no longer looked upon as a block of marble to be shaped by a master craftsman, but rather as a living organism which evolves according to its immanent principles. It is obvious that Apollonius holds the same views.

Agathodämon finds it more difficult to formulate his concept of God because God is for him identical to the impenetrable mystery of Nature (XXXV, 409-410). In attempting to explain the ineffable he retraces his long search for God. The account of his life sounds similar to Wieland's own. First, Apollonius studied various philosophic systems, vainly seeking Nature's innermost secret. Frustrated, he abandoned himself to excesses of the imagination until he recognized Nature's deceptions. There followed periods of vacillation between religious belief and rational skepticism. Ultimately he returned to Nature and to his own ego in an attempt to delineate the unifying and harmonious forces of the external world and to understand the unifying force of his own feelings, sensations, ideas, premonitions, and desires. He endeavored to comprehend that which unifies the external world with his internal, spiritual one. In these endeavors, in tracing the individual elements to a common source, he would lose himself in the oneness of infinity. In such a state he would fall, as Kymon said, like a drop of water into a boundless ocean. Upon awakening from overwhelming visions, he would again find himself within the accustomed confines of finiteness, would sense his oneness with creation, intuit the presence of God, and become once more aware of what it means to be human.

> ... das allgemeine Leben der Natur drängt sich wieder warm an mein Herz, ich webe in allem was webt, und fühle mich in allem was athmet; die Fantasie schliesst ihre unsichtbare Zauberwelt wieder vor mir auf; die Unsterblichen nahen sich meinem Geiste, und mit süssem Schauern umfasst mich die Gegenwart des allgemeinen Genius der Natur, des liebenden, versorgenden Allvaters, oder wie der beschränkte Sinn der Sterblichen den Unnennbaren immer nennen mag, und ich bin -- mit einem Worte, wieder was ich seyn soll, ein Mensch, gut und glücklich, und verlange nicht mehr zu seyn als ich seyn kann und soll. (XXXV, 411)

There can be no doubt that this experience, this insight, is anything but rational. The emotive language itself reflects the irrationality of Apollonius' view: [20] "warm," "Herz," "webe in allem," "fühle mich in allem," "Fantasie," "unsichtbare Zauberwelt," "mit süssem Schauern," etc. We have here, as Hatfield says, a delayed echo of Werther's impassioned pantheism. [21] Wieland has finally been able to reconcile the disparate forces of his nature as best he could. [22] The reconciliation is not the same as Archytas', [23] for Agathodämon realizes -- as does Peregrinus -- that ultimate felicity and harmony are not possible in this world. He also realizes that "to be a man" means to accept the irreconcilability of human limitation and human striving for the Infinite. [24] He does not desire to be more or less than human ("und verlange nicht mehr zu seyn als ich seyn kann und soll"). Acceptance of the human condition is the key to the peace he has found. Ultimate perfection and fulfillment (mystical union with the One) are reserved for the afterlife; his intuitive visions assure him of the reality of man's ultimate destiny. Thus, like Peregrinus, Apollonius does not fear death. Rather, he welcomes it with open arms as a dear friend who comes to lead him to his cherished goal (XXXV, 289).

The key to Wieland's epistemology, therefore, is actually given in the Delphic adage, "gnothi seauton," which was also a slogan of the eighteenth century. [25] Agathodämon reiterates this claim and substantiates the validity of the conclusions drawn in the foregoing analyses. This novel underscores, furthermore, the two essential elements of Wieland's epistemologic theory: das Dämonische and innere Form. We have seen that the daemonic plays an important role in Peregrinus Proteus, but the significance of inner form was left unstressed. Because the daemonic, or "deus in nobis," is common to all men, it can be considered the only valid standard for evaluating human behavior. [26] Nevertheless, each person's inner form necessitates and legitimizes an individual expression of the daemonic. In Agathodämon both aspects are emphasized and depicted in their reciprocity. In Apollonius' complementation of philosophy through religious belief, a final reconciliation of the head and the heart is achieved. [27]

NOTES

1. Gruber, 53, 283-284.
2. Keil, 226 (letter of 11/26/1796).
3. Karl August Böttiger, Literarische Zustände und Zeitgenossen (Leipzig: Brockhaus, 1838), I, 161.
4. Friedrich Beissner, "Neue Wielandhandschriften," Abhandlungen der Preussischen Akademie der Wissenschaften, 13 (Berlin: W. de Gruyter, 1938), 15-16.
5. Strich, I, 203.
6. Sengle, p. 486; Wulff, p. 171. Johanna Mellinger, Wielands Auffassung vom Urchristentum mit hauptsächlicher Berücksichtigung seines Romans "Agathodämon" (Marbach: A. Remppis, 1911), pp. 39-48, discusses some differences between Herder's and Wieland's religious thought. She contends that there can be no direct influence of "Vom Erlöser der Menschen" on Wieland's novel because Herder's essay appeared a year or two after Agathodämon (pp. 45-46).
7. Sengle, pp. 488-490.
8. For a consideration of the epistolary and dialogic form, see Eva D. Becker, Der Deutsche Roman um 1780 (Stuttgart: Metzler, 1964), pp. 166-185.
9. See Mellinger's study. Fritz Martini, "C.M. Wieland und das 18. Jahrhundert," Festschrift für Paul Kluckhohn und Hermann Schneider (Tübingen: J.C.B. Mohr, 1948), p. 256, indicates that Wieland turned more decisively to Christianity because of the conflict between empirical reality and the idealistic longing of his fantasies.
10. Cf. also XXV, 17. There are many parallels between Wieland's philosophy and that of Friedrich Heinrich Jacobi. They are similar not only in their concepts of human nature but also in their views of Nature, the nexus God-Man-Nature, inner form, and God as the source and end of all philosophy. Cf. F.H. Jacobi: Philosoph und Literat der Goethezeit, ed. Klaus Hammacher (Frankfurt: Klostermann, 1969); esp. the essays by Marco M. Olivetti, "Der Einfluss Hamanns auf die Religionsphilosophie Jacobis" and Valerio Verra, "Lebensgefühl, Naturbegriff und Naturauslegung bei F.H. Jacobi." There is a definite need for a thorough study of the personal and intellectual relationship between Wieland and Jacobi.
11. Cf. Strich, I, 204. He suggests that mythology in Agathodämon is the result of an "inner necessity which forces man to take himself as standard and model."
12. The Pythagorean element in Wieland's philosophy was of course not new and had been noted by his contemporaries. Herder, for example, saw its continuity from "Natur der Dinge" through Archytas and Agathon to Agathodämon. Böttiger, I, 198.
13. Buddecke, pp. 100-115, also demonstrates that the eventual goal of man's striving should be the subordination of the animal to the spirit: "Ziel der Entwicklung ist nicht mehr das schön geordnete, harmonische Verhältnis aller menschlichen Kräfte ... sondern die unumschränkte Herrschaft des 'unsichtbaren Ichs,' die dem Menschen ein 'bloss geistiges Leben' zu führen ermöglichen soll" (p. 115).

14. Cf. a similar appraisal of the dream as such in "Musarion," XII, 58; Aristipp, XXXVII, 95-105; Wulff, p. 86. See Müller-Solger for a study of the dream-fantasy motif in Wieland's works.

15. Böttiger, I, 162.

16. Cf. also Aristipp, XXXVII, 152-154.

17. Martini, "C. M. Wieland und das 18. Jahrhundert," pp. 256-257, recognizes the irrationality and subjectivity of Wieland's belief. See also Reichert, p. 16.

18. Mellinger discusses some differences, pp. 23-28, et passim.

19. Cited by Melitta Gerhard, Der deutsche Entwicklungsroman bis zu Goethes "Wilhelm Meister" (Bern & München: Francke, 1968), pp. 106-107, n. 4. Gerhard demonstrates the unconscious influence of this concept on the shaping of Agathon (see esp. pp. 104-107). See also Aristipp, XXXVII, 324-330. Here "inner form" stresses the important function of relativity in the author's philo-sophic scheme. At the conclusion of "Aristipp" the legitimacy of the various philosophies (particularly Platonism, Cynicism, and Cyrenaic hedonism) is explicitly stated. The implication is that the individual's "inner form" deter-mines which system is best suited to the attainment of the common goal of eudaemonia.

20. Karl Heinz Kausch, "Die Kunst der Grazie," Jahrbuch der deutschen Schiller-gesellschaft, No. 2 (Stuttgart: A. Kröner, 1958), pp. 16-25, demonstrates that Wieland's style is designed to excite the emotions. The effect evoked by the language is the prime concern. This use of language is paralleled by the func-tion of all art: aesthetic evocation. See also B. Munteano, "Constantes Hu-maines en littérature: l'éternel débat de la 'raison' et du 'coeur,'" Stil- und Formprobleme in der deutschen Literatur, ed. Paul Böckmann (Heidelberg: C. Winter, 1959), pp. 66-67, for a discussion of the aesthetic effect.

21. Henry Caraway Hatfield, Aesthetic Paganism in German Literature from Winckelmann to the Death of Goethe (Cambridge: Harvard University Press, 1964), pp. 42-43.

22. Ibid., p. 43; Reimer, p. 110, refers to this reconciliation as a synthesis of Agathodämon's rationalism with the sincere religious Schwärmerei of Christ.

23. Reimer, pp. 117, 121, 141-142, indicates that Archytas' attempted synthesis of mind and heart emphasized the rational element, whereas Agathodämon's attempted synthesis of these two forces underscores the irrational element. Archytas believed man has the power within himself to achieve this synthesis and to live a happy life. Agathodämon depends upon an outside force to realize this harmony. Reimer considers Agathodämon's irrational synthesis more satisfying (and I might add, more convincing) to the reader.

24. Cf. also Wieland's supplement to "Das Leben ein Traum" (1771), VII, 204-228, esp. 214-215.

25. By positing the Delphic adage as a central theme in Agathon, Peregrinus, and Agathodämon, we see Wieland as a link between the author of Simplicius Simplicissimus and the author of Wilhelm Meister.

26. Cf. Müller-Solger, p. 312.

27. Mellinger, p. 24. Cf. Sommer, pp. 40-41.

The expressed intent of this study has been to determine Wieland's concept of Truth and man's ability to know it. The predominant philosophic influences on Wieland in this regard were exerted by Plato and Shaftesbury. Truth was ultimately conceived as the morally and aesthetically Good, Beautiful, and Virtuous. The heart -- man's moral and aesthetic "sense perceptor" -- was interpreted as a sixth and infallible sense. This guide was seen to negotiate reliably the labyrinthine contortions of the dual reality of human existence, which can so easily confuse Verstand and Vernunft.

The distinction between Schwärmerei and enthusiasm is at the heart of this study. Don Sylvio, Agathon, and Peregrinus Proteus seem to form a trilogy devoted to an elucidation of this important differentiation. All three heroes are called Schwärmer, but only Peregrinus enjoys the specific epithet "sincere" (XXXIV, 185). Don Sylvio, Agathon, and Peregrinus apparently represent stages of evolution in the concept of enthusiasm. [1] Don Sylvio has been described as "still devoid of idealistic self-awareness" (p. 65). Agathon concluded his life in a utopia, having failed in his idealistic endeavors in the world. [2] Peregrinus realized that the attainment of his ideals could only be effected by destroying his body. Don Sylvio's adventures led to an awareness of society; Agathon's ended in an esoteric society; Peregrinus' experiences caused him to reject the company of men. At the core of each of these "aberrant" individuals is the desire to bring about a major change in the world. Each stage in the development of the Schwärmer motif brings with it a greater awareness of the incompatibility of ideals to life in society. Peregrinus seems to reflect the psychogenesis of the sincere visionary depicted in distinct stages in Don Sylvio, Agathon, and himself when he describes his own process of refinement.

Das, was du meine Schwärmerei nennest, bekam allmählich eine andere Richtung. Je mehr Gewalt die Einwirkungen der äussern Sinnenwelt über mich erhielten, je stumpfer wurde der innere Sinn für die geistigen Erscheinungen der fantastischen Ideenwelt, in welcher ich ehemals gelebt hatte [Don Sylvio's disenchantment]. Anstatt dass einst das Ziel aller meiner Wünsche gewesen war, unter höhern Wesen das Leben der Geister zu leben, und mich bei lebendigem Leibe zum Dämon zu entkörpern, -- fühlte ich jetzt kein dringenderes Bedürfniss, als von aller Verbindung mit Menschen, deren ganze Art zu seyn in ewigem Widerspruch mit meinem Ideale von Harmonie und Schönheit stand, je eher je lieber befreit zu werden, um in einer kleinen Gesellschaft unverfälschter, durchaus guter Menschen zu leben, an deren Anschauen meine Seele immer reines Wohlgefallen haben, und über die ich die ganze Fülle meiner Liebe, ohne Furcht vor Täuschung und Reue, ohne Gefahr von ihren Leidenschaften und Sitten angesteckt zu werden, ergiessen könnte. [Agathon's Tarentum] Mit Einem Worte, Lucian, die magische Schwärmerei meiner frühern Jugend ging unvermerkt, eine Zeit lang wenigstens, in eine moralische über, welche mich zwar wieder neuen Illusionen der Einbildung und des Herzens aussetzte, aber doch zugleich dem, was in meinen Augen Vollkommenheit des Menschen ist, näher brachte, und vielleicht ein Mittel-

zustand war, durch welchen ich nothwendig gehen musste, um auf den gerade-
sten Weg, der zu jener Vollkommenheit führt, zu kommen. (XXXIII, 264-265)

Don Sylvio's fantasy world and Agathon's moral idea can be seen as necessary stages
in a direct line of development culminating in Peregrinus' refined concept of enthusiasm. The state of perfection alluded to is none other than the reunification of the
human soul with the Godhead. This state is, of course, Peregrinus' eudaemonia.
As long as man is on earth and bound to his body, he is subject to error; that is,
to Schwärmerei. Any belief that perfection is possible in this life is delusion. Peregrinus is the epitome of the enthusiast because he realizes that his ideals are not
of this world. He is inspired by God to return to God. [3]

Wieland introduced the Schwärmer as the logical focal point for the dispute concerning the nature of Truth, right perception, and the fantasy-reality nexus. At the
conclusion of the first work, the aberrant individual is cured of his extremism and
naiveté. He is thereby prepared to become a purposeful and functional member of
society. Die Geschichte des Agathon is an intensification of the author's concern
with gnosiology. Decisive in this work is the definition of ultimate Truth in moral
and aesthetic terms (i.e., the Highest Good). The dichotomy of the individual and
society in Don Sylvio has been refined in Agathon to indicate as well the dualism of
spirit and flesh. Because man is related to the divinity through the spirit, man's
base nature must be subjugated to the spirit.

The sum effect of Agathon's disillusionments with his preconceived notions of
theurgic religion, human love, and society is to drive the hero from the mainstream
of life and to induce him to join the monastery-like community in Tarentum. However, one point remains undisputed: despite all disappointments Agathon does not
renounce his ideals, does not become a cynic or a skeptic. Yet it must be stressed
that his excessive idealism is gradually tempered by the demands of practicality,
reason, and sense experience. With respect to the concept of Schwärmerei the hero
progressed from naive, abstract religiosity to concrete human asceticism. But it
has also been seen from a consideration of the various versions of the novel that
Wieland was never really satisfied with the solution of the phenomenon of Schwärmerei in the novel.

Peregrinus Proteus presented a vindication of the sincere fantast. Peregrinus was
fully aware of his "abnormality" but never conceded to the social and practical
demands of existence. In this work there is no longer the requirement of a delicate
balance of the rational and irrational forces in the perception of Truth. Gnosis is
the only type of binding knowledge of which Wieland will admit. Social and empirical
reality have become minor concerns for him. We have seen that the author repeatedly stated that we cannot doubt what has passed within us. But the notion of intrinsic
experience and the necessary co-concept of personal integrity advance, in this
novel, to the forefront of Wieland's thinking.

In the course of the three novels, then, the author changed his philosophic position.
In Don Sylvio the aberrant individual had to recognize his abnormality and accede

to the normative influence of society which was his only assurance of felicity. In Peregrinus Proteus the protagonist adheres to his "aberrancy" because, for him, it is the only path to Truth. Wieland has become completely honest with himself. Thus he cannot depict an idealistic solution to the human dilemma. The reconciliation of subjective ideals and empiric reality as depicted in Tarentum is no longer possible. The poetic reconciliation of the disparate forces of spirit and flesh in Agathon was the necessary conclusion of the history as originally conceived. Peregrinus' life lends itself to a more realistic depiction of the consequences of inordinate enthusiasm. In order for Peregrinus to realize his destiny and attain his exalted goal, he must pass from the mundane world to the transcendental one. This transition could only be accomplished by his death, which for the sincere visionary is not an end but a beginning. The metaphysical world is shown to be man's true raison d'être; only in the next-world can man enjoy complete bliss and perfection. At the conclusion of this work enthusiast and rationalist accept one another as equals. This mutual respect seems to evince Wieland's reluctance to establish any universally binding norm. The sole criteria for Truth have become intrinsic experience and personal honesty. The brief examination of Agathodämon evinced the accuracy of these findings.

The development in the three novels (with respect to the titular heroes) has been from the youth to the man in his prime to the mature and wise sage. The mutation in the content of Schwärmerei has been from harmless fancies to humanistic idealism to transcendent Truth. (This development is counterpoint to the humanization process that Agathon's idealism underwent.) This transformation is manifest in a leitmotif common to all three novels: Sympathie.

In Don Sylvio the term described the physical attraction between Don Sylvio and Felicia, between Pedrillo and Laura, etc. The attraction between Don Sylvio and his sister also revealed the deeper spiritual significance of the phenomenon. But the spiritual connotation of Sympathie enjoys a much greater emphasis in Agathon. There is still the physical attraction (Agathon-Danae), but this bond of Sympathie is soon overshadowed by the spiritual affinities, which are most apparent in Danae's evolution from a hetaera to a schöne Seele, and in the unifying force of Archytas' court. In Peregrinus Proteus the phenomenon has been superseded by das Dämonische. This term is particularly indicative of the increased spiritualization of the enthusiast's desires. From the first, Peregrinus is intrinsically drawn to the True, the Good, and the Beautiful. The daemonic in man is a vestige of the divine and embodies the concepts of previous existence, instinct, intrinsic experience, and insatiable longing. All these characteristics are essential to Wieland's epistemology.

The evolution of the content of the Sympathie motif indicates the increasing spiritualization of love as explained by Diotima: the dreamer advances from love of corporeal beauty to love of spiritual beauty and, finally, to love of the Source of all beauty. Thus Don Sylvio and Agathon were merely stages in the development to Peregrinus Proteus, who is himself a representative of the elusive quintessence of human nature: das Dämonische.

This metamorphosis of philosophic content is reflected in the author's style. The use of polyperspective, dialogue, dialectics, psychological excursions, and the ironic humor of an omniscient author in <u>Don Sylvio</u> emphasized the aberrancy of those characters who did not comply to a single, universally accepted norm. In the evolution of <u>Agathon</u> the normative standard is retained, but the "corrective" force of the stylistic elements has been reduced. The omniscient author has gradually receded farther and farther into the background, which is stressed by the philosophic vacillation between Hippias and Archytas until a final decision is reached. The conflict between the individual and the group is given a poetic solution. In <u>Peregrinus Proteus</u> style and structure indicate a total lack of a social norm or of an empirical standard. The novelistic form itself, therefore, shows that truth and reality have become problematic. 4

The structure and style of the novels were marked by an emphasis of the subjectivity and relativity of views of which the chameleon is symbolic. The <u>Romanwirklichkeit</u> is a mixture of fantasy and reality, just as each individual perception of the world is an intermingling of the two. Thus Wieland's poetic reality is both indicative of his theory of knowledge and is representative of his concept of Truth, since its content is the Good and the Beautiful. 5 If we consider the essential emotionality of Wieland's apparent epistemology and of the aesthetic experience per se, then the relationship between poetry and the author's theory of knowledge is especially close. The technique of indicating the various perspectives can be seen as a logical consequence of the author's gnosiology. The spiritual side of human nature; that is, <u>das Dämonische</u>, is the guarantee that ultimate Truth is the same for all men. If the individual is truly sincere, then he can know himself. Self-knowledge is thus a necessary step toward gnosis. 6

Our considerations have repeatedly led us back to the starting point: the observer. Only through introspection can man hope to discern his <u>raison d'être</u> and to decipher the sacred hieroglyphics of Nature. The world is but an imperfect reflection of the Divinity, as is man. By hearkening to the vibrations of his heart man can best realize all that he -- as a unique individual -- is capable of becoming. The intellect is ancillary to the heart, for its function is to clarify man's moral and aesthetic intuitions. Thus the honest <u>Schwärmer</u> is not reviled. Once he recognizes his innate limitations he will become an enthusiast. (This is particularly true of Agathon and Peregrinus, for they were god-inspired.) The normative influence of Archytas has given way to the subjectivism of Peregrinus and Apollonius. Wieland gazed too deeply into the mysteries of Nature not to have learned that the demands of the "inner form" are more valid and binding than the claim of a universal social standard. The subjectivity of the fantast is just as valid as the subjectivity of the rationalist as long as personal integrity and intrinsic experience are observed.

Viewed in these terms the title of this book -- <u>Fantasy and Reality</u> -- does not imply a dichotomy of irrationality and empirical actuality but rather suggests an epistemologic unity of complexities for Wieland. In <u>Don Sylvio</u> the author demonstrated that the fantastic and the empiric are easily amalgamated. In <u>Agathon</u>, <u>Peregrinus Proteus</u>, and <u>Agathodämon</u> the irrepressible influence of the fantasy was manifest. Wieland seems to assert that the head is restricted by phenomena but that the heart can soar effortlessly on the wings of premonition. When the intellect is used to complement the imagination man is able to pare the vagueness from his intuitions and achieve clarity of knowledge. Christoph Martin Wieland's life, work, poetic theory, and epistemology are permeated separately and collectively, as it were, by the ceaseless interaction of fantasy and reality. In the conjuncture of the two ultimate Truth can be known.

A significant by-product of this investigation is an implicit stress of the affinities between the stereotyped Wieland and the early Romantic school. In the course of the several analyses notable parallels have come to light. For example, there is the general predominance of irrational forces determining the course of man's life, there is the same sense of the endless, the same orientation to the unremitting Absolute, the same mystical view of death as a release (Novalis, Hölderlin). Even on the question of poetics Wieland and the Romanticists are closer than is normally presumed. Wieland's <u>Romanwirklichkeit</u> approximates Schelling's and Friedrich Schlegel's concept of the role of art in the revelation of the <u>Weltseele</u>, since art blends <u>Geist</u> (fantasy) and <u>Natur</u> (empiric reality) for Wieland as well. For the Romanticists the <u>Ich</u> became origin, catalyst, and object in their striving for the Absolute. In Wieland's view too the ego serves as the source of impulse as well as the key to understanding the divine Totality. It is to be hoped that future studies of Wieland will turn more and more to a critical appraisal of the stereotypes of Wieland and thus contribute to a more accurate picture of him as a responsive contemporary of the Classical-Romantic era.

NOTES

1. However, in a letter to Gessner (<u>DB</u> I, 5; November 11, 1763), Wieland also defended Don Sylvio as an "ehrlichen Phantasten." The ascertainment that not Don Sylvio's fantasms but rather his upbringing was the object of satire in that novel, plus our new understanding of the "ehrlicher Schwärmer," underscores the evolution of enthusiasm as it has unfolded before our eyes.

2. In her overview of the eighteenth century, Barbara Schlagenhaft, pp. 3-9, indicates that the idyll and utopia are the last refuge of disillusioned idealists.

3. Lucian and Dionysius further illuminate the essential difference between <u>Schwärmerei</u> and enthusiasm as manifested in the person of Peregrinus. Lucian claims that he never mocked virtue. Rather, his derision was directed at "the false or exaggerated presumptions of perfection which have not been imparted to mortal man" (XXXIV, 154-155). The wanton refusal to note the limitations of one's abilities is in Lucian's opinion <u>Schwärmerei</u>. Lucian and Peregrinus disagreed, of course, on the limitations. Dionysius underscores the nature of enthusiasm by citing Christ as an example of the true enthusiast: "Er war ein <u>Enthusiast</u> im erhabensten Sinne dieses ehrwürdigen Wortes, welches durch Vermengung mit Schwärmerei, Fanatismus und Magismus so häufig entheiligt wird: aber seine <u>Lehre</u> war zu einfach, sein <u>Sinn</u> zu lauter, die <u>Vollkommenheit</u>, zu welcher er einlud und die er an sich selbst darstellte, zu rein und gross, als dass es sich nur denken liesse, sie könnte jemals das Antheil von Hunderttausenden und Millionen seyn" (XXXIV, 101-102).

4. Eva Becker, pp. 163-164, has demonstrated this for the German novel written around 1780.

5. Even the titular heroes in all four novels were exceptionally handsome men who subsequently became beautiful in spirit.

6. Steven R. Miller's study, <u>Die Figur des Erzählers in Wielands Romanen</u> (A. Kümmerle: Göppingen, 1970), which unfortunately became accessible to me only after this manuscript had been finished, also approaches Wieland from an epistemological point of view and substantiates many of my findings regarding the source of Wieland's personal tone and style. However, Miller's intent is to argue the relevance of the author's concept of <u>historical truth</u> as an interpretive tool; he does not consider the broader epistemological problems of the possibility and limits of knowledge, the question of absolute Truth, or the function of man's cognitive and intuitive faculties as I have attempted to do. Nevertheless, Miller's work is to be commended for its evaluation of the influence of the concept of historical truth on Wieland's writing an aspect long neglected.

BIBLIOGRAPHY

Primary Works

The Attic Nights of Aulus Gellius. Vol. II. Translated by John O. Rolfe. Loeb
   Classical Library 200. 1927: rpt. Cambridge: Harvard University Press, 1960.

Gellert, Christian Fürchtegott. Lustspiele. 1747: rpt. Stuttgart: J.B. Metzler,
   1966.
Goethe, Johann Wolfgang von. Werke. 143 vols. Published by order of the Grand
   Duchess Sophie of Sachsen. Weimar: Hermann Böhlau, 1887-1912.
                                              /
Jacobi, Friedrich Heinrich. Auserlesener Briefwechsel. 2 vols. Edited by
   Friedrich Roth. 1825-27, rpt. Bern: Herbert Lang, 1970.

Lessing, Gotthold Ephraim. Gesammelte Werke. 2 vols. Edited by Wolfgang
   Stammler. München: Hanser, 1959.
Lucian. Vol. V. Translated by A.M. Harmon. Loeb Classical Library 302. 1936;
   rpt. Cambridge: Harvard University Press, 1955.
Lukian. Sämtliche Werke. Vol. II. Translated by C.M. Wieland. Edited by Dr.
   Hans Floercke. Klassiker des Altertums. Vol. VIII. Erste Reihe. München &
   Leipzig: Georg Müller, 1911.

Michel, Victor. "Lettres de Sophie de la Roche a C.M. Wieland: Precedees d'une
   étude sur Sophie La Roche." Annales de l'Est: Memoires 8. Nancy, Paris,
   Strasbourg: Berger-Leveault, 1938.

Plato. Symposium. Translated by Benjamin Jowett. New York: Bobbs-Merrill, 1956.

Schiller, Johann Christoph Friedrich von. Sämtliche Werke. 5 vols. Edited by
   G. Fricke, H.G. Göpfert, H. Stubenrauch. München: Hanser, 1960.

Wieland, Christoph Martin. Sämtliche Werke. 53 vols. Edited by Johann Gottfried
   Gruber. Leipzig: Göschen, 1818-28. Vols. 50-53 contain Gruber's biography
   of Wieland.
-   Sämmtliche Werke. 36 vols. Leipzig: Göschen, 1855-58.
-   Werke. 5 vols. Edited by Fritz Martini and Hans W. Seiffert. München:
   Hanser, 1964-68.
-   Ausgewählte Werke. 3 vols. Edited by Friedrich Beissner. München: Winkler,
   1964-65.
-   Ausgewählte Werke. 6 vols. Edited by Wolfgang Jahn. München: Wilhelm
   Goldmann, 1964-.
-   Geschichte des Agathon. Frankfurt & Leipzig. 1766-67; rpt. Edited by Klaus
   Schäfer. Berlin: Akademie Verlag, 1961.
-   Ausgewählte Briefe von C.M. Wieland, an verschiedene Freunde in den Jahren
   1751-1810 geschrieben und nach der Zeitfolge geordnet. 4 vols. Zürich: n.p.,
   1815.

Wieland, Christoph Martin. Auswahl denkwürdiger Briefe. 2 vols. Edited by
Ludwig Wieland. Wien: Carl Gerold, 1815.
- Neue Briefe C.M. Wielands: vornehmlich an Sophie von La Roche. Edited by
Robert Hassencamp. Stuttgart: J.G. Cotta, 1894.
- Wielands Briefwechsel. Published by the German Academy of Sciences in
Berlin, Institute for German Language and Literature. Vol. I: Briefe der
Bildungsjahre (1. Juni 1750-2. Juni 1760). Vol. II: Commentary to Vol. I.
Edited by Hans W. Seiffert. Berlin: Akademie Verlag, 1963.
- Wieland und Reinhold: Originale Mittheilungen als Beiträge der Geschichte des
deutschen Geisteslebens. Edited by Robert Keil. Leipzig & Berlin: Verlag
Wilhelm Friedrich, 1885.

Secondary Works

Abbé, Derek Maurice van. Christoph Martin Wieland. London: Harrap, 1961.
Anchor, Robert. The Enlightenment Tradition. New York: Harper & Row, 1967.
Anger, Alfred. Literarisches Rokoko. Sammlung Metzler 25. Stuttgart: J.B.
Metzler, 1962.

Bach, Matthew G. Wieland's Attitude toward Woman and Her Cultural and Social
Relations. New York: Columbia University Press, 1922.
Becker, Eva D. Der deutsche Roman um 1780. Germanistische Abhandlungen 5.
Stuttgart: J.B. Metzler, 1964.
Beissner, Friedrich. "Poesie des Stils: Eine Hinführung zu Wieland." Wieland:
Vier Biberacher Vorträge. Wiesbaden: Insel Verlag, 1954.
- "Neue Wieland-Handschriften." Abhandlungen der Preussischen Akademie der
Wissenschaften 13. Berlin: Walter de Gruyter, 1938.
Blackall, Eric Albert. The Emergence of German as a Literary Language 1700-
1775. Cambridge: Cambridge University Press, 1959.
Blanckenburg, Ch.F. Versuch über den Roman. 1774: rpt. with an afterword by
E. Lämmert. Sammlung Metzler 39. Stuttgart: J.B. Metzler, 1965.
Bobertag, Felix. Wielands Romane: Ein Beitrag zur Geschichte und Theorie der
Prosadichtung. Breslau: Grass, Barth und Comp., 1871.
Bodmer, Johann Jakob. Critische Abhandlung von dem Wunderbaren in der Poesie.
1740; rpt. Stuttgart: J.B. Metzler, 1966.
Boeschenstein, Hermann. Deutsche Gefühlskultur: Studien zu ihrer dichterischen
Gestaltung. Vol. I: Die Grundlagen 1770-1830. Bern: Paul Haupt, 1954.
Böttiger, K.A. Literarische Zustände und Zeitgenossen. 2 Vols. Leipzig: F.A.
Brockhaus, 1838.
Borcherdt, Hans Heinrich. Der Roman der Goethezeit. Stuttgart: Port, 1949.
Breitinger, Johann Jakob. Critische Abhandlung von der Natur, den Absichten und
dem Gebrauche der Gleichnisse. 1740; rpt. Stuttgart: J.B. Metzler, 1967.
- Critische Dichtkunst. 1740; rpt. Stuttgart: J.B. Metzler, 1966.
Bröcker, Luise. "Das Zweiseelenproblem bei Goethe und Wieland." Diss. Münster
1947.

Brüggemann, Fritz. "Die Weisheit in Lessings Nathan." Gotthold Ephraim Lessing. Edited by Gerhard and Sibylle Bauer. Darmstadt: Wissenschaftliche Buchgesellschaft, 1968.

Bruford, W. H. Germany in the Eighteenth Century: The Social Background of the Literary Revival. 1935; rpt. Cambridge: Cambridge University Press, 1965.

Budde, Fritz. Wieland und Bodmer. Palaestra LXXXIX. Berlin: Mayer & Müller, 1910.

Buddecke, Wolfram. C. M. Wielands Entwicklungsbegriff und die Geschichte des Agathon." Palaestra 235. Göttingen: Vandenhoeck & Ruprecht, 1966.

Burger, Heinz Otto, ed. Annalen der deutschen Literatur. 2. Aufl. Stuttgart: Metzler, 1971.

- Dasein heisst eine Rolle spielen: Zwölf Studien zur deutschen Literaturgeschichte. München: Hanser, 1963.

- "Deutsche Aufklärung im Widerspiel zu Barock und 'Neubarock.'" Formkräfte der deutschen Dichtung vom Barock bis zur Gegenwart. Göttingen: Vandenhoeck & Ruprecht, 1963.

Butler, Eliza Marian. The Tyranny of Greece over Germany: A Study of the Influence Exercised by Greek Art and Poetry over Great German Writers of the 18th, 19th and 20th Centuries. 1935, rpt. Boston: Beacon Press, 1958.

Cassirer, Ernst. The Philosophy of the Enlightenment. Translated by Fritz A. Koeln and James P. Pettegrove. Boston: Beacon Press, 1955.

Copleston, Frederick, S. J. A History of Philosophy: Modern Philosophy. Vol. VI, Part. 1: The French Enlightenment to Kant. Garden City, N.Y.: Doubleday, 1960.

Craig, Charlotte. Christoph Martin Wieland as the Originator of the Modern Travesty in German Literature. University of North Carolina Studies in the Germanic Languages and Literatures 64. Chapel Hill: University of North Carolina Press, 1970.

Doering, Heinrich. Ch. M. Wieland nach den zuverlässigsten Quellen dargestellt. Sangerhausen: Verlag Jul. Rob. Rohland, 1840.

Elson, Charles. Wieland and Shaftesbury. New York: Columbia University Press, 1913.

Ermatinger, Emil. "Das Romantische bei Wieland." Neue Jahrbücher für Klassisches Altertum, Geschichte und deutsche Literatur. Vol. XXI, No. 3. Leipzig: Teubner, 1908.

- Deutsche Dichter: 1750-1900. Eine Geistesgeschichte in Lebensbildern. 2nd. ed. rev. Bonn: Athenäum, 1961.

- Die Weltanschauung des jungen Wieland. Frauenfeld: Huber, 1907.

- Wieland und die Schweiz. Frauenfeld und Leipzig: von Huber and Co., 1924.

Das Fischer Lexicon: Philosophie. Edited by Alwin Diemer and Ivo Frenzel. Frankfurt a/M. Fischer Bücherei, 1970.

Friese, Otto. Die drei Fassungen von Wielands Agathon. Diss. Göttingen, 1910. Göttingen: W. Fr. Kaestner, 1910.

Gerhard, Melitta. Der Deutsche Entwicklungsroman bis zu Goethe's "Wilhelm Meister." 2nd ed. Bern & München: Francke, 1968.

Gottsched, Johann Christoph. Versuch einer critischen Dichtkunst. 4th ed. 1751; rpt. Stuttgart: J. B. Metzler, 1968.

Greiner, Martin. Die Entstehung der modernen Unterhaltungsliteratur: Studien zum Trivialroman des 18. Jahrhunderts. Reinbeck bei Hamburg: Rowohlt, 1964.

Gruber, J.G. Wielands Leben mit Einfluss vieler noch ungedruckter Briefe Wielands. Vols. 50-53 of Wielands Sämmtliche Werke. Edited by J.G. Gruber. Leipzig: Göschen, 1828.

Grudzinski, Herbert. Shaftesburys Einfluss auf Chr. M. Wieland. Diss. Breslau 1912. Stuttgart: Metzler, 1912.

Hafen, H. "Studien zur Geschichte der deutschen Prosa im 18. Jahrhundert." Diss. Zürich 1952.

Hallberg, L. E. Wieland: Etude littéraire. Paris: E. Thorin, 1869.

Hamann, Emil. Wielands Bildungsideal. Diss Leipzig 1907. Chemnitz: Hugo Wilisch, 1907.

Hamlyn, D.W. "The History of Epistemology." Encyclopedia of Philosophy. Vol. III. New York: Macmillan, 1967.

Hammacher, Klaus, ed. F.H. Jacobi: Philosoph und Literat der Goethezeit. Frankfurt: Klostermann, 1969.

Hampson, Norman. The Enlightenment. Baltimore: Penguin, 1968.

Hatfield, Henry Caraway. Aesthetic Paganism in German Literature from Winckelmann to the Death of Goethe. Cambridge: Harvard University Press, 1964.

Hirzel, Ludwig: Wielands Beziehungen zu den deutschen Romantikern. Bern: 1904.

Jacobs, Jürgen. Wielands Romane. Bern & München: Francke, 1969.

Jahn, Wolfgang. "Nachwort." Die Abenteuer des Don Sylvio von Rosalva. München: Goldmann, n. d.

Kahler, Erich. "Untergang und Uebergang der epischen Kunstform." Neue Rundschau, 64 (1953), 1-44.

Kaiser, Gerhard. Geschichte der deutschen Literatur. Von der Aufklärung bis zum Sturm und Drang 1730-1785: Gütersloh: Mohn, 1966.

Kausch, Karl Heinz. "Die Kunst der Grazie: Ein Beitrag zum Verständnis Wielands." Jahrbuch der deutschen Schillergesellschaft. Vol. II. Edited by Fritz Martini, Herbert Stubenrauch, Bernhard Zeller. Stuttgart: Alfred Kröner, 1958.

Kayser, Wolfgang. Entstehung und Krise des modernen Romans. Stuttgart: J. B. Metzler, 1968.

-    Die Wahrheit der Dichter: Wandlung eines Begriffs in der deutschen Literatur. Reinbeck bei Hamburg: Rowohlt, 1961.

Kimpel, Dieter. Der Roman der Aufklärung. Sammlung Metzler 68. Stuttgart: 1967.

Kistler, Mark O. "Dionysian Elements in Wieland." Germanic Review 40, (1960), 83-92.

Kluckhohn, Paul. Die Auffassung der Liebe in der Literatur des 18. Jahrhunderts und in der deutschen Romantik. 3rd ed. Tübingen: Max Niemeyer, 1966.

Köster, Albert. Deutsche Literatur der Aufklärungszeit. Heidelberg: Carl Winter, 1925.

Kurrelmeyer, Wilhelm. "Gil Blas and Don Sylvio". Modern Language Notes. 34, (1919), 78-81.

- "The Sources of Wielands Don Sylvio." Modern Philosophy, 16 (1919), 637-648.

Kurth, Liselotte E. Die zweite Wirklichkeit: Studien zum Roman des 18. Jahrhunderts. University of North Carolina Studies in Germanic Languages and Literatures 62. Chapel Hill: University of North Carolina Press, 1969.

Lange, Victor. "Ausklang des achtzehnten Jahrhunderts." Spätzeiten und Spätzeitlichkeiten: Vorträge, gehalten auf dem II. Internationalen Germanistenkongress 1960 in Kopenhagen. Edited by Werner Kohlschmidt. Bern und München: Francke, 1962. /

- "Erzählformen des Romans im 18. Jahrhundert." Zur Poetik des Romans. Edited by V. Klotz. Darmstadt: Wissenschaftliche Buchgesellschaft, 1965.

- "Zur Gestalt des Schwärmers im deutschen Roman des 18. Jahrhunderts." Festschrift für R. Alewyn. Edited by Herbert Singer and Benno von Wiese. Köln: Böhlau, 1967.

Lovejoy, Arthur O. The Great Chain of Being: A Study of the History of an Idea. 1936; rpt. New York: Harper & Row, 1960.

Markwardt, Bruno. Geschichte der deutschen Poetik. Vol II. Aufklärung, Rokoko, Sturm und Drang. Berlin: Walter de Gruyter, 1956.

Martens, A. Untersuchungen über Wielands "Don Sylvio" und der übrigen Dichtungen der Biberacher Zeit. Diss. Halle-Wittenberg 1901. Halle: E. Karras, 1901.

Martini, Fritz. "Wieland, Napoleon und die Illuminaten. Zu einem bisher unbekannten Briefe." Un Dialogue des Nations. München: Max Hueber Verlag, 1967. S. 65-95.

- "Wieland-Forschung." Deutsche Vierteljahrschrift, 24 (1950), 269-280.

- "Wieland und das 18. Jahrhundert." Festschrift für Kluckhohn und Schneider. Tübingen: J.C.B. Mohr, 1948.

- "Wielands Stellung in der deutschen Dichtungsgeschichte des 18. Jahrhunderts." Deutschunterricht, 8 (1956), 87-112.

- "Nachwort." C.M. Wielands Werke. Vol. I. München: Hanser, 1964.

Mayer, K. Otto. "Die Feenmärchen bei Wieland." Vierteljahresschrift für Litteraturgeschichte, 5 (1892), 374-408, 497-533.

Mellinger, Johanna. Wielands Auffassung vom Urchristentum mit hauptsächlicher Berücksichtigung seines Romans "Agathodämon." Diss. München 1910. Marbach: A. Remppis, 1911.

Meyer, Hermann. Der Typus des Sonderlings in der deutschen Literatur. München: Hanser, 1963.

Michel, Victor. C.M. Wieland: La formation et l'évolution de son esprit jusqu'en 1772. Etudes de Littérature Etrangère et Comparée 10. Paris: Beivin, 1938.

Michelsen, Peter. Laurence Sterne und der deutsche Roman des 18. Jahrhunderts. Palaestra 232. Göttingen: Vandenhoeck & Ruprecht, 1962.

Miller, Norbert. Der empfindsame Erzähler. Untersuchungen an Romananfängen des 18. Jahrhunderts. München: Hanser, 1968.

Miller, Steven R. Die Figur des Erzählers in Wielands Romanen. Göppinger Arbeiten zur Germanistik 19. Göppingen: A. Kümmerle, 1970.

Minder, Robert. "Reflexions sur Wieland et le Classicisme.": Un Dialogue des Nations. München: Max Hueber Verlag, 1967. S. 33-42.

Müller, Jan-Dirk. Wielands späte Romane: Untersuchungen zur Erzählweise und zur erzählten Wirklichkeit. München: Fink, 1971.

Müller-Solger, Hermann. Der Dichtertraum: Studien zur Entwicklung der dicterischen Phantasie im Werk Christoph Martin Wielands. Göppinger Arbeiten zur Germanistik 24. Göppingen: Alfred Kümmerle, 1970.

Munteano, B. "Constantes Humaines en Littérature: L'éternel débat de la 'raison' et du 'coeur.'" Stil- und Formprobleme in der Literatur. Edited by Paul Böckmann. Heidelberg: C. Winters, 1959.

Oettinger, Klaus. Phantasie und Erfahrung: Studien zur Erzählpoetik Christoph Martin Wielands. München: Fink, 1970.

Otto, K. "Wielands Romantechnik." Diss. Kiel, 1922.

Preisendanz, Wolfgang. "Die Auseinandersetzung mit dem Nachahmungsprinzip in Deutschland und die besondere Rolle der Romane Wielands (Don Sylvio, Agathon)." Nachahmung und Illusion. Edited by H.R. Jauss. München: Eidos, 1964.

Promies, Wolfgang. Die Bürger und der Narr oder Das Risiko der Phantasie: Eine Untersuchung über das Irrationale in der Literatur des Rationalismus. München: Carl Hanser, 1966.

Ranke, Ernst Constantin. Festgabe zum neunzigsten Geburtstag Leopolds von Ranke: Zur Beurteilung Wielands. Marburg: n.p. 1885.

Ratz, Alfred E. "C.M. Wieland: Toleranz, Kompromiss und Inkonsequenz." Deutsche Vierteljahresschrift, 42 (1968), 493-514.

Rausse, Hubert. Geschichte des deutschen Romans bis 1800. Kempten & München: Joseph Ksel, 1914.

Reed, Eugene E. "Leibnitz, Wieland and the Combinatory Principle." Modern Language Review, 56 (1961), 529-537.

Reichert, Herbert W. "The Philosophy of Archytas." Germanic Review, 24 (1949), 8-17.

Reimer, Gerhard Johann. "The Schwärmer in the Novelistic Writings of Christoph Martin Wieland." Diss. Michigan State University, 1968.

Ridderhoff, Kuno. "Sophie von La Roche und Wieland: Zum hundertjährigen Todestage der Dichterin (11. Februar 1807)." Gelehrtenschule des Johanneums zu Hamburg. Hamburg: Lütcke & Wulff, 1907.

Schelle, Hansjörg. "Unbekannte Briefe C.M. Wielands und Carl Leonhard Reinhold aus den Jahren 1787 bis 1792." Lessing Yearbook III. München: Hueber, 1971.

-      "Das Wieland-Museum in Biberach an der Riss und seine Handschriften." Jahrbuch der deutschen Schillergesellschaft. Vol. V. Edited by Fritz Martini, Herbert Stubenrauch, Bernhard Zeller. Stuttgart: Alfred Kröner, 1961.

Schelle, Hansjörg. "Wieland-Museum und Wieland-Archiv: Rechenschaftsbericht 1962-1970." Jahrbuch der deutschen Schillergesellschaft. Vol. XIV. Edited by Fritz Martini, Herbert Stubenrauch, Bernhard Zeller. Stuttgart: Alfred Kröner, 1971.

Schindler-Hürlimann, Regine, Wielands Menschenbild: Eine Interpretation des Agathon. Zürich: Atlantis, 1964.

Schlagenhaft, Barbara. Wielands "Agathon" als Spiegelung aufklärerischer Vernunft- und Gefühlsproblematik. Erlangen: Palm & Enke, 1935.

Schönert, Jörg. Roman und Satire im 18. Jahrhundert: Ein Beitrag zur Poetik. Germanistische Abhandlungen 27. Stuttgart: J. B. Metzler, 1969.

Schroeder, Friedrich Wilhelm. Wielands "Agathon" und die Anfänge des modernen Bildungsroman. Diss. Königsberg 1904. Königsberg: Hartung, 1904.

Seiffert, Hans Werner. "Wielandbild und Wielandforschung." Wieland: Vier Biberacher Vorträge. Wiesbaden: Insel Verlag, 1954.

Sengle, Friedrich. "Der Romanbegriff in der ersten Hälfte des 19. Jahrhundert." Arbeiten zur deutschen Literatur 1750-1850. Stuttgart: J. B. Metzler, 1905.

- "Von Wielands Epenfragmenten zum Oberon: Ein Beitrag zu Problem und Geschichte des Kleinepos im 18. Jahrhundert." Arbeiten zur deutschen Literatur 1750-1850. Stuttgart: J. B. Metzler, 1965.

- "Wieland und Goethe." Arbeiten zur deutschen Literatur 1750-1850. Stuttgart: J. B. Metzler, 1965.

- Wieland. Stuttgart: J. B. Metzler, 1949.

Seuffert, Bernhard. "Prolegomena zu einer Wieland Ausgabe." Abhandlungen der Königlich preussischen Akademie der Wissenschaften. Vol. I: 1904; Vol. II: 1905. Berlin: G. Reimer.

- "Wielands höfische Dichtungen." Euphorion, 1 (1894), 520-540, 693-717.

- "Wieland: Vortrag bei der Gedächtnisfeier der Goethegesellschaft, gesprochen von Bernard Seuffert." Jahrbuch der Goethegesellschaft. Vol. I, Leipzig: Insel-Verlag, 1914.

Singer, Herbert. Der deutsche Roman zwischen Barock und Rokoko. Köln & Graz: Böhlau Verlag, 1963.

Sommer, Cornelius. Christoph Martin Wieland. Sammlung Metzler 95. Stuttgart: J. B. Metzler, 1971.

Sommerfeld, Martin. "Romantheorie und Romantypus der deutschen Aufklärung." Deutsche Vierteljahresschrift, 4 (1926), 459-490.

Stamm, I. S. "Wieland and Sceptical Rationalism." Germanic Review, 33 (1958), 15-29.

Stanzel, Franz K. Typische Formen des Romans. 3rd ed. Göttingen: Vandenhoeck & Ruprecht, 1964.

Steinmetz, Horst. "Der Harlekin: Seine Rolle in der deutschen Komödientheorie und -dichtung des 18. Jahrhunderts." Neophilologus, 50 (1966), 95-106.

Stern, Guy. "Saint or Hypocrite? A Study of Wieland's 'Jacinte Episode.'" Germanic Review, 29 (1954), 96-101.

Sternberger, Julius. Wielands Jugendjahre. Arbeiten Göttinger Bibliothekare 3. Göttingen: Ludwig Häntzschel & Co., 1935.

Stettner, Leo. Das philosophische System Shaftesburys und Wielands Agathon. Bausteine zur Geschichte der deutschen Literatur 28. Edited by Franz Saran. Halle (Saale): Max Niemeyer, 1929.

Strich, Fritz. Die Mythologie in der deutschen Literatur: Von Klopstock bis Wagner. Vol. I Halle (Saale), 1910: rpt. Tübingen: Max Niemeyer, 1970.

Teesing, H. P. H. "Wielands Verhältnis zur Aufklärung im Agathodämon." Neophilologus. 21 (1936), 23-35, 105-116.

Vormweg, Heinrich. "Die Romans Chr. M. Wielands: Zeitmorphologische Reihenuntersuchung." Diss. Bonn, 1956.

Weilguny, Hedwig. Das Wieland-Museum im Wittumspalais zu Weimar. Berlin & Weimar: Aufbau Verlag, 1968.

Wellek, Rene and Austin Warren. Theory of Literature. New York: Harcourt, Brace and World, Co. 1956.

Wölfel, Kurt. "Daphnes Verwandlungen: Zu einem Kapitel in Wielands Agathon." Jahrbuch der deutschen Schillergesellschaft. Vol. VIII. Edited by Fritz Martini, Herbert Stubenrauch, Bernhard Zeller, Alfred Kröner, 1965.

Wolff, Hans M. Die Weltanschauung der deutschen Aufklärung in geschichtlicher Entwicklung. 2nd ed. Bern & München: Francke, 1963.

Wolffheim, Hans. Wielands Begriff der Humanität. Hamburg: Hoffmann & Campe, 1949.

Wulff, Margrit. "Wielands Späte Auseinandersetzung mit Aberglauben und Schwärmerei." Diss. University of Texas, 1966.